THE MISSING MADONNA

A NOVEL

BY

DAVID MAIDMENT

This book is dedicated to my fellow workers – staff and volunteers – at Amnesty International, and especially those who work for justice and the rights of those suffering from threats of violence and are forced to leave their country as refugees.

It is also dedicated to those who campaign in particular for vulnerable children threatened with violence in their homes, on the streets and in institutions that should be protecting them. All royalties from this book will be donated to the Railway Children charity, www.railwaychildren.org.uk.

Previous titles:

The Child Madonna, Melrose Books, 2009

Copyright © David Maidment 2012

ISBN: 978-1-291-04447-8

The right of David Maidment to be identified as the author of this work had been asserted by him in accordance with the Copyright, Designs and Patents Act 1988.

This is a work of fiction. Names and characters are the product of the author's imagination and any resemblance to actual persons, living or dead, is entirely coincidental.

All rights reserved. No part of this publication may be reproduced or transmitted in any form or by any means, electronic or mechanical, including photocopy, recording or any information storage and retrieval system, without the prior written permission of the author, nor by way of trade or otherwise shall it be lent, re-sold, hired out or otherwise circulated without the author's prior consent in any form of binding or cover other than that in which it is published and without a similar condition including this condition being imposed on the subsequent purchaser.

Acknowledgement:

I am greatly indebted to author John Houghton, fellow member of the Association of Christian writers, for the considerable help and advice that he has given to me during the concept and writing of 'The Missing Madonna' and other books in the 'Madonna Trilogy'. Also to Dr Andrew Pratt and Marjorie Dobson, who encouraged me to persevere with the publication of the first book of this series and have continued to offer advice and support.

Author's Note:

The name 'Jesus' is a Greek translation of 'Yahoshua' (shortened version 'Yeshua') commonly rendered in English Bible versions as 'Joshua'. I have therefore used this name throughout.
His full Aramaic name was 'Yahoshua ben Yosef', ie 'Joshua, son of Joseph'.

'Mari' or 'Mary' is a shortened version of 'Mariam' or 'Mariamne'. I have deliberately used the variation 'Mari' throughout as a reminder that this is a work of fiction.

Part 1

Rachel's Children

'In Ramah was there a voice heard, lamentation, and weeping, and great mourning, Rachel weeping for her children, and would not be comforted, because they are not.'

(Jeremiah 31, verse 15; Matthew 2, verse 18)

Chapter 1
Rachel, BC 6

They've gone! She wasn't at the well this morning. I called at her house when I'd got the water back home, and found the place shut up. There was no sign of her or her infant or her husband. I tried Rebecca who lived next door to Mariam and her family.

'No, Rachel, I haven't the faintest idea. They were at home all yesterday and didn't say anything about going away to me. I chatted with Mari for several minutes and she didn't mention a thing. I heard noises about midnight, but I just thought one of their animals had got loose.'

I hitch Ben onto my hip and the two of us go together to investigate again. Rebecca knocks loudly on the wooden door. Nothing. No sound. We push the door and it opens. Their donkey's not there and the chickens are gone as well. We enter the living space and it's bare. I'm a bit nervous about going in any further. I feel we're trespassing without any proper invitation.

'Come on, Rachel. Don't stand there looking as though you've seen a ghost. What you waiting for?'

'Should we ...?'

'If there's anything wrong, they'll be glad. If there's no-one here, it doesn't matter, they won't know!'

So I follow Rebecca into their room. A few pots and implements stand in the corner, but we can't see any sign of food ready for preparation, and the usual odour of cooking is absent. We push into the backroom which Joseph uses as his workshop. There's a strong smell of fresh wood. I still feel as though we're intruding where we shouldn't be, but Rebecca charges ahead and peers out into the small courtyard at the back. There are unfinished orders all over the place - a table, a couple of ploughs and a lot of timber stacked untidily as though Joseph's put things away quickly, expecting to continue his labours this morning. I nearly trip over some odd cuts of timber that are lying untidily on the ground.

'Careful, Rachel, don't drop the lad. Give him to me.'

'It's alright, I've got him now.'

I'm wracking my brain to think of what might have happened. I look at all the half-finished implements and furniture around.

'They can't have gone far,' I say, 'Joseph would never have let his customers down by leaving orders unfinished.'

'A bit of a mystery,' says Rebecca, 'but they'll probably turn up tonight. Perhaps the boy was taken ill and they've gone to seek help in Jerusalem.'

'Mari would have told me, I'm sure. If Joshua had been ill, she'd have come to me and sought my help here in the village before tackling the trek into the city with a sick child.'

Ben begins to fidget, so I put him down for a moment and he toddles off on unsteady steps over the uneven earthen floor. He starts to take too much interest in some of the planks of wood and I grab him before they can collapse on top of him. Then I notice that Joseph's tools are missing. Normally they are laid out on the workbench, in regimented rows, he's so proud of them. But there are none visible. I poke around but can't see any. This is really strange. Unfinished carpentry and no tools to be seen.

We give up and I return home. I try to get on with the household chores but I'm worried, it's not like Mari to go off like that without saying anything to me. After all, we have been the best of friends ever since she'd settled in Bethlehem with her husband and brand new baby some eighteen months ago. Mari is my own age - well nearly so - I am just a year older at sixteen - but we both have toddlers the same age and Josh and my Benjamin are inseparable. Mari is so bubbly, she tells me all sorts of things, secrets that I'm sure she makes up sometimes with that fertile imagination of hers.

My husband, Nathan, whom I married three years ago, six months after my 'bat mitzvah', is doing some repairs to the walls in Jonah's fields.

'Wait till your Dad gets home, then we'll ask him,' I say half to Benjamin and half to myself.

It'll be dusk before he gets back and I can ask him if he knows anything; perhaps Joseph confided in him. I try to forget Mari's disappearance and get on with my own tasks. I must sweep out the house and I leave Ben playing with a stick he picked up on the way home - Mari and Joseph's house is in the next street to ours, next door to Rebecca and her husband, Andrew. Rebecca is several years older than me and she has a ten year old girl whom she's left in charge of her young children, a couple of boys and a six month old baby girl.

When I've finished the essential cleaning and have washed Ben's soiled clothes, I can relax for an hour or so before I need to start the meal for Nathan. This is my special time with Benjamin. He enjoys my full attention and we play together. He loves hiding his face from me - he thinks he is totally hidden; he thinks if he can't see me, I can't see him. Then we have time for hugs and he sits on my knee while we practise the few words he can say. Mari's Joshua is a very clever little boy, he can say twice as many words as my Ben can, but I think my Ben can do more steps unaided than Joshua before he falls over.

'Ben, what's that you're saying?'

It sounds like a shushing noise, I don't think he wants me to be quiet. Well, I'm not making any noise!

'Ben, say it again!'

'Shusha!'

'Oh, you mean Joshua? You want to play with Joshua?'

'M'm.' He's nodding. I think that means 'yes'.

'Well, he's not here, darling. I don't know where he is at the moment. We'll find him soon, I expect. Let's look for him tomorrow and ask him to come and play with you.'

I can't help wondering where Mari is though, Ben is missing Joshua already - he keeps saying 'Shusha' which is his word for his friend. I'm wondering if the visitors they had the other night have anything to do with their disappearance. It was weird. Several expensively dressed men - well, some of them looked like foreigners in very exotic robes - called at Mari's house late in the evening. I didn't see them myself, but Rebecca told me about it. She said they stayed a long time, and that it was nearly midnight before they left. You'd think at that sort of time they'd have been guests for the night, but Rebecca said they left in a bit of a hurry and didn't stay in the village at all. I wonder if there's any news yet. Perhaps I'll just go round to their house a last time before it gets dark. I take Ben with me and we go round to Mari's house again. It is still shut up and silent.

Rebecca sees me and calls out, 'No. Not a movement all day. I can't understand it. A couple of men came round earlier to ask Joseph to do some work for them, but I was unable to suggest where he might be. They said they'd come back tomorrow.'

We give up and go back home because I must get the meal going. Nathan'll be tired and ravenous because he's been doing heavy work in the fields all day. At last Ben is beginning to grizzle and yawn, so I can lay him down for a nap while I get on with my work. I don't know how Rebecca manages with four youngsters although I think her eldest, Miriam, gives her a lot of help with the little ones. I keep wondering when I might conceive our next child, Nathan is very amorous and his mother keeps hinting to me that another baby must be surely on the way soon. Perhaps there's something wrong with me. After we got married it was nearly eighteen months before Ben was born, and Nathan's parents were asking him almost every day if I was pregnant yet. They made it very clear to me that it was my role to produce a son and heir as soon as possible. Even my mother seemed concerned and used to tell me what to eat and drink, which food promotes fertility and even advised me on what position to adopt during love-making to make conception a greater possibility. It was a great relief to them - and to Nathan and me because they were getting us anxious too - when a healthy boy was born. I'd have been just as happy with a girl - look how useful Miriam is to Rebecca - but all the others seemed to think it much more important that a boy comes first. Anyway, Benjamin came along and life without him would seem very strange and empty now.

The cooking pots are bubbling nicely when I hear Ben begin to stir and before he can cry, I'm picking him up and making soothing noises to him. His dark brown eyes open wide and he gives me a beautiful grin and I leave my chores for a few minutes to cuddle him and feel his soft skin against my cheek. Nathan's mother says he looks like Nathan, but I'm not so sure. He has my big eyes and curly dark hair and my mother says he's very like me when I was that age. I've heard the two grandmothers both arguing about this, not that I think it matters because I'm quite content if he grows up looking like my handsome husband. Anyway, it's not his looks that matter, if he has Nathan's good nature and honesty I'll not complain. I never cease to thank my parents for finding someone as good as Nathan for me. Some of my friends have not been so lucky. When we meet each morning at the well I hear some of them complaining, and Martha last week had a black eye, which she said had been caused by her husband, who often gets drunk and beats her up if she hasn't done everything just as he likes it.

I've been keeping an eye on the lane outside and spy my husband coming. I pick up Benjamin and together we rush out to meet and greet Nathan, who sweeps us both into his arms and gives us a joint hug before he kisses me. Some people think it's indecent to show affection in public like this, but I don't mind, I like it. It means Nathan really loves me or he wouldn't risk criticism by behaving in such a manner. I don't think my father really approves of such a display of affection, I've never seen him show any outward signs of his care for my mother although I'm sure he loves her really. It's just that he's rather formal and stiff and finds it hard to unbend like Nathan and some of the younger men nowadays.

Nathan takes Benjamin from my arms and they tussle together playfully while I pour water from the largest pot so that Nathan can wash and freshen himself before our meal. I tip most of the stew I've been cooking into a dish for my husband and put some into mine, although I'm not feeling terribly hungry.

'Here we are, I hope that's enough for you. Ben can have a bit of mine.' I take a small mouthful to test how hot it is, then I look up at Nathan.

'What have you been doing today?'

'We're still tackling the broken walls between Andrew's field and mine. He helped me today, we should have it finished by tomorrow. I don't want Jonah's goats trampling all over our crops again as they did last week. What have you been up to today?'

'I think Ben has another tooth coming.'

I'll not say anything about the disappearance of Mari and her husband until the meal's over and we've got Ben to sleep for the night. I give Ben a little of our food cut up small, but after the meal I'll breast feed him as he is not yet weaned. I love this time. At first I was a little uncomfortable and sore, he was such a greedy baby, but now he sucks so peacefully and we share a lovely intimate time together. I know Nathan just likes looking at us, I don't know whether he's just admiring his family or feasting his eyes on my bare breasts with eyes of lust, the naughty man! I know he likes looking at me when I'm so immodestly dressed, he tells me constantly how much he loves my beautiful body so that I would find it hard to reject his avid love-making even had I wanted to.

After we've cleared away the remnants of our meal and I've fed Ben, I rock him gently in my arms and sing a lullaby to him. His eyes are heavy and I lay him down in his cradle that Nathan had Joseph make for us. I watch him lying there for a long time, his eyelids flickering, his breathing light and steady, he looks so small and vulnerable and I feel so responsible for him, it is a huge task. I have to nurture him until one day he is a strong and handsome man like my husband. Nathan joins me and puts his arms around my shoulders, then bends and kisses the sleeping child on the cheek. I copy his movement and bid the little boy good night and sweet dreams before we both return to the table and begin to chat in low voices so as not to disturb the child. I can't wait to tell him my news.

'Nathan, Mari and Joseph have disappeared. I mentioned it to Rebecca today and we went right into their house. There was no sign of them. Do you know where they've gone?'

'No, my sweet, I expect they've just gone to visit someone. Haven't they got some relatives in Ein-Karem? I've heard Mari speak of an elderly cousin there.'

'Well, perhaps. But when we went into their house all Joseph's tools had gone. You know, the ones he uses for his work. Rebecca and I couldn't see any sign of them. When I visit Mari I usually peep in and show Ben to Joseph and they're always lined up in a neat row on his bench. There was no sign of them today.'

'Perhaps he's gone to fix something in the house they're visiting.'

'But he wouldn't take all of them, surely?'

'Why, are you worried about them?'

'I don't know. Ben's already missing Joshua, I think. And if they've taken Joshua to a physician in Jerusalem because he's ill, then I'm worried that he may have some disease that Ben could pick up.'

'Alright, Rachel. If you're really worried about them, I'll ask round. Someone will know. They won't have just disappeared without telling anybody.'

Nathan decides to call on some of his friends to see if any of them know what has happened. He pulls on his cloak, for the sun has dropped and the temperature is falling quite rapidly outside. While he is gone, I watch over Ben asleep in his cradle, humming softly to myself. I should be doing something useful, I know, but when we are alone like this I just want to sit and watch him, thinking about the miracle that

Nathan and I could have created such a wonderful new human being. He looks so vulnerable there, sucking his thumb, so trusting that we will look after him. He stirs occasionally, the thumb slips out of his mouth, a little wriggle and a huge sigh escapes him, then he snuggles back, and the thumb engages with his mouth once more, a few vigorous noisy sucks, and then he is sleeping peacefully.

Nathan is back after an hour or so.

'What have you found out?'

'Nothing, Rachel. It really does seem rather odd. I tried everyone. I bumped into Rebecca's Andrew, right outside Joseph's house. I thought if anyone, he'd know. But he hadn't a clue.'

Nathan is shaking his head, putting on a puzzled expression.

'Rebecca came out and told me, I guess, only what she'd already told you earlier today. Then I saw Matthaeus and Simeon. They didn't know anything either.

Nathan purses his lips. 'I'm a bit dry, love. Can you get me a cup of wine? My back's aching. It was hard work today.'

He pauses long enough for me to fetch the drink.

'There seems to be some concern. It turns out that Joseph promised at least a couple of the men that their farm equipment would be ready tomorrow morning and they are relying on that promise and Joseph has never let anyone down before.'

'I'm sure Joseph wouldn't forget something like that. He's most reliable. Mari is always telling me how upset he gets if he can't finish things by the time he's promised people.'

'Several apparently saw him at work yesterday and a couple chatted with him and he gave no inkling then that he was thinking of going away, even if only for a short period. A number of the men had glimpsed strangers who called on Joseph after nightfall yesterday although in the darkness they could not give any description of them that would identify who they were or where they came from.'

Nathan takes a sip from his cup and licks his lips.

'Someone wondered if they had got tangled up with the terrorists around Galilee.'

'Never,' I interrupt most indignantly. 'He'd never get caught up in anything like that.'

'Well, how well do you know Joseph? You know Mari well enough, but you don't know Joseph's views on everything, do you?'

'Mari's never given me any clue about such a thing.'

'Well, she wouldn't, would she? If he had been mixed up in some political action against the Romans, they'd both keep it quiet, wouldn't they?'

I shake my head. I can't believe that. It's ridiculous.

'There are groups up in Galilee who are fighting Herod's soldiers and anyone who's thought to be a collaborator with the Romans. Anyway,' he says smiling, 'like you, everyone I spoke to thought this most unlikely and not in Joseph's character, but Mari's family comes from that area and he's said very little about their life there before settling here.'

He suddenly seems to have a brainwave.

'Perhaps the strangers were from one of those groups come to put pressure on Joseph or tell them something that has happened affecting their relations in Galilee.'

'I still don't believe that. I'm sure Mari would have dropped a hint. She's told me plenty of things, some of which seemed a bit strange. But nothing of that sort.'

'Well, the general view of those I spoke to was that those men had brought some bad news, perhaps from Mariam's home village, and that they have had to go there in a hurry. Perhaps there has been a death in the family. There's surprise, though, that Joseph has not confided this to someone or made apologies to the customers awaiting their orders.'

'I think Mari would have told me if she'd had bad news. She'd want me to share her worry if it was that sort of thing.'

'Unless, of course, Joseph himself was involved with the terrorist groups, something he would certainly not have told us here. If there was even a whisper or rumour of this sort, it would soon reach the ears of one of Herod's spies. He wouldn't last long then!'

This conversation makes me more alert than usual and after we have gone to bed and Nathan has made love to me even more ardently than usual, I lie awake instead of falling asleep in his arms, and let all sorts of thoughts flit through my mind, so that eventually when I try to stop them and go to sleep, I find I can't. I toss and turn for a bit and then think about Mari and her boy. I met Mari for the first time at the well when we both were carrying babies - hers was less than a month old. She seemed very young, I guessed she had been married as soon as the law permitted, and I found out soon enough that she was fourteen, just a year younger than me. She'd been quite ill at first after the birth, and had lost a lot of blood, picked up an infection and become very weak.

Rebecca had told me there was a new girl who was sick - she'd been helping the husband look after her and had been fetching water for both of them. Anyway, when she had regained her strength, we met at the well and hit it off straight away. Despite the fact that she was still recovering from her fever, she seemed very cheerful and chirpy - in fact, she seemed a lot of fun and not at all like some of the women who just seem to want to criticise each other and revel in any scandal or gossip going. She was certainly not a shy girl and despite her lack of experience, she seemed very confident with the child. I found out later that she had been left in charge of her cousins and younger sisters and brother a lot when she was only a young girl and was quite used to caring for babies. Indeed, although older, I was the one who asked the questions and found myself more often seeking her advice about baby things than I did of my mother.

She was also a very religious girl. She often brought God into her conversations quite naturally in a way I was unused to. He seemed very real to her, whereas Jehovah and his activities seemed just words I'd heard many times in the local synagogue, things that happened long ago about which the rabbi would drone on in a most boring way while my mind was elsewhere. She didn't try to lecture me on this in any way, she just spoke about God as though he was very personal and full of meaning for her. I must say that I envied her in this. I used to press her to tell me about her life before she came to Bethlehem. I knew she came from Galilee, I could tell that by her slight accent, she said she was from a tiny village called Nazareth. I must admit I'd never heard of it, but she said it was near the city of Sepphoris and I'd heard the men mention that place although it really meant nothing to me. She was at first reluctant to tell me any more about her life there except that she had two younger sisters and a brother and that her mother was a widow.

Gradually as we'd got to know one another better, she opened up a little. She told me about her uncle, Eli, who was a Pharisee, who took responsibility for them and gave them a home, but I got the impression she didn't get on too well with him. Then one day, after I'd told her all sorts of intimate things about Nathan and our courtship and life together, she told me something that was quite shocking. She said that she and Joseph were not properly married, only betrothed to one another. They'd had to come to Bethlehem for the census because of Joseph's family registration and had intended to go back to Nazareth and get married then, but for a number of reasons she wouldn't tell me, had stayed in a house Joseph had rented here and set up his carpentry business in which he'd been trained by his long-dead father. She wouldn't say, but I feel that she didn't want to go back because of some rift or problem with this Eli she talked about. I then realised of course that she must have conceived Joshua out of wedlock, possibly before she was even betrothed, and that was obviously the reason she could not return. There must have been some terrible scandal. She would have been ostracised and possibly even threatened, so had escaped with Joseph before they could harm her and the baby.

Although this scenario had seemed the most likely, I found behaving in that sort of loose and immoral way something I could not associate with the Mari I knew. And I didn't think from what I knew of him, and what Mari said, that Joseph was the sort who would have seduced a young girl and certainly not raped her. Then one night, after we'd been at a celebration together, Mari asked me if I could keep a secret. I think perhaps the wine had made her lose any inhibitions she might have had. She astonished me by saying that she'd been a virgin; that Joshua was a miracle and she'd been visited by a messenger from God who told her she'd have a baby and that he would be the promised Messiah. She said Josh's real name was Yahoshua as she'd been instructed by the messenger but they normally called him Joshua to bring less attention to him as knowledge of who he really was could bring danger to the family. I didn't believe her, of course, she'd gone right over the top. I could understand her not wanting to admit that she and Joseph had made love before they were married, but this seemed too far-fetched an excuse to be credible.

I didn't know quite what to make of her after that. She sensed my disbelief, although I found it too difficult and embarrassing to tell her outright that I didn't believe her. Somehow the openness and intimacy between us disappeared after that, there was a thin wall of wariness that inhibited the freedom with which we'd previously talked. We still met up regularly and chatted about the growth of our babies and all the things that mothers do about their children, but I never asked her anything else about her former life and she never volunteered anything more about Joshua being the Messiah or about being a virgin. I was sure she wasn't still a virgin anyway, even if she was not properly married. We'd both talked about when we might expect another baby on the way and there was nothing Mari said that made me think that the next child she had would be miraculous!

As I lie awake and ponder all these things, my imagination begins to weave all sorts of scenarios about Mari and her child.

Suppose what she'd said is true! What if Joshua is the future Messiah? After all, the rabbis and scribes are always going on about the coming Messiah who will drive the hated foreigners out of Israel. If what they say is right, someone has to be mother of the Messiah. Why not Mari? Well, my rational mind replies, she's hardly from the sort of background to give birth to a prince or warrior, is she? I know Joseph comes from the family line of King David, but then so do several men here in Bethlehem, as this is the village that is sacred to him and his descendents. Perhaps that's why they came to Bethlehem. If that was the case, then who were the strangers who visited them yesterday? Has someone in authority got wind of who they are and come to warn or threaten them? Is that why they've disappeared in such a hurry?

I begin to imagine more and more exotic scenarios in my tired and confused brain, while another part of me tries to calm me down, to question why I am getting myself so het up about it when she's just a friend. What has it really got to do with me? Does it really have anything to do with my life and that of my slumbering family beside me? I get up and have a look at Benjamin sleeping peacefully in his cradle. I watch my husband breathing more heavily in a deep sleep, drink a quick draught of water and get back onto my bed and must have fallen asleep at last.

Chapter 2
Rachel

There is still no sign of Mari's family today. Nathan checked first thing this morning and said their house was still deserted.

I go down later and there is quite a crowd. I hear raised voices and see that a couple of men are complaining bitterly that implements they need, and that Joseph had promised for today, are not ready. One of them is really quite angry.

'Don't you go on at me, young man! There's no point in you complaining to me. I know no more than you about what's happened!' Rebecca's voice is strident above the general din.

The men push into Joseph's house and begin to root around the half finished pieces of furniture and farm equipment and both eventually emerge brandishing what looks like an oxen's yoke and a rudimentary plough, but they are rough and some splinters of wood protrude.

'I'll have to bloody well finish this myself now,' I hear one of the men mutter. 'If Joseph thinks he's going to get paid for this, he'd better think again.'

The men eventually make off, still grousing, and the gaggle of women outside the house begins to disperse. I look at Rebecca and she shakes her head.

'Still no sign of them. I'm baffled. It's just not like Joseph to let his customers down, especially that Simon from the other side of Jacob's Field. He's had a long trek and he comes regularly. There's no way Joseph would have forgotten he was coming this morning unless there's been some emergency.' She looks at me with a worried frown.

'Either Joshua has been taken seriously ill and they've gone looking for a physician in Jerusalem or Mari's had bad news from Galilee and they've gone to her home in a hurry. But I'd have thought they'd have at least told one of us.'

Rebecca's expressing what we all feel. Eventually everyone drifts away back to their own homes. I walk with Rebecca's daughter, Miriam, to the well. She immediately picks Benjamin up and starts bouncing and tickling him and he chortles with laughter. He loves Miriam who always makes a fuss of him. I carry her water pot while she carries him and she plays in the dust with him while I draw water for both of us. There are a couple of other women there and there is only one topic of conversation. However, I don't learn any more. Just the same old guesses as to what must have happened.

So we go home and carry on as normal, although Mari and Joshua's disappearance is never far from my mind. The silence from Joseph's house seems eerie, I'm so used to hearing the noise of hammering or sawing echoing in the distance as I go about my chores. Although Ben has been happily occupied by Miriam, after his afternoon sleep his first words to me sound like 'Shusha' and I guess he's missing Joshua as most days the two toddlers are inseparable.

When Nathan comes in from the fields I greet him and look at him expectantly.

'I've come back via Joseph's house. There's still no news of the family; no-one has heard anything.'

I think this very strange. There is always someone who can be relied on to have heard whatever news or gossip is going the rounds.

'No, Rachel. Absolutely nothing! Some men blame the strangers that were seen after nightfall at Joseph's home a couple of days ago, but that's pure guesswork and they admit as such.'

Benjamin seems very fretful at bedtime. I worry that he might be sickening for something, he's usually so jolly and we have a lot of fun as I give him his last feed and change his soiled clothes. I wonder if it's because he's missing his friend, or whether he has picked up some bug from Joshua. Anyway, I eventually get him to sleep and have a few minutes with Nathan before we go to bed too. I think Nathan may be too tired at first to make love, but he curls himself around me and oh, what can I say …? I just let myself go and forget everything. Afterwards I just sink back and think that it's so lovely and I'm so lucky really to have such a gentle and gorgeous man for my husband. I know from the gossip at the well that not many women are so fortunate. I hear all their complaints then; some of them seem very resentful or bitter sometimes, I can't imagine what it must be like to be married to someone who does not respect you and neglects or even abuses you physically, which some women seem to be quite open about. I think I'd be too ashamed to admit such things if I were to suffer like that – heavens above, what am I even thinking about? I just can't imagine Nathan ever treating me like that.

After we have lain quietly for a while, I wonder if he will embrace me again, but he turns and I realise he's quickly asleep. I listen to his regular breathing for some time and I suppose I must have drifted off to sleep soon as well, but it doesn't seem many minutes before I wake with a start and hear Ben crying. I'm alarmed for it is several weeks now since he started sleeping right through the night and my first thought is that he must be ill. I pick him up and he doesn't seem particularly hot. In fact his eyes open wide and he grins at me as I lifted him from his cradle – I'm at once relieved that nothing seems to be wrong and annoyed at the little devil that he seems to be enjoying waking me up. I think that perhaps he might be soothed if he takes a little milk so I put him to my breast and settle myself as comfortably as I can. After he's taken his fill – not very much in truth – I rock him and wait for those eyes to close. They stare at me for a time, then begin to blink, but every time I make to put him down the movement stirs him and his eyes open once more.

I find my mind wandering as I rock him. I keep looking over to the huddled form of my husband, still rising and falling gently as he breathes in such a restful rhythm and I wish Ben at this moment would take a hint from his dad. It seems strange, now that we are so settled, that just three years ago it was so difficult for us to come together. I used to see him quite often accompanying his father, who was a scribe in the synagogue, when the white robed man would stop at my father's market stall to buy vegetables to take home for his evening meal. In fact I'd noticed him when I must have been barely ten years old and dreamed about the young man who was already showing signs of adulthood and whom I knew had celebrated his 'bar mitzva' the previous year. I know I used to go all gooey inside looking forward to the time of day when his father would come by on his way home from the synagogue and I'd be devastated if Nathan did not accompany him. I used to be shy at first and I'd blush and go hot all over if I thought he was looking at me, then I'd feel silly, because I thought that he'd never be able to take me seriously.

He used to tease me a lot and I loved that because it meant that he'd noticed me. I would play up to him, goad and egg him on, and he'd chase me around the stall and try to grab me while his father and mine haggled over the price of my father's vegetables or occasionally over a chicken we'd slaughtered. My father used to shout and tell me not to be so silly, but I would ignore him. Then one day, Nathan sat down and talked to me, just like a friend, and I'd felt so grown up and when they'd both gone I started to dream that one day he'd marry me. Little did I think it would really happen!

I don't know how long it was before Nathan's father noticed that his son spent time talking seriously to me and even began to seek me out at other times and stop to chat. My father warned me one day – I must have been coming up to my twelfth birthday by then – that I must not set too great a store by my obvious friendship with Nathan. I mustn't begin to get any ideas ... But it was already too late as far as I was concerned. I used to long for the times I saw Nathan returning home from his lessons at the synagogue, I longed so hard that it hurt! And I began to think he really liked me too, not just as a childhood friend, but something more special. I could see his eyes light up, he started to show off to me and made it obvious that he wanted me to see just how grown up he was and ready to get married and start a home of his own. Then one day he beckoned me to leave my father's side and whispered that his mother and father had told him that he mustn't be seen alone with me any more, that it was unseemly and he should keep himself for a girl they would choose to be his wife …I cried myself to sleep that night.

'Oh, shush, my darling Benjamin, do go to sleep. Shut those gorgeous eyes and let me dream on about your great big handsome dad. Shush, my love, go to sleep, let those eyes close, shush …'

Then that thrilling moment when he said he loved me and wanted me to be his wife and made me promise to keep it a secret. 'Why can't we tell everyone?' I said, and he told me that his parents disapproved because I was only the daughter of a tradesman and his father was from a family of scribes and that he couldn't ever marry me. So he used to come and whisper where we could meet without his family knowing. I don't know how he managed to keep our assignations secret – nor how I managed to keep it a secret as well as I was so excited. He's always told me that his father never found out until I was of age and he'd asked my father formally if he could marry me. My mother guessed long before where I was going and she would admonish me and say that no good would come of it, I'd be disappointed in the end. She used to warn me that I must be careful and not let him take advantage of my youth and innocence. He would leave me and if he'd taken my virginity they'd not be able to find me a proper husband. I knew she was wrong about that, Nathan never pressed me, he never even tried to kiss me, let alone anything more, but he held my hand and I so wanted him to take me in his arms and, silly me, I think I'd have let him do anything, I was so infatuated.

'Oh, Benjamin, do go to sleep. I'm tired, I can't keep my eyes open, why don't you let your eyes shut, then we could both go back to bed. Come on, let me rock you, that's it, quiet, now, shush, my darling, shush …'

I think he's gone, at last.

Chapter 3
Rachel

It's stupid. Ben's asleep now and I'm in bed beside my sleeping husband. I'm tired and I should have dropped straight off to sleep myself, but now I can't. I'm lying here on my sleeping mat, I'm hot and now my mind is too active and thoughts are whirring round my head. I feel guilty that I should be so happy, leaving my mother alone to look after poor Ishmael. I used to carry him around, acting as his poor crippled legs, and when he was with me he could play and join in with the other children. Now he can only leave the house when my mother takes him out and she hasn't the time and the other children laugh at his twisted legs and I could hit them, but I have Ben to look after now and he takes all my time and energy.

I vividly remember when I told my parents that Nathan wanted to marry me. My mother actually laughed. 'Who'll look after Ishmael?' was her first response. 'You're not serious, are you?' was her next. 'Rachel, you're only thirteen. You can't think of leaving your home so soon. And anyway, what makes you think Nathan's parents will permit it?'

When she saw I meant it, I could tell that she was worried about how they'd manage at home. 'How will I be able to keep up my sewing if I'm having to cope with Ishmael's needs every few minutes? You all need my income as well as your father's if we are to have proper meals and clothes.'

My father raised his voice for the first time I ever remember and rebuked her.

'If what Rachel says is really true and Nathan is seeking her as his wife, we should seize this opportunity. She won't get a better offer than this. It's a golden chance to raise the family up in the world, to be related to a family from the synagogue.'

Afterwards, out of my mother's hearing, he told me that I mustn't be disappointed. He thought it was doomed to failure, he warned me Nathan's parents would never allow it, but he would not stand in my way if I really got the chance.

And so it became public. Nathan let it be known among his friends that he was seeking me as a wife and of course this became common knowledge immediately, putting his parents under great pressure to agree. They could continue to argue that I was of the wrong tribe, my parents were not Levites as they were, and that Nathan should maintain the purity of their family line, but in those days the traditions were already breaking down, especially in the growing city of Jerusalem. I know Nathan's father wanted him to become a scribe in the Temple there, and marrying out of the line would jeopardise his chances, but Nathan had already confided to me that he had no wish for a scribe's role.

'It's boring and I want to remain in the fresh air undertaking honest toil and growing crops and herding sheep and goats like most of the other boys. I want to keep my friends I see in the synagogue every day and be like them, not get shut away in a stuffy old office at the back of the Temple.'

Nathan said that when he first told them of his intention, his mother and father were strongly opposed to the marriage, and it took nearly three months of arguing before they began to realise that he was not going to back down. At last they caved in and sent for my father and decided to make the best of it and told him that they were willing to consider a betrothal only on the grounds of the friendship Zechariah and my father had formed over many years of meeting daily at the market stall. So I got what I wanted and was betrothed immediately after I became of age. I remember the excitement I felt when Nathan told me that his parents had given in and were going to allow us to get married. His mother pretended to be pleased and told everyone that we had known each other since we were both tiny children and had always been intended for each other despite the difference in our families' status.

I'm still wide awake. I don't know why, but I suddenly feel anxious about Benjamin. I get up and peer at him. He's completely still, I can't hear him breathing, and for a second I panic. Then I hear him sigh and relief floods over me. Now I'm up I go and get a draught of water to see if it will settle me.

Back in bed, my thoughts continue to disturb my peace. It's too hot, I toss and turn. Looking at my son reminds me of the things my mother-in-law kept on at me about when we got married. She certainly made it her business to instruct me in my wifely duties.

'Your first priority is to produce a son for Nathan and a grandson for us. And look after my son as we have always done. He's used to good food properly cooked. I hope your mother has taught you well.'

It was clear to me that only having a boy would establish my status as their son's wife. When they found that Nathan had eventually made me pregnant they were delighted although I know my own mother was very worried on my behalf because I was still only fourteen and small and she was concerned that I would find it difficult to give birth. It is true that I suffered a lot during the later stages of my pregnancy, becoming very tired and struggling to carry out all my duties, especially the fetching of water. Nathan was most considerate and even fetched water after dark so that he would not be ridiculed – he didn't want his mother especially to have any reason to criticise me.

The birth itself was agony – I never believed anything could be so painful despite everything my mother told me. The labour went on for hours – they say it often is with the first child – but eventually dear Benjamin came into the world and when they put him in my arms and told me that he was a healthy boy, I was so relieved and proud. Martha even kissed me and told me that I was a good wife to her son!

My mother was with me throughout the labour assisting the midwife, although she found it difficult looking after Ishmael at the same time. The midwife got cross when he kept getting in the way, falling over when he tried to stand and look closely at what was happening, although at that stage there was little to see. In the end poor Ishmael was banished to squat in the corner and threatened with dire punishment if he moved again before the baby appeared, not that I remember as I had other things on my mind. Mother told me that afterwards. At one stage my mother cried and said that she had expected it to be my older sister, Rhoda, who she'd have been helping first in childbirth.

Rhoda! Why has my older sister come into my mind now? I still miss her, especially at times like this when I'm lying awake. Tears are forming in my eyes even as I think of her. Just when she was reaching marriageable age and my father was beginning negotiations to find her a suitable husband, she'd fallen sick with a nasty fever and died within a couple of days. I remember being shocked and frightened when Rhoda was taken so ill. She'd looked after me when I was little and I couldn't believe I'd never see her again. And seeing my mother and father crying, that was strange and unnerving. I'd never seen a grown-up cry before and it made me very confused and added to my own grief. Even now I find I'm crying. Why? It must be at least five or six years ago. I thought I'd got over it.

All these thoughts are whirling through my mind and I suppose at some stage they merge with my dreams in sleep. I remember struggling and screaming and clinging to my sister as her body lay wrapped in a white cloth, but I'm not sure if this ever really happened. My mother told me later that she was worried that I'd never allowed myself to grieve properly for my sister's death, that I'd bottled it up and that my face had just clouded over whenever her name was mentioned, that I'd never cried but just seemed withdrawn.

Suddenly I'm caught up in the riot in Jerusalem and we are being tossed around by the soldiers, they have my sister and are throwing her in the air, then they grab me and toss me to the sky and I am falling, falling … Now I'm awake again. My shift is soaked in sweat. I remember the fear. It must somehow have been about the time I was in Jerusalem with my father and I saw the fight. I don't know what caused it – but I saw the soldiers come and slash at people with their swords. I saw one man with his arm bleeding and another screaming, blood pouring down his face. My father grabbed me and pushed us through the throng and I remember bouncing in his arms as he ran out of the city and didn't put me down until we were outside the city wall and on the road back to Bethlehem. I'm sure my sister wasn't with us, so I've no idea why she was in my dream.

I'm not sure why I've woken up again - whether it was my dream or whether Benjamin stirred and alerted me - I'd better get up and look. Why am I so agitated for him? I can't see anything wrong, he's alright I think. He seems to be sleeping peacefully now. I don't know what time it is. It's pitch dark and I can't hear any movements outside. I must try to sleep again or I'll be tired all tomorrow.

The dream has disturbed me. As I lie down again, the events of that horrific day - it must be over seven years ago now because I was only eight or nine then - come flooding back to me. The sheer panic I felt as we got surrounded by soldiers and the crowds trying to escape from them trampling each other, people falling over and getting crushed, while my father lifted me up and tried to escape from the throng. And the noise - the cracks of the soldiers' whips, the screams and bloodcurdling shrieks of people the swords had slashed, the total confusion. I've never really understood what it was all about. I've only been into Jerusalem twice since - I'm scared to, in case I get caught in a riot again.

'Rachel,' my father used to tell me, 'don't be so frightened. I've been to Jerusalem many times quite safely. There are always Roman soldiers about, they try to keep the peace. I've never seen crowd violence before or since.'

Then other bad things come into my mind - I don't know why I'm feeling so morbid with my gorgeous son and husband both sleeping so peacefully beside me. I remember the time that I was ill - I must have been about seven years old I think - and they thought I was going to die. I remember my mother holding my wrist and squeezing it so tightly that it hurt and when they thought I was asleep, I heard her talking to my father.

'I'm frightened that we're losing Rachel. Please go quickly and find another physician straight away. I can't bear the thought of losing our other daughter.'

I've never told them that I overheard, and I puzzled for a long time why they thought they'd lost me when I was lying in the bed in front of them! And then my mind flits to the time, just before I got married, when I had to rescue Ishmael from a group of soldiers. He'd been attracted by their uniforms and one of them was on horseback and he'd gone too close to have a look. One of the soldiers yelled at him to get out of the way and because of his legs he wasn't quick enough and one soldier picked him up and flung him into a ditch and was going to strike him when I yelled and rushed to stop him, putting myself between the soldier and the boy. I remember shouting that he was a cripple and how dare he hit him and afterwards when the soldiers had gone, I trembled all over and nearly fainted. Miriam's father brought us both home and told my mother how brave I'd been and mother was so polite to him, then scolded both of us when he'd gone for being so foolish and warned us to stay away from soldiers.

Still I can't get to sleep. It's as if my whole life is flashing through my head. Some say this is what happens when you are dying. I'm not dying, am I? Why am I so disturbed? Why are all these fears flooding back to me. It's stupid, I'm so fortunate. I suppose I'm afraid that suddenly everything good might be taken away from me.

And now my thoughts roam to the time of the great famine when it was so difficult to buy bread and everyone was hungry, how worried my mother and father were and how thin we all got. I can remember crying a lot because the hunger pain was so bad and Rhoda telling me not to be such a baby, we were all suffering just the same and no-one else was crying.

'Be thankful for once that the Romans are here,' I heard my father say to a neighbour. Apparently they'd arranged relief supplies from their country far away across the sea where they had grain to spare. That was the only time I ever heard him say anything good about the Romans, although he didn't usually say much out loud like some of our neighbours did, always complaining about what they were doing in Jerusalem and also about our King Herod who wouldn't stand up for us but was too much a friend of the Romans.

I don't know how much longer I was thinking like this, or when I finally got to sleep, for before I realise it, I hear movements and see the beams of light shafting into the room and watch Nathan as he slips from his cover and begins to dress ready for the fields. It's my duty to get up and prepare something for him to eat before he goes out. I feel sleepy still and hope that Benjamin does not wake until Nathan's away so I can concentrate on my husband first. Ah well, at least it's daylight now and I can banish all those dark thoughts from my mind. I wonder if there's any news of Mari and Joseph yet. Perhaps someone at the well this morning will have found out something.

Chapter 4
Rachel

I'm so tired that Nathan is up and about before I come round. I'm still trying to open my eyes when I sense him leaning over me.

'Well, lazybones, didn't you get much sleep last night? Did Ben keep you awake?'

'Didn't you hear him? No, of course you didn't – you were snoring away. I don't know how you manage to stay asleep when Ben's so restless.'

'It's from healthy exercise in the field making sure you lot get fed properly.'

'I know, Nathan. I'm not complaining. But the little devil kept me awake half the night, then I couldn't get to sleep afterwards. I had lots of dark thoughts that wouldn't go away. I don't know why I worry so much when everything is going so well. I'm feeling a bit more lively now. I'll get up and get your food.'

'I'll help you. Ben's still asleep at the moment. If I get ready quickly I can be off before he wakes, then you can look after him at your leisure without me getting in the way.'

Nathan helps me prepare the food he'll take with him to the field. As he kisses me goodbye and slips out into the dawn, I wonder if he still enjoys the outdoor life rather than the softer option of becoming a scribe as his father had planned for him.

Last week his father had a go at him in my hearing.

'Nathan,' I overheard, 'there's still time for you to change your mind. I could get you a scribe's job assisting Mordecai, despite you not marrying a Levite. He owes me a favour for what I did for him a few months ago.'

'No, Father, leave me in peace, would you! I'm fed up with you trying to persuade me every time we meet. You know I'm happy in the fields and I intend to stay that way.'

'But you could better yourself, boy. It took our family a long time to be accepted in the Jerusalem Temple. Why give up all this now? Think of your son! You're sacrificing a career opportunity for him too in years to come.'

'Father, drop it will you! Just get it into your head that I don't want to be a scribe!'

'You're too headstrong. We've given in too much to you. We should never have allowed you to marry beneath you. A different more suitable wife wouldn't allow you to get away with neglecting an opportunity like this.'

'Leave Rachel out of it. She's a good woman, worth far more than some of the daughters of the priests and scribes you'd have preferred for me.'

'Don't talk to me like that. I'm your father, you owe me respect!'

'Then show me some respect too. You forget I'm a man now with a wife and son and I'll make my own decisions!'

I had never heard Nathan lose his temper with his father before, and after his still angry father had left, Nathan realised that I'd overheard everything.

'I'm sorry, Rachel,' he'd said to me afterwards, 'my father is much too concerned with his own status. I think my mother nags him about it. I don't care about such things. You're my beloved wife and I'm going to provide for you and our children ...' (he actually said 'our children!' We only have one at present but he thinks any time now we may add to our family). 'It's a healthier life than staying indoors all day and just copying out old parchments.'

I know his father says that one day he could become a teacher for the younger boys - he would be able to teach Benjamin when he is older - and I think that would be nice too, but Nathan won't have it and so I keep quiet.

Ben is awake soon after his father has left and I bathe him and let him suckle a while before giving him a little of the more substantial food I've prepared. Then it is time for us to go and fetch the day's water. I can carry two vessels now that

Benjamin can walk which means that I don't have to return in the afternoon for a refill unless I have guests for our evening meal - sometimes my mother and father call and join us. Nathan's parents only came to our house for a meal once, although we regularly are invited to join them in their home.

It's a slow business to get to the well though, because Ben is interested in everything and we never quite go in a straight line! This time he picks up a stick and wants to poke every stone and flower to see what's underneath. We have to stop outside old widow Sarah's house to see her chickens - they're just like ours, I tell him, but to him they are a fresh distraction and he wants to wait until the red-combed cockerel emerges from the back yard into view.

We eventually get to the well and find ourselves at the back of a queue of women waiting to draw water. Luckily there are many children playing around and Benjamin dashes off to play with other toddlers.

'Miriam, Naomi, Judith, make sure the little ones don't fall over or get into mischief,' calls out one of the women.

This frees us women to share the latest gossip, and because there's not much other news at the moment, Mari and Joseph's disappearance is still the topic of much speculation.

'I heard Mari's mother had died,' says old widow Bethan.

'Nonsense,' says another, 'the girl's taken Joshua to dedicate him to the Temple but they refused him and she can't face us.'

'Where on earth did you hear that?'

'Oh, old widow Sarah said that to me yesterday evening.'

'And you believed that old bat? She lives in a world of her own imagination. I don't take seriously anything she says.'

'I don't know about all that,' says Susannah. 'There are now at least half a dozen upset men waiting for the implements Joseph had promised to supply. Unless he comes back soon with a good excuse, he'll lose all his trade.'

They know I was particularly friendly with Mari so I get pumped for everything that I can remember that might have any significance at all.

'Come on, Rachel,' Susannah wheedles. 'You must know. You're always together. Surely she told you something.'

'Well, I know she has her family in Nazareth in Galilee – you all know that anyway - and that she has a widowed mother and younger siblings. Perhaps her mother is ill or her uncle Eli who is a priest at the synagogue there has died because he must be getting to a good age.'

She had been brought up by this priest apparently after the death of her father.

'There was a rumour that her father was a freedom fighter living in the hills above the Lake Genneseret, one of a band that was taking on the Romans and Herod's soldiers, but he'd been killed in an encounter with them.'

Someone pipes up, 'Perhaps Joseph is a secret fighter too and had to escape.'

'You don't know what you're talking about. That's complete nonsense, that is, Joseph is the last person to engage in such an enterprise especially with his young wife and toddler to look after.'

Then under further questioning I stupidly let out that she thought that Joshua was a special child and that leads to a flurry of questions which I can't stop. Having already said too much, they won't stop until they've dragged everything from me that Mari ever said, most of which I don't believe anyway.

'Come on, Rachel,' they say. 'You can't stop there. You do know more. Why does she think Joshua is a miracle?'

'Well, one night she told me… Well, no, I can't say that. I don't believe it.'

'What don't you believe?'

'I think she must have been drunk when she said it. We'd both been at a wedding celebration.'

'Come on, Rachel, you can't leave us up in the air like this. What did she tell you?'

'Well, she claimed that she'd been told that he was the promised Messiah.'

'What?!'

They're all agog now.

'What on earth makes her think that?'

'She said she'd been a virgin until Joshua was born.'

Everyone falls about laughing. That's just too much and poor Mari's name is dragged through the mud.

I feel ashamed now that I've let my friend down and I'm worried what she will say to me if she returns now and finds I've blabbed all her secrets to everyone in the village. Because that is what will happen now - the story will go round like wildfire and get exaggerated (if that's possible).

'Stop, don't go on so. Mari only told me this once and I didn't believe her, I thought she was teasing me. She was always saying things like that, things that seemed odd, and I thought she just had a vivid imagination and was a born story-teller.'

'You're making excuses for her. She's a weird one, she is.'

Another adds, 'She's always bragging about what her Joshua can do. I bet she's trying to convince us all that he's a cut above us.'

'You're being cruel. Mari doesn't brag about him. And anyway, even if she did, she'd have good reason. You're all just jealous of her.'

'You've got to admit that she does say some odd things sometimes.'

'No, she just used to tell Joshua all sorts of wondrous stories - I thought they were complete fiction, just stories to amuse Joshua. It seemed to me that they were a bit too complicated and outrageous for such a small child. But I used to listen because she was so enthusiastic and would get carried away …'

'You really believed her, didn't you? I didn't think you were such a fool.'

'No, don't interrupt me. Let me finish. It was as if she was really there when she told them. Her eyes used to light up and she would be so happy, then she used to hint at dark things that had happened to her, but she would never tell me what, however much I tried to get her to confide in me.'

It doesn't matter how much I protest now, the stories about Mari will fly around the village and when - or if - she comes back she'll have a tough time explaining what really happened and not be the butt of ridicule. Anyway, in the end no-one believed what she'd apparently said about herself.

'It's all too silly for words,' says Susannah. 'If the girl said things like that, she was obviously drunk.'

'I'm surprised you took her seriously,' says Rebecca to me. 'Are you sure she wasn't pulling your leg? She's never said anything remotely like that to me and I've chatted to her every day since she settled here.'

'I expect you're right,' I say, grasping the opportunity to try to undo the damage I've done to Mari's reputation. 'Much more likely that she and Joseph have gone to Galilee because of some unexpected family crisis there.'

'That's the most likely reason,' agrees Rebecca, 'though why she failed to confide in us is a mystery.'

It's the general view that it must have been at Mari's instigation because Joseph has no known living relatives and in any case this is his home village. And it's assumed that it was Mari who had pushed Joseph into such a rapid departure without telling anyone - everyone was sure that Joseph would have wanted to stay to finish his commitments.

'Mari would have been impatient if she got news late at night. I bet she pushed Joseph into leaving immediately. I think she usually gets her way. Despite her little size, she's a strong character although she's much younger than Joseph.' It's Susannah again, thinking she knows Mari. I'm not so sure she's right there. Joseph is a quiet one, but he can be quite firm.

Just when I think they are going to let the matter drop, someone, Martha I think it is, suddenly says, 'What did you make of the strangers who came to their house a couple of nights ago?'

Everyone shakes their heads.

'I didn't see anyone. My husband said no-one knew who they were or where they were from and they'd come and gone under nightfall.'

'My husband said they must have been messengers from Mari's home village with the news that had caused their sudden departure.'

Eventually the interest lapses and we get on with the tiring job of hauling up the water and carrying it back home. This was the bit I most dislike. The full water pots are heavy and although I try to balance them using a yoke on each shoulder - one that Joseph had made for me and refused to accept any money for, a gift he said, because of my friendship and welcome to Mari - they drag and cause my shoulders to ache and Benjamin will keep running off and holding me up when all I want is to get home and have a rest before attending to washing clothes and preparing the evening meal. I get quite cross with Ben when he runs off with one of the older girls – I'm not pleased with her either because she's encouraging him, and I make a mental note to ask her mother to tell her not to keep playing with the boy when it's time to go.

At least by the time we get back the sun is high in the sky and Benjamin begins to look tired after all his exertion and goes back to sleep without too much opposition. I take a draught of water to quench my thirst and mop my brow to remove the sweat and lie down on my mat for a few minutes respite. My unwise babbling to the other women bothers me even more now and I feel a traitor to Mari in letting on so much. After all, it was only once that she had told me about the story of Joshua being the Messiah and that she'd never had intercourse with any man before he was born. Even as I think about it, I begin to wonder if I've made it up. We'd talked late into the night on one occasion and we were flushed with wine after we'd attended the wedding of a girl in the village and perhaps our heads were spinning a little and I misunderstood what she'd said.

Afterwards when I'd tried to get her to say more, she'd clammed up and tried to get me off the subject as if she was embarrassed to have ever mentioned it. And now I've opened it up to everyone. Will she ever forgive me? Can we still be friends? I began to feel sorry for myself. Then I turn and see Benjamin sleeping so peacefully. At least I have him and Nathan whatever Mari thinks. It would be a pity to lose that friendship, but as long as I have my own family, that is what's important. And I turn over and wait for Benjamin to stir…

Chapter 5
Herod

'The bloody foot, I can't bloody stand it. Joachim, come here, come and bathe this wretched leg.'

I sit up on my haunches and glare at my night servant who has done nothing to deserve the look I give him. He scurries off, with a hurried 'Yes, of course, your majesty,' and is gone to fetch some water and soothing ointment. It isn't midnight yet and eight long hours stretch out before me, hours of darkness and black pain and despair. I groan as the movement I make shoots arrows of fire through my leg up through my hips and to my stomach. Haven't they anything that can blot out this throbbing nightly agony other than render me comatose with one of their hideous filtres? Sixty-seven years old, the Jew's scriptures say that our span is threescore years and ten, so I've just under three more years to endure and I don't know that I can make it - what's more, I'm not sure now that I want to. Everything's fallen apart these last few years, there's little more I can accomplish in this gruesome state. I can give a few more orders perhaps, things will happen because I say so, but there is little I shall accomplish with my own hands or actions.

Joachim reappears with a bowl of steaming water and puts it beside the bedroll. He bows and murmurs the necessary 'Your majesty' again under his breath and begins to wipe the warm damp cloth gently over my swollen tortured rotting flesh. I wish he'd say something to take my mind off the parlous state I'm in, but he won't say anything except in response to my command or invitation and I'm too full of my woes, too tired to think of anything else. I can't concentrate, it's bad enough during the day when I have government business to conduct. It's months since I slept for more than a couple of hours during the night watch.

At last he's finished his task, the stinking ointment will give a little temporary relief from the worst pain, but it'll be a miracle if I can snatch a few minutes' sleep. He takes up his position outside the hanging robes of my ante-chamber so he is in earshot should I need him further, and I am alone. Alone with my thoughts because, as I suspected, I can't bloody sleep.

Huh, my thoughts! What a damned mess they are now. I was Caesar's choice for this throne and now I can't even sit on the crappy thing in comfort. He still expects me to keep control here and I can't control my own fractious family. Oh Alexander and what's your bloody name … Aristobulus, I can't even remember my own son's name now … what was I thinking? Oh, yes, why, oh why, did you plot against me? What did you intend to do? Were you going to dispose of me and then divide the kingdom among yourselves? Would one of you do as I did and murder your brother to have it all for yourself?

Oh, gods' truth, give me strength, I can't stand it. They should chop it off, can't be worse. A one-legged king. I'll play the fool and let that idiot rule in my place. Can't do any worse. Let him take the blame!

And Aristo, you bloody rogue, what were you going to do about big brother Antipater? If you had murdered me, then you surely would have done away with him too. No wonder he was my informant on your treacherous plans. What had turned you away from me? I gave you so much, you were the favoured sons of my favourite wife, you could have had so much anyway without taking such an extreme step against me. Did you really think I'd leave you nothing? That I'd let Antipater rule over the whole kingdom as the Romans granted me? The Romans would never have allowed that, Antipater has not proved himself to the Emperor as I did on numerous occasions. They'd have split the kingdom up even if I had not decreed it. Instead you were impatient, you wanted too much too soon. You were too like your mother, Mariamne, who wanted her own way. I'd have given her almost anything except the throne itself, which she wanted for her young brother. So she named you after him. Have you inherited her loathing of me despite the love I bestowed and still had for her and you? It was you, Aristobulus, wasn't it, that poisoned the mind of your brother Alexander, and got him to plot with you. Yes, he was popular with my troops, perhaps with him on your side you'd have got away with it.

So you made me do it. Don't throw that hurtful look at me, don't look at me, I tell you! It's no use you denying the treachery you'd planned. Antipater told me everything, I wanted to spare you from torture, but you wouldn't admit to what was so bloody obvious. So I had to get Alexander to confess, you forced him to the torture by your stubbornness. He was reluctant to admit that you were the instigator… Where's that bloody servant, where's anybody? What the hell am I talking about … I know, I know you were even… even what? Is he listening to me behind the curtain? I didn't want to see you die, but you insisted that I watch your execution. I thought at least I'd get your confession and plea for mercy. Then you were fucking defiant looking at me in that hurtful way before I shut my ears and ordered the execution to continue. Ugh, your head rolled from the block, your eyes still open staring at me. Be gone, you damned ghost, don't think you can haunt me now. Your curse will not wound me further. You think you're making me suffer now, but I tell you, my limbs were already in travail before this wretched day dawned. I'd have stopped the execution of Alexander had I known your obstinacy, but that act had already been carried out in the barracks, I could not bear to watch that. I was a fool to think Alexander was wholeheartedly in this plot, I should have spared his life at least. So he is on my raddled conscience now. So, Aristobulus, what of your vile brood now? Shall I fuck your wife and bugger her gaggle of sons, are they already vipers in the nest? Will your treachery and my butchery poison the mind of the boy Agrippa? Will he one day inherit or will he try to avenge himself on Antipater and suffer the same fate as his father?

'Aaagh! By Zeus and Jehovah, it's too much. I cannot take much more.'

I try to move just then and the pain sears through my right leg. If I stay still my limbs ache and I get bedsores. Joachim comes running but there is nothing he can do.

'Get out! Don't listen to my every breath.'

The wretched man would eavesdrop on the thoughts revolving round my head if I gave him the chance. There was a time I'd have kicked him round the courtyard for such presumption. It's been over a year now since I fell from the blasted horse and injured this leg. The physicians just thought I'd pulled a muscle. Then, when it swelled and discoloured, they said it was a blood clot. What did they do? Nothing! They argued amongst themselves and all the time the leg got worse. Bah, they pretend to know, they look so thoughtful, but it's just superficial. They haven't a fucking clue. I should kick them out and get one of the Galilean self-promoted miracle workers to have a go. They couldn't do any worse. And if they failed, I could execute them for their failure and their preposterous claims, killing two birds with one stone, so to speak, undermining the blasphemous rabble which follows them and creates difficulties for my soldiers there.

Oh, Alex! Why did you listen to your brother? You'd have made a fine successor! You were the only one who understood the troops, who had their respect. You were the only one who could hold on to the lands we Herod clan have gathered from the Romans. You were the only one who might have earned the trust of Octavian, what chance now Antipater? That self-serving thug, he knew what he was doing when he denounced you and Aristobulus. He was securing his own succession, because he knew he'd have a bloody fight on his hands. He knew the army would have preferred you. I'll have to watch him like a hawk. If he thinks I might have other ideas, he'll see me off by bribing one of those incompetent mendicants to slip me some poison under the pretext of another soothing filtre. So what if I did pass him over for one of my other sons? Which of them is worthy of the role? Herod Antipas? He's weak, he'd barely hang on to Galilee if I bequeathed that god-forsaken state to him. His brother Archelaus? A better bet perhaps, I'm not sure he's ruthless enough, the others will do for him unless he gets in first and I can't see him doing that. Philip? Maybe. Olympias, Phasael and the others? They're too young, unknown quantities at the moment, and I haven't got much time.

'Ye gods, this ruddy leg hurts! Anyone, help me!'

'Yes, Sire?'

'Oh, it's you. Ignore me. You can't do anything unless you're a miracle-worker. Are you a fucking miracle-worker?'

'No, Sire.'

'Then go away and don't bloody pester me!'

Soon I'll be gone. Thank the gods! Hope this leg doesn't chase me into immortality. Don't want. Just let me feel nothing, that's all I ask. I've done my bit. What sort of legacy will this lot leave for history? Can I trust any of them to enhance the name of Herod, build on the achievements I've made? I've been friends with the greatest of the age, Octavian, the Caesar Augustus, and before that, Marc Antony. In Caesar's honour I've built a great harbour and fort at Caesarea and the Emperor honoured me with his presence at its dedication. I've built the Jews their Temple, outdoing that of Solomon, although the Pharisees and Sadducees squabble over its management and ritual. What thanks do I get? Most Jews think it blasphemous that it was built by a foreigner, although they all flock to it at festivals. I've kept the peace, the Romans have improved the city, I've got the taxes to the Romans without any insurrections here despite the crippling rates imposed for the new works undertaken.

I'm still awake. I guess not an hour has yet passed. I can't think straight, yet sleep will not come. I'm drowsy, then the throbbing pain brings me to full consciousness. The thoughts

I'm having reverberate round my brain. As I toss, then wince, and try to lie still once more, my mind revisits the argument raging through my head, Alexander and Aristobulus and Antipater and Antipas and Archelaus and Philip. Where are all the women who bare these sons? Why aren't they here with me, soothing my brow, my brain? Why won't they come near, while away the night hours with me? Why is the only one that I feel near me Mariamne, whom I had executed nearly twenty five years ago? If she were here now she would be a screaming nagging hag, but I can only remember the voluptuous woman who captivated me and I fucked night after night until I was satiated with her. I know she hated me yet she put up with my nightly demands, she allowed her lusts to merge with mine. Perhaps she ignored the person that I was, treated me as a sex object bent to her own desires, it didn't matter, I adored her. And she bore my most favoured sons, Alexander and Aristobulus and now I've fucking killed them.

For a while I drift into a light doze and Mariamne does come to me, eyes glinting, shedding her diaphanous robes letting me touch her exquisite skin, and then under my very eyes that skin ages, becomes rough and wrinkled and her face looks at me, an aged crone, then the skin falls away from even that hideous spectacle and becomes a leering skull. I awake dripping sweat, groaning aloud in pain and horror.

Antipater. My thoughts fill with him again. The more I think about him, the less confident I feel about his motives and the future in his hands. I don't trust him. His betrayal of his brothers was too enthusiastic, he revelled in their downfall. Perhaps he fabricated part of the evidence for his own ends. I cannot bear the thought that perhaps Alexander was innocent. Yet he confessed under torture. Surely if he had been innocent he would have withstood that test? He was a brave soldier, surely torture would not have broken him so that he made a false confession? I will set spies to watch Antipater's every move. They will report to me each day all his activities, his friends, they will inveigle themselves into his company and feign friendship with the monster. And if I find so much of a hint of treachery, intents upon my person, I'll have him follow his brothers to the block. I'd better draw up contingency plans should that occur. I'll make other wills. Perhaps Herod Antipas should inherit after all, or perhaps I could split the kingdom, put Archelaus in charge of Judea, and place Antipas and Philip into the more remote regions giving Archelaus a chance to establish himself in Jerusalem and gather sufficient allies to hold off any open rebellion or intrigue from the others.

I'm getting confused now, my mind is going round in circles, whatever I start to think breaks up and I see the snags before I've thought it through. I'm too tired to contemplate such strategic things properly at this hour, yet I can't stop my mind being occupied by such matters for other matters are mundane, are trivia. The only other thing I am aware of is my bloody pain and I'm trying to divert my brain away from this pointless indulgence. My advisors seek to influence me, but I know they split into factions, how do I know which one to trust? They already see my end approaching and they are scrambling around trying to guess which of my sons to ally themselves with. Well, the ones that chose Alexander or Aristobulus are flailing around now in the darkness, if they jump to Antipater perhaps they'll regret that too. They were busy reminding me yesterday that my end is foretold anyway, the superstitious buffoons. Well if they're right, I'll see I take them with me. They spoke of a prophecy foretold in the Jewish scriptures that the longed for Messiah will arise after seventy-seven generations from the first man. Then they tell me, the bastards, that I'm of the seventy-sixth generation, so I needn't worry about my succession after all. What fools! They think I'm too weak to condemn them for such blasphemy? It only needs a word from me to my faithful guards, they do not realise how near the edge they are treading. Another word out of place and I'll have them strung up for the birds to pick to pieces.

And they think that no-one will regret my passing? I'll fucking show them. I'm making a list of everyone who's offended me these last few years and I'll leave instructions in my will for all of them to be brought to the hippodrome. They'll think they've been invited to some bloody boring ceremony as my memorial, they'll not dare to absent themselves. And when they're there and waiting for something to happen, my guards will slaughter every single one of them. No mourning at my death? We'll see about that. Half of Jerusalem will have lost someone, there'll be plenty of funerals, plenty of wailing. I've got over two hundred on the list already. At least Antipater will have no qualms in carrying out my instructions. He'll enjoy the carnage, that bloodthirsty son of mine, that'll ensure no Jew dares to oppose him. Making peace with the Romans after that might be a bit more tricky, but that'll be his problem, not mine.

Only Joachim knows of the whereabouts of this list. Perhaps I ought to take Antipater into my confidence. He'll want to spare one or two of the courtiers who have been his supporters, I'm fooling myself if I think he'll sacrifice them too. I'll add those bumptious Jewish priests who keep feeding me this prophecy nonsense, and those ones that advised me the other day when the Persian astrologers came with some fairy tale about a new king being born. I ask you, all this bloody way and they got it fucking wrong! I've had no children now for nearly four years and the last one was a runt of a girl anyway. Then they have the gall to tell me that it could be this Messiah, this scion of the seventy-seventh generation who is going to drive the Romans out, ha ha! What with, I ask? A rabble of home-grown terrorists from upper Galilee? They're nothing more than crude and greedy bandits preying on rich men who've given support to art, culture and education, things they despise.

Nonsense though it is, it could be bloody dangerous. It'll give some fool the idea that he can mount a challenge against me using this so-called Messiah, if they can convince some

Jews that they've got a miraculous baby somewhere. Perhaps even one of my sons will try it on, offering to be regent until the boy comes of age and then having him executed or assassinated under some pretext. When one of the astrologers asked us where a king could be born if not in our royal palace, some idiot priest quoted an obscure scripture that mentions the crap town of Bethlehem. That wretched peasant village of all places, five miles from here, anyone of any worth soon comes to the city here. Then they quote their ancestor David who apparently came from that place, they think he's the king to end all kings and it must be seven or eight hundred years since he lived. What did he achieve that I haven't? Why don't they honour the king they've got, instead of worshipping some corpse that's been rotting in the grave for centuries? Did David give them a magnificent Temple? No, that was his son, Solomon, and the one I've built is bigger. Did he build cities like Caesarea and foster trade that has made many Jews rich beyond compare with ancient times? No, of course he didn't. Did he maintain the peace and prosperity of his country? No, he was always fighting wars with neighbouring tribes. The Jews don't realise the debt they owe to me and the Romans for the prosperity and civilisation we've brought to this country.

'Joachim, Joachim!'

He comes running.

'Yes, your majesty?'

'Bathe my bloody leg again and get me some more of that filtre preparation that is meant to dull the pain.'

He hesitates. He knows that too much of that stuff will make me even more confused and delirious, but I don't care, it will shorten the hours until daylight. He wants to warn me, but he dare not. He does not trust my temper. He fears I'll add his name to the list I've entrusted to his care. He obeys my command. For a few precious minutes I can feel the balm and hope for oblivion for a short while. Then he is finished. But nothing happens. My mind will still not rest. Those astrologers were instructed to return to me to tell me if they'd found this so-called baby king. That was days ago, surely they should have returned by now? Huh, perhaps they're still looking, still searching, frustrated because there's nothing to find.

This thought will not go away now. Why haven't they returned? Have they really found the prophesied child? Would they tell me if they had? I don't trust them, why should they trust me? I'll have a search made for them, force them back to explain to me, I don't care who they are, they can't treat me with such lack of respect.

'Joachim, Joachim!'

'Yes, your majesty?

'Fetch Uriah!'

'But it's well past midnight, your majesty.'

'I don't fucking care, wake him if necessary and bloody well bring him here.'

Uriah claims to be my chief advisor, that's what he tells others any way. I make a pretence of listening to him sometimes, then do what I will. And he pretends that it was him who advised me so. It's a long time before Uriah appears and I'm getting impatient.

'Uriah, organise a search for the astrologers who claimed they'd come to honour the birth of a king.'

'Your majesty, this has already been done. When they failed to return here within two days, I organised such a search immediately.'

'Well, why haven't you bloody well brought them to me, then? What did they have to say?'

'Your majesty, we couldn't find them. We searched everywhere. We've tried all the inns. There were rumours that they had left the same night after taking our advice earlier in the day, and we had soldiers set off in pursuit along the way to Jericho and the East, but although they went over 50 miles, there was no sign of them and no-one admitted to seeing any strangers.'

'They fucking tricked you. Foreigners in a strange country and they managed to deceive you. I'm surrounded by nothing but fools. Get out of my fucking sight. You're flaming useless.'

I'm glad to see the wretched man is frightened, he doesn't know whether I'll have him punished now or later. Poor bloody fool, I'll just add him to my list. He backs out nearly tripping over his own feet.

So, they tricked me. Why? Was that because they found nothing and were too humiliated to come back and own up to their frustration, months of travelling for nothing, an absurd wild goose chase? But if, as Uriah said, they left the same night, they must have found something. They would not have given up so easily. What did they find? And if they found a baby they convinced themselves was this prince, why did they not return to me? Who told them to leave quickly? Is there some truth in this ancient prophecy after all? Or at least enough similarity for them to think it is the truth, which could be just as dangerous. We must nip it in the bud. How?

I'm trying to think this through but I keep falling into a light doze. Then my fevered imagination merges with dreams, horrible dreams in which my sons and Mariamne laugh at me, and accuse me of being cuckolded, that one of my wives has born a son I know nothing of. Then the mothers of Bethlehem are swarming all over the palace all crying out 'this is the one, this is the one' until I'm shouting at them to stop the fucking noise.

Joachim comes rushing in.

'Sire, you called out. What do you want? Can I bring you something?'

'Go away, Joachim, it's alright. I was just dreaming.'

I've got to do something to get to the bottom of this. I can't leave the uncertainty to fester on. I can call the commander of my forces in the morning and question him about the search they've made, but what will that tell me? Only the same as Uriah reported. He certainly had no motive to hold back anything he knew. He's too frightened of me. So what do I know? The astrologers said they saw a sign back in their own country. That must have been several months ago, then they would have had preparations for the journey and they must have been travelling for several weeks. So when would the baby, if there was one, have been born? How old would he be now? Probably about nine months, perhaps a year or even more, perhaps eighteen months at most. And how many boys of that age would there be in a town like Bethlehem?

'Joachim!'

He comes quickly like a faithful dog, ever willing to be kicked. It is less boring for him if I keep him occupied.

'Joachim, how big is Bethlehem. How many inhabitants?'

'It's not too large, Sire. Between five hundred and a thousand I should think, including women and children. Do you want me to fetch Uriah again?'

'No, that is near enough.'

'Do you want anything else, your majesty?'

'No, not for the moment.'

Five hundred, let's say a thousand to be on the safe side. How many children will that be? At least half I would guess. And how many will be babies? A tenth of those? Up to fifty. And half will be girls, so that leaves twenty five baby boys. And up to two years old to be sure? Another twenty five perhaps. Fifty children and any of them could be a threat if this story gets around as it will. Have I got that right? I can't trust my brain to calculate with accuracy at the moment. Does it sound right? Fifty out of a thousand. Twenty five out of five hundred. A hundred if Joachim has underestimated the size of the village. Does it matter? One would be bad enough.

Thoughts are festering in my mind. Why not get it over quickly? I could be tormented for days if this uncertainty remains. Easy enough after all. My Idumean troops will not hesitate, they've always been loyal and they have no family links to this Judean village. What are a few lives hardly started, worthless peasants? I'm saving them from a life of bloody poverty and drudgery. They should thank me. Shall I consult Uriah again? A recipe for indecision that would be - he'll remonstrate with me, if he has the courage, he'll warn me that I will alienate not just the Jews in that village but the message will spread. What does that matter? Most Jews don't like me anyway. The influential ones know where their favours lie and they won't complain. And the Romans, they couldn't care less. They'll just see the actions of a strong king able to keep order and ensure his own succession. No problems there. Oh, hell and damnation! This abominable pain gets no better, I can't be bothered to think this through any further. I'm the fucking king, they'll do what I ask and ask no questions either.

'Joachim, Joachim.'

'Yes, your majesty.'

'Fetch Judah, the commander of my guard. Don't look so quizzical. Now, at once!'

'Yes, Sire.'

What if it is barely two hours past midnight? Soldiers are paid to be on their guard. He should be alert, not sleeping. He could sort it out by dawn and be back inside the barracks before crowds begin to come onto the streets, and it'll take a day before the news of any backlash begins to filter through to the city. I'll have a few extra troops patrol the main thoroughfares just in case of any trouble.

He doesn't take long and I'm pleased to see he's in full uniform, no quick panic leaving details unattended to.

Judah salutes.

'Your majesty, what is your wish? Is there some emergency that needs my immediate attention?'

'Yes, Judah. I want you to take handpicked men from your company and put down a potential challenge to my authority before daybreak.'

'Where, Sire? How big is the danger? Are there many men involved and are they armed?'

'There's rumour of a baby born in Bethlehem village that is claimed to be a king, the Jewish Messiah. I want him killed.'

'A baby? Surely a baby's no threat to you, Sire?'

'It's not the baby, it's his potential followers if we let the story grow. There's plenty of Jews only too willing to believe the ancient prophecies. They can make trouble and I want to pre-empt it, deal with the problem before it escalates.'

'But how do we find this baby? Do you know his identity and location?'

'No, we don't know his identity. We know he comes from Bethlehem, we know astrologers from Persia heard rumours and came looking for him and were despatched to Bethlehem by the priests, and they didn't stay long there so they must have found the child.'

'So what do you want me to do? Get all the villagers to parade the children and bring any likely looking specimens back to you to scrutinize?'

'No, kill them all. Put them to the sword. All the boys. All those less than eighteen months old. No, make that two years old, to make sure.'

'But Sire …'

'Don't 'but' me, soldier. Those are your orders. Obey them. And tell your troops unless they wipe out any possible pretender to my throne I'll have them crucified like common criminals.'

'When, Sire?'

'Now, now, how many times must I say this? Why do you think I've got you out of bed at this hour? To wait for a fucking cosy chat about it in the morning? Get to it. I want a report on my desk before the midday meal or there'll be trouble. And it had better be that the task has been accomplished. I'm holding you responsible for that. And you can get more troops out patrolling the streets in Jerusalem and cordon off the road from Bethlehem, prevent anyone from the village getting through for a couple of days. Any trouble will have died down by then. See to it. Now soldier, now!'

'Yes, Sire, if that is your will.'

'It is my fucking will, soldier. Just do it!'

Chapter 6
Bethlehem

The village is silent and in darkness. It is still, no breath of wind. Although the sun has not yet risen, there is a glow in the east and the warmth of the coming day is already seeping into simple homes. The first cock crows will soon be heard and then there will be shadowy movements as men begin to prepare for labour in fields or workshops and women start preparing food and emerging to fetch water from the village well.

On the outskirts of the village a hundred soldiers have just halted on the Jerusalem road. They have marched in full combat order since they were roused at the third hour and are now being briefed. Their commander orders a detachment of fifty soldiers to advance into the village, weapons at the ready, and the men move off silently and begin to enter houses in the first street. There are muffled sounds of movement, the occasional shout quickly stifled and figures slowly appear. The second draft of soldiers moves forward to meet them and pens the emerging figures, encircling the increasing number of men, young and old, stumbling into the open. Gradually the narrow road fills with men and youths shuffling into the pre-dawn twilight. They seem confused, frightened. They have not been given any reason for this rude awakening, this apparent military arrest. More and more men appear, escorted by the soldiers, their weapons drawn and threatening any who would seem reluctant. Women start to appear at the doors of their houses, scared women, believing their menfolk to be taken prisoner, fearing perhaps that some act of terrorism has been traced to this village and that all their men are under suspicion and threatened with interrogation and torture.

Eventually, as the first shafts of sunlight suddenly streak the stony ground, the soldiers march their prisoners to the end of the village to the white walled, now pink flushed, synagogue and push the men inside, a hundred men, and more, perhaps nearly two hundred. Once all are crammed inside, the large entrance doors are barred and a detachment of some dozen soldiers are left to guard the entrance. The village men, hitherto mainly silent, now begin to cry out in protest as they find themselves cut off from their guards, shouts more confused than angry, puzzled calls, fearful of what will happen next. Someone calls out that they can see flames and a short-lived panic ensues until another vouches that it is only someone with a lamp. Their calls for explanation meet no answer from the troops guarding the entrance. They maintain their vigilant stance barring exit from the largest building in the village.

Meanwhile the second detachment of fifty soldiers has spread out through the village and taken up strategic positions so that all the streets and lanes are covered and any woman who tries to follow out onto the street is quickly ordered back into her home. These fifty are strengthened by a couple of dozen now released from their round-up of the men, while others are ordered to the edge of the village where the refuse is thrown and lies still smouldering where each night it is burnt to deter the vermin that would otherwise infest it. These soldiers now begin to dig a pit in the soft earth alongside the stinking rubbish, then, when it is deep enough, await their next orders.

The commander now gives the order for all the remaining women and children to be herded into the village square where several of the lanes converge.

Chapter 7
Rachel

I'm woken up by a loud crashing at our door and a figure stumbles into our room. My husband stirs and this intruder grabs him and yanks him from my side. Nathan cries out in alarm. What on earth is going on? The noise has woken Benjamin and he starts crying. I try to rise but I'm still half asleep and my head starts spinning and I have to sit down again quickly. I become aware that Nathan and this intruder are grappling with one another. Are we being attacked? Have robbers come to steal our few possessions? I'm frightened.

Instinctively I shout to my husband, 'Don't resist, let them have whatever they want, don't fight and get hurt!'

Then I see the glint of metal and realise that the intruder is a soldier.

'You, come with me!'

Who is this ruffian addressing? The door swings open and from the pale dawn light I see that it is indeed a soldier and he has hold of Nathan. What's happened? What's he done? He's being led away.

My panic gives me courage and I yell, 'Hey, you, soldier! What's going on? Why are you taking my husband? Where are you taking him?'

'Rachel, look after Benjamin …' That's as far as Nathan gets before he's propelled out of the house and the door slams behind him.

I'm really panicking now. I want to follow Nathan to see what is happening. Has he been arrested? Why? He hasn't done anything wrong. But Benjamin is crying now. I ought to go to him. I'm torn. I pick Benjamin up but the suddenness of my movement doesn't reassure him and he's still wailing when I shove open the door and peer out to see what's going on.

Help, there are soldiers everywhere! Are we being attacked? Has our town been invaded?

'Woman ... yes, you, get back inside your house!'

I'm pushed back in by a soldier and the door is slammed in my face. Benjamin screams even louder and I'm scared stiff. What are they going to do to Nathan? Are they going to kill him? What are all the soldiers here for? Are they going to kill all our men?

I'm trying to comfort Benjamin but I'm sure he picks up my fear and he does not stop crying. What shall I do? What can I do?

Before I can make my mind up the door crashes open again and another soldier enters.

'You, woman, you've got to come out into the village square with your children. How many children have you got?'

I see now, from his uniform, that he's one of King Herod's guards. Why are our own soldiers doing this to us?

'Woman, I'm talking to you. Have you any more children or is this all you've got?'

'Yes. Just this one, just Benjamin.'

The soldier peers into every corner of the house, then grabs me by the shoulder and pushes me to the door.

'Where's my husband? What have you done with my husband?'

I get no answer but find myself in the street and there are huddles of women everywhere carrying crying children. Other children are clinging to their mothers' skirts. Many of them are crying too. We are all being herded into the square. There are Herod's guards everywhere, manhandling the women. Some are protesting and shouting at the soldiers. One woman who is screaming abuse at a soldier gets a vicious slap to shut her up. None of our men are in sight. Where are they? What's happened to them? I can only see women and children here.

There is no explanation. We are all huddled together in the market square. There are hundreds of us – it looks as though all the women of the village are here. But what have they done with our men?

I see Rebecca with Miriam and her children.

'What's happening?' I shout at her. 'What have they done with our husbands?'

'I don't know. They just grabbed Andrew without any explanation.'

'They've taken them to the synagogue.'

'And they've locked them in. They're going to burn the place down with all the men inside!' yells another voice. Screams of panic engulf us, especially when one woman says she can see flames in the direction of the synagogue.

'No, it's just the soldiers' torches,' shouts another.

'But they've arrested every man in the village. Are they going to kill them all? Is it revenge? Has someone killed Herod or attacked the palace and they're arresting everyone? Has someone in this village committed treason?'

Most of the children, woken early and suddenly from their slumbers, are crying, and the women are trying to quieten them, fearful of the consequences if the children's howls offend or upset the sullen troops. By the time all of us are crowded in a huddle on the square the sun has risen and the sky is a clear deep blue. We await events with trepidation. We have no idea what will happen next. Will our village be torched in retribution for some criminal act perpetrated elsewhere of which we are ignorant? What will happen to our men? Are they in danger of being carried away to execution?

We watch as a bevy of soldiers are going round all of our houses, peering inside. What are they looking for? Are they searching for anyone who may have been left? They've found old widow Sarah and they're pushing her towards us – poor thing, she can hardly walk. She's protesting, but the soldiers with her have no mercy, they're virtually dragging her now.

They must be searching every house to ensure no-one has escaped or been overlooked, no children have been left asleep on their beds, no-one is hiding.

A tall soldier, who's obviously in charge, barks out an order which I can't understand, and the guards start separating the older children from their mothers. Miriam is pulled away from Rebecca and her younger siblings and she starts shouting and the children renew their howling. When Miriam tries to wriggle free from the soldier's grasp, he slaps her hard across her cheek and threatens another blow, so she tears herself away from the youngsters and is pushed towards a group of older children. These soldiers roughly handle the children, pulling to one side all those children who are older, those who do not need their mothers to hold or comfort them. In some cases where a girl is holding a younger child, the baby is separated from the arms of its sister and thrust into the arms of the mother, even if she is already struggling to hold another child. The children are pushed to one side of the square where half a dozen soldiers are enough to keep them under control. Several of the children are weeping, some are calling out for their mothers and all are frightened and cower from the soldiers who have unsheathed their daggers and threaten any child who shows any signs of breaking out from the ranks.

They start marshalling us in small groups and immediately another soldier comes up to us and takes away a number of smaller children, all of whom try to cling to their mothers and recommence their howling for they are all extremely frightened – as I am. We haven't a clue what is going on. The men are apparently imprisoned in the synagogue, and now the children – at least all those who are walking – seem to have been separated out and are being held by a group of soldiers on the far side of the market square. Surely they're not going to harm them? What danger could any of those children be to Herod's guards? Surely they're not going to punish them for anything any adults may have done? Or are they punishing us by hurting our children?

Then the soldiers come back to us and start asking us the age of all the children we're still holding - any aged three or over are turned away and sent to stand with the older children, and more childish screams rend the air as a couple of three year olds are wrenched away from the mothers they have been clinging to. I just can't understand what's going on. No-one is giving us any explanation at all. We women have been left in our groups – the soldiers have been counting us out and each group of ten of us has a couple of guards making sure we do what we're told. In my group four of us are holding babies or toddlers. Then the women who have no children with them are ordered to go and join the children the other side of the square. I see the same is happening in the other groups of women. We are just left with women like me who have a baby or toddler in our arms. Are they going to send us back to our homes while they do something awful to the others?

'What's happening now?'

It's Barthaeus's wife, Miriam, who shouts at the soldiers as they start trying to get us on the move again. 'Where are we going now? What are you doing with us?'

'They're sending us back home,' exclaims Susannah, 'what about the other children?'

'No, they're not!' It's Ripah who senses that things are taking a different turn. 'Look, they're rounding us all up and wanting us to move that way.'

'Why? That track doesn't lead anywhere. Only up to the rubbish dump.'

Benjamin is struggling in my arms now. He wants to get down and walk. He's stopped crying and seems curious. And he's spotted the soldiers and is excited. He wants to go up to one and touch his long boots. Then I see one of the other toddlers has started trotting away from the crowd and immediately a soldier swoops on him and almost flings him back into the arms of his mother. The boy screams in alarm and I hold Ben even tighter.

We are being ordered to move. The file of women begins to walk, bewildered, along the pathway leading to our refuse tip. I can't make sense of it. Nearly all the soldiers seem to be accompanying us. Why are they singling us out? What have we done?

'Come on, woman, move!'

I get a prod in my back from a guard and I see his dagger is unsheathed. Others round me are threatened too, so we all begin to walk slowly in the direction we are being forced to go. I'm trembling with fear. I'm still worried about what has happened to Nathan. At least they haven't separated Benjamin from me, that's my only comfort. Many of the babies and children are still crying, but Ben is wide awake now and still wants to get down and play, but I hold him tight lest he run away and gets threatened like the other toddler.

We eventually begin to assemble at the desolate sight where we bring our refuse. It stinks, even at this hour of the day. Why are we here – what on earth are these soldiers intending to do? Then I see it, there's a great gaping hole at the edge of the tip with earth piled high. The soldiers must have been digging this for there are spades lying on the ground. Oh my God, are they going to kill us and bury us here? Surely not, there's far too many of us – there must be fifty or sixty of us plus our children. Perhaps they're going to pick out someone and make an example to punish the village for a crime that's been committed, but why us? What have we done?

Something's happening. I can hear more crying and protests coming from the women at the front of the crowd. I can't see what's happening at first, then the message comes rushing down the line.

'They're making us strip the children.'

'What did you say?'

'I said, they're making us strip the children. Take their clothes off.'

'Why? Why are they stealing the children's clothes?'

'They're not stealing them, silly. But I don't like what's happening. I'm getting a nasty feeling about it.'

I clutch Benjamin closer to my breast. I'm squeezing him so hard that he looks at me in surprise and begins to whimper.

All of a sudden we're surrounded by soldiers and they are telling us to hurry up and remove all the children's clothes.

There is a howl of astonishment and fear at this order and some of the women make a futile attempt to escape but are manhandled back to the tip. If the women are slow to comply, soldiers grab the baby or toddler and roughly tear the clothes from the child. I see what is happening to some of the others, so I begin reluctantly to remove Benjamin's shift and undergarment. He looks at me quizzically and says 'wee, wee?' The soldiers are now examining the naked babies. As soon as any girl child is exposed, she is thrust back into the arms of one of the women, but boys are passed from hand to hand to the group of soldiers standing round the freshly dug pit. Some of the soldiers are trying to shield what is happening from us, but a glimpse of blood is seen by one of the women.

'They're killing the babies!'

A horrendous scream rents the air.

I can hardly look, but I catch sight of a soldier with blooded hands severing the neck of one of the babies with his dagger. Howls of rage and pain shatter the air. Any semblance of order disintegrates. Soldiers are now fighting the women who are finding superhuman strength to hold on to their offspring at all costs. It dawns on me now why they told us to strip the children. They are only taking the male babies. Some women have not yet realised that the soldiers are selecting only the boy children for slaughter. Each child is becomes a human tug of war. Clothes are ripped. Children are being torn from their mothers' arms. Girl children and babies are now just being dumped by the roadside, dropped even. Their mothers are lost in the fray. We can all see what is happening, the soldiers have stopped trying to hide it from us. Babies are being strangled or even dashed against the rocky ground before the bodies are thrown into the pit. Some soldiers are thrusting their daggers into the corpses.

Those of us near the back of the crowd see all this, and it is unreal – I'm paralysed with fear and can't move. What is happening over there is so terrible that it seems to have nothing to do with me, until suddenly we are surrounded by the soldiers who are attempting to take our children from us. One soldier suddenly attempts to grab Benjamin from me and I hang on to him with all my strength. I'm pulled by the man into the thick of the crowd which is now a heaving, writhing, struggling mass, and Ben is screaming for me. I hug him for all I'm worth, but suddenly there is a ripping sound and my own shift is torn from my shoulders. In shock I relax my hold for a second and he is gone.

'Ben, Ben,' I scream and I'm knocked to the ground. As I try to scramble up to claw after him, I'm suddenly smothered, and I feel my remaining clothes being ripped apart. I'm writhing on the ground, my only thoughts are about regaining my boy, but he is gone and I'm being pinned here by a great brute of a man. Then I feel his hands clamping my thighs and I realise what he is doing. He's going to rape me. 'No, no!' I scream again, but my voice is going. In the pandemonium, no-one will here me and there's little I can do. If Ben is gone, what does it matter? They can kill me too. I give up. I'm battered as I lay there on the stony ground. My head hurts. I think I'm lying in blood, mine or that of children. I've vomit in my mouth, my nose, my hair. The brute is ramming into me, it's agony but I just want him to finish me off. 'Kill me, too,' I whisper, but he doesn't hear me. When he's finished with me, he kicks me between my legs and I double up in pain, nearly passing out.

When, I come round, I realise I'm not alone in my plight. It's total chaos all around me. Women with bloodied hands and clothes are screaming and wailing. Some of them have been stripped naked. I see other mothers being raped by blood-lusted soldiers who take them without pity or care. My stomach heaves again and more vomit adds to my degradation. A soldier hauls me to my feet and slings my torn shift back over my shoulder, but it slips leaving me exposed. I look around, scarce believing what has happened. I push through the throng of women calling for their children, and see blood everywhere, and naked limbs, bodies of babies thrown on the ground and in the pit. Even as I watch I see a soldier dash the head of a screaming child against a rock and sling him into the grave that had been dug. Where is Benjamin? I must find Benjamin, but the soldiers shove me back.

I claw my way forward again. I'm on my knees now. I get to the edge of the pit, and stare horrified at the pile of butchered tiny corpses lying in a heap. My head swims. My Benjamin is in there, but I cannot see him. I must have fainted clean away, because I can remember no more …

Chapter 8
Herod's Guards

'Attention! Attention! Company, withdraw!'

The commander's voice sounds above the din.

'Form ranks!'

His face is furious. The soldiers detach themselves from the broken and dishevelled women, many of whom are lying in the dust, sobbing or howling in grief at the loss of their children and their own violation.

Several of the soldiers are hastily trying to adjust their uniforms, trying to shield themselves from his gaze. While they struggle to come into line, he stares at the scene of desolation that is revealed. Many female babies are lying on the ground screaming, a couple with bones broken in the struggle, other naked toddlers are wandering around in total shock looking for their mothers. Some women have broken through the protecting lines of soldiers and are howling in grief and rage as they stare down at the bloody corpses of their children lying on top of each other where they've been thrown, twenty, thirty tiny lifeless bodies, it is not even possible to count the twisted limbs entangled with each other.

Then a couple of women, wild in their despair, plunge past the harassed soldiers and throw themselves into the pit, scrabbling at the mound of innocent flesh into which they've fallen.

'Get them out of there! You, there, get those women out of there!'

They are immediately hauled out, and other women hold them and smear themselves, their faces and hair, with the children's blood.

'Form a protective barricade round the pit! Go!'

The soldiers scramble into position. Several are still belatedly buttoning up their tunics. The commander gives them a long hard look. The women are forced back and start trying to reunite themselves with their female children. The commander is still noting which of his soldiers is in disarray and has some outward sign of having been involved in violations and rapes. He is aloof, seems from his look of disdain to have been less than enamoured with the order he has had to carry out. There are other soldiers too who are exhibiting signs of shock, while some now are looking sheepish or guilty as the enormity of their behaviour and the displeasure of the commander seeps into their consciousness.

'Front rank, you are to fill the pit. The rest of you will stand guard until all the women have left this area. Move!'

The soldiers begin to throw the fresh earth to cover the corpses of the children, and the women are ignored or turned to go back to their homes. Slowly they begin to drift in that direction, most are now sobbing, even those whose children, being female, were spared. They are reunited with the older children in the village centre and there are fresh screams and tears as the children see the state of their mothers and begin to learn what has happened to their tiny brothers.

The soldiers now round up the women and children who have not yet gathered themselves together. Some hang around searching for clothing or waiting to see if they can get back to the pit.

'Go home,' the commander tells them. 'There's nothing more you can do here. Go and find your other children. What's done is done.'

Someone cries out 'Why, why, what have we done to deserve this?'

No-one answers. The soldiers are silent now as if shaken by the act that they have perpetrated. A couple of soldiers even seem moved to tears although they turn away and hide any possible sign of weakness from the women and their commanding officer.

The commander details a platoon of the guards to escort the women back to the village.

'Make sure the women enter their houses. Do not let them congregate on the street. When you have done that, release the men in the synagogue and return here at the double.'

When at length the women and surviving children have been shut in their village homes and parted forcibly from each other to reduce the communal tension and suppress any sign of resistance or rioting, the commanding officer gives the order for the troops guarding the exit to the synagogue to fall back into their ranks, and the entire company beats a hasty retreat from the village before the men spill out and find out what has happened while they've been incarcerated in the synagogue. The troops march in rapid time back along the Jerusalem road, a small detachment at the rear covering their back in case any of the men decide to pursue the departing soldiers to attempt to wreak vengeance for the massacre and violations that have taken place.

The soldiers regain their barracks at a little after the third hour as the heat of the day is becoming oppressive. Before they can be dismissed however, the commanding officer decides to address the men:

'Soldiers of Herod's bodyguard, you have completed the task entrusted to us by orders of the king himself. What had to be done has been done. It was distasteful and against all our instincts, but the king has said that it was to protect the established authority and prevent a more severe repercussion from the Romans which would have an even more horrendous impact on families throughout Judea.'

The officer pauses and then adds in a softer and less confident tone:

'Most of you did what you were ordered to do, that and no more. You were instructed not to tell anyone the reason for the actions you have carried out as Herod will not tolerate the rumours of the birth of a possible usurper of the throne, and I trust that you have obeyed this edict as, if the story of a Messiah's birth continues to go the rounds among the priests and populace, Herod will have his revenge and some of you will not be spared.'

One or two soldiers blanch at this statement and it is possible to surmise that there have been one or two loose tongues.

'However, a few of you lost all discipline during the round up of the women and rapes and violations were committed. I will have no truck with that, such behaviour was both deplorable and inexcusable. I will be carrying out an investigation and those found guilty of such behaviour will suffer a military flogging. I will expect no cover ups and if those who witnessed such obscenities will not give evidence against their guilty colleagues, they too will be sentenced to the same punishment.'

The company stirs uneasily and it is clear that some in the ranks would protest, but the commander raises his arm to pre-empt any expression of mutiny.

'If Herod were informed of your behaviour, I would not attempt to assess his reaction. It could be ridicule, it could be that he would overturn the punishment, but I would not gauge his mood - he could order the execution of those involved, such is the unpredictability of his actions. And if he chose to hand out such penalties, there is nothing I could do to save any of you. So accept what I have decreed. The orders we had were unpleasant in the extreme, but there was no obligation to inflict the shame of rape and violation on the innocent women of the town. The repercussions of this behaviour will be felt for some time, you have not made our difficult and unpopular role here in Jerusalem any easier. Now go to your barracks and cleanse yourselves so that you are not seen by others with the blood of children staining your apparel. And from the ninth hour this afternoon, I will speak to each soldier individually about their role in the action carried out today. Dismiss!'

The commander completed his investigation two days later and two non-commissioned officers were reduced in rank for not controlling the men under their command, three men were flogged and were thrown out of the company of Herod's bodyguards altogether, and nine further soldiers were flogged but allowed to retain their occupation and rank. The floggings were all carried out in the parade ground in the barracks in front of all ranks of the King's Guard.

When the sentences had been carried out, the commander ordered the remainder of the Guard to assemble.

'Men of Herod's bodyguard, this unpleasant but necessary action, ordered by the King to prevent insurrection, is now complete. Your comrades who took a disgraceful advantage of the situation, let themselves and the company down and you have just witnessed the consequences. I order you, at the command of King Herod, to forget the whole episode. The King does not wish knowledge of this exercise to be known to the public, as it might create further unrest. I will depute a number of you whom I can trust to patrol the city. You will be augmented by further militia. The Roman garrison has been informed and you will all listen to the talk of the populace and will quell any subversive rumours or unrest that the elimination of the children might engender.'

The ranks of soldiers, unnerved by the punishments they have just witnessed, stir uneasily.

'I shall now report the successful completion of our orders to the King. The King's Guard, attention! Dismiss!'

Chapter 9
Rachel

I've somehow arrived at the door of my house. I'm in a trance, a nightmare. I want to wake up. Everything is a blur, I cannot see through my tears. I'm stiff and ache, every muscle in my body is screaming, but I am silent. I feel a hand on my shoulder and a push, and I'm stumbling inside into the shadow. I have nothing in my hands except a piece of cloth. It is streaked with blood. My blood? Benjamin's blood? I cannot care, I shudder.

The room is empty. Benjamin's cradle is in the corner. It is empty.

I grab the woollen blanket from his tiny bed and bury my head in it. I wipe my eyes, the blanket is smeared with blood. I touch my face, there is blood on my mouth, my nose. I have a nosebleed. I do nothing to stop it, I let it flow. I wish I were dead.

I keen.

I cuddle the soiled blanket.

'Benjamin, Benjamin, Ben,' I cry out in my despair. I cannot stop. His name echoes from my lips repeated over and over again.

'Oh Benjamin, Benjamin, Benjamin …oh Benjamin,' I scream. I howl.

I rock the blanket and cry at it, and my voice trails off repeating this now meaningless phrase to me for it is no more.

'Ben, Benjamin, Ben, Ben …'

My voice chokes, I can hardly speak. My mouth is going through the motions whilst my head spins. Everything is blurred. Suddenly I feel sick and stumble to the door and empty my entrails on the threshold. I stumble back into the darkness and fling myself on the ground. I don't feel anything more - the hurt is already too great.

'Benjamin,' my disembodied voice slurps into the dust. Then eventually, a new sound.

'Why?'

'Why? Why? What have they done with you? My lovely baby boy. Benjamin, I love you so much it hurts. Why did they …?'

I do not hear the door open or see the streak of violent light that arrows across the floor and strikes my crumpled form. I do not feel the arm on my shoulder gently shaking. I do not hear the words.

'What has happened? Rachel, for pity's sake, tell me what has happened? Where is Benjamin? What have they done to you?'

I cannot answer. I feel his arms tightening their grip around my shoulders. He is trying to pull me up but I am limp and he lets me slip once more to the floor.

'Rachel, Rachel, you must answer me. What has happened? Why are all the women crying? What have the soldiers done to you?'

I still cannot answer. I am dumb. I shake my head and burst into tears again. He notices the blood flowing from my nose and cradles me in his arms and tries to stem the flow with a piece of his garment. I rock in his arms, fresh tears convulsing my body.

'Rachel, calm down. Tell me what is so wrong. Where is Benjamin? Please answer. Where is he?'

'You can't.' That is all I can manage.

'Why not, Rachel? Tell me where he is and I will fetch him. Is one of the older children looking after him?'

'You can't, you can't, he's dead.' I blurt it out. There is a shocked silence.

'Oh my God, my God. What did you say? It can't be true. Tell me it's not true. What on earth has happened?'

'He's dead. They killed him. They killed all the children.'

'No, Rachel, I saw many children as I came here from the synagogue. Rachel, please tell me, what happened.'

I try to say words but nothing comes out. Eventually. I gasp 'Nathan!' He props me up against this chest and strokes my face in anguish.

'The soldiers killed him, Nathan. They killed all the babies. All the boys. They just tore them from our arms. They murdered them. I saw it. They threw him in a pit.'

He lets me howl, he does not try to soothe or stop me. I feel his muscles tighten, he is becoming angry. He wants to get up and go out in search of someone to strike, but he cannot and will not leave me like this. He rocks me in his arms. He is crying now. I do not know how long we lay here in each other's arms weeping for our loss.

My nosebleed has stopped. I drag myself to the waterpot in the corner and splash some of the tepid liquid round my face. I realise Nathan has slipped out. He is gone. The room is empty.

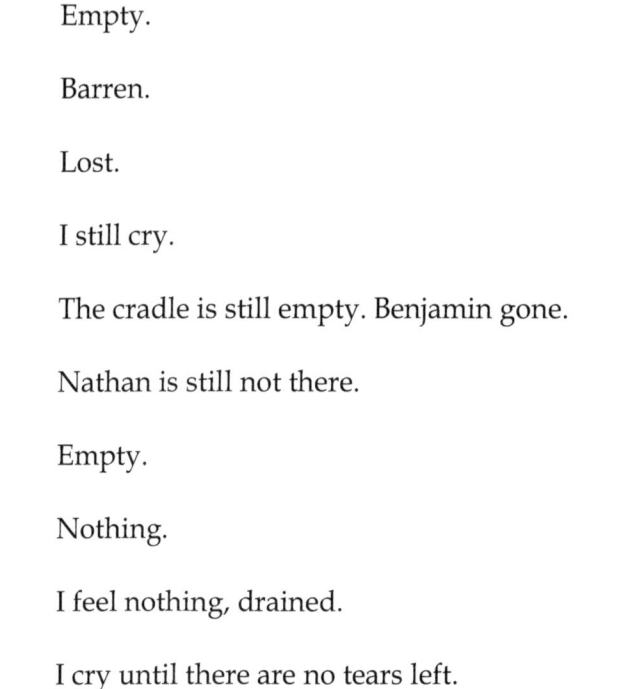

Empty.

Barren.

Lost.

I still cry.

The cradle is still empty. Benjamin gone.

Nathan is still not there.

Empty.

Nothing.

I feel nothing, drained.

I cry until there are no tears left.

A long time. It's a long time. A long time to feel empty. I hurt. I hurt all over. My arms hurt where they tore him from me. I clung to him, but the brutish soldier was so strong. Benjamin was screaming. My last memory of him is his sheer terror, his face twisted and contorted. I saw him, once he'd been wrested from my arms, being flung to another soldier.

The nightmare continues. I saw nothing further because the first soldier continued to struggle with me, he was still pulling at my shift. Then he knocked me to the ground and nearly smothered me, I thought he was going to kill me too. But I heard his rasping breath, felt his violent movements and realised too late that he was attempting to rape me. I suddenly lost all my strength and gave in. I felt him enter me and crush all the breath from my body. His movements were violent, I felt a jabbing pain between my legs, then he shouted and it was all over so suddenly and I just lay in the dust, half naked. The image won't go away. It's seared on my brain.

The tears are flowing again now.

I do not know how long I stayed there, numb and scared. One of the other women helped me to my feet and drew the shift around me to attempt to make me decent. Then Benjamin's absence overwhelmed me, I called him, but everyone was shouting the names of their children, I could not make my voice loud enough above the tumult. I ran in all directions, in circles, looking for my boy, in vain. I saw the soldiers in a huddle and I shouted at them, 'What have you done with my boy?' but they wouldn't answer. I tried to pass through their lines to see what they were guarding, but they shoved me back and wouldn't let me through. One said:

'Lady, I shouldn't look there. It is no sight for a woman.'

Then I saw that several of the soldiers were smeared with blood, and glimpsed bloody daggers in belts of some of Herod's troops and realised the brutal truth. At first I did not accept it, my mind revolted at the reality of the deed, I kept shouting 'No, it can't be.' Other women were screaming the same, everyone was angry. Some soldiers shrank from our abuse. Others began to hit us, to drive us away from the scene. One man struck me in the face, that must have caused my nosebleed. Then we turned and rushed at the soldiers and took them by surprise, enough to create a gap and we saw. We saw the pit and bare flesh, butchered red, piled in the red earth. We screamed again, then the ranks of soldiers closed and the gruesome sight was shielded once more. Hideous sobs shook our bodies, I could see nothing through the avalanche of tears, and we felt arms, gentle at first, then more insistent, guiding us back towards the village.

One woman was shouting.

'Why have you done this dreadful thing? What have we done to earn such retribution? Is this Herod's doing?'

But the soldiers would say nothing, just pressed us to walk back to the village.

'What have you done to the other children and our men? Have you murdered them too?'

The hysterical voice struck panic in us all, but we soon came across the older children in a huddle, frightened, confused, and when they saw our state, the blood, some began to cry. A couple of older children realised that many of the babies and toddlers were missing and started asking the obvious questions and soon the truth was admitted and children began to scream and wail. At least some women have other children, even if they are distressed. I have no-one, I am childless, empty. I cannot remember re-entering my house, whether I found it myself or whether someone led me here.

But I do not tell Nathan all this. It's just in my mind replaying over and over again. I try to shut it out, but it won't go. I want to be nothing, nowhere, but I can't escape this wretched body.

What can I do here? Where has Nathan gone? Why is he so long? I begin to imagine further horrors; that he has pursued the soldiers and struck at them and been cut down and that even now his body is lying in the dirt beside the road. I want to stir myself and get up and run out of the house and search for him, but my body is too shocked, too weary, and I remain slumped on the floor. Have I ceased to care? I worry that my feelings for my own husband are so dead. Why did he leave me so soon, why is he not here to comfort me?

I stumble out of the room into the blinding sunlight. There are other movements, sounds of distress all round me, but I am only vaguely aware of this. I am being drawn up the dusty slope towards the refuse tip where the outrage was carried out. I cannot help myself, that is where I am going. I trip over stones and rocks as I cannot see where I am putting my feet, blood flecks appear on my toes but I cannot care, I'm still smeared with blood from the multiple violations. I find myself at the stinking site and see men frantically scrabbling at the loose soil with their bare hands. I join a gaggle of other weeping women and watch through misted eyes. Nathan is there. There are about a dozen men digging, throwing up clods of soil wildly in all directions.

Eventually the men draw back from their labour and stare unbelieving into the void they have created. We women surge forward and push alongside them. They do not seek to restrain us, it is useless. There are tiny limbs poking through the disturbed earth. The men are exhausted and are no match for the frantic women who break through their ranks and start pulling the bloody corpses from the ground. I am staring at this horror, I cannot move. Nathan sees me at last and comes over, laying his hand on my shoulder. He cannot speak. There is nothing he can say to console or comfort me. We just watch in anguish as, one by one, the bodies of the children are lifted from their murdered graves, limp flesh is passed from man to woman as each family claims its own. Someone has a nameless child in their arms, is looking round for someone to claim the lifeless body.

Nathan exclaims, 'That's Benjamin, my son. Give him to me.'

He tries to hand the soiled child to me but I recoil. Then his head lolls towards me and through the streaks of blood, I see it is indeed my Ben. I burst into tears again as I clutch at him, trying so hard not to drop him in my anxiety that he should not be hurt. I do not realise that it doesn't matter now. I am so gentle, I cuddle him close to my breast and realise I can hold him against my bare flesh for I have not bothered to cover up after a soldier's assault ripped all pretence at modesty from my frame. His tiny body is still warm. His eyes are open but they are glazed in terror. I cannot look at them, I close them gently and kiss his eyelids and wash them with my tears.

Somehow we've got home. I do not remember how. I still cling to the tiny body as though I'm expecting him to wake and cry at any moment. I feel Nathan gently wresting him from my arms and bathing him, and wringing out the pink water at our doorway. I feel Nathan bathing me, lifting my torn tunic from my body, and laying me down on my bedroll beside my recumbent son. He makes me drink and closes my eyes. I am weeping inside now, I don't know if tears are still coming.

Then he is gone.

I haven't told him yet I was raped.

Chapter 10
Rachel

We have buried the children. Twenty seven tiny boys, one only a few days old. My son, Benjamin, was one of the oldest. He was twenty months old, already a personality I had grown to know and love. Rebecca stood next to me when we buried Benjamin, she tried to comfort me, but she was lucky, her six month old was a baby girl and she had not been harmed. How could she feel what I was going through? But at least she was there as a friend. Where was my other friend, Mari? How come she had been so lucky to be away? Would she reappear any time now with her Josh, with some innocent explanation for her disappearance? Did she know anything about the raid, had someone given her the tip? If so, why didn't she warn me?

My mother and father and Nathan's parents were there of course also. My father said little, his face was set in stone. My mother tried to console me but she could hardly contain her own grief. Nathan's mother was beside herself, her hopes dashed overnight, Nathan had to spend all his time trying to minister to her to prevent her total collapse. He could pay little attention to me.

Bethlehem is a sombre place today, there have been so many burials, so much wailing. The sounds of mourning are echoing round the village each hour of the day. No-one is looking at each other, all are isolated in their grief. Those who have not lost children feel guilty, why have they escaped, they think, as they clasp their girls and older boys around them, holding them extra tightly lest they escape.

The men do not know what to do, how to cope. They are frustrated because they cannot comfort their wives or manage their own grief. There is angry talk, talk of revenge, but it is powerless because they do not know whom to blame or why. They know soldiers carried out the deed, but soldiers work under orders. Was it the Romans? Or Herod? Or the religious authorities carrying out some cruel sacrifice to a cruel God? Youths are throwing stones and rocks. They cannot throw them at the soldiers because they are not there. They throw them instead aimlessly at sheep and dogs and get curses from the shepherds attempting to take the flocks to their normal grazing grounds. Some want to go to Jerusalem, but the men restrain them, saying that there will be danger there and the village should suffer no more loss.

'Why?' is on the lips of everyone. 'What have we done to deserve this?' We know there are rebels, bandits even, who cause grief to the Romans and our king, Herod, their lackey. But no-one is aware of anyone in our village who has links with any of them. Joseph's name is mentioned with suspicion because he and his family have escaped the massacre, but although his wife, Mari, is a stranger from Galilee, he is known here. He grew up here as a boy, all know him and they cannot believe him to be either a rebel or one of Herod's spies.

'Perhaps Mari is the culprit. She comes from Galilee and the activities of rebels and bandits are much greater in the north. Perhaps her family is to blame.'

So prattle the tongues of a couple of the women. But why wreak revenge and even punishment on a village a hundred miles away that has so little contact? And if she is the cause, why has she been the only one with a young boy to escape?

'Perhaps she didn't escape,' said Rebecca.

'Perhaps the reason for her disappearance and that of Joseph and Joshua is that Herod's men or the Romans have arrested the whole family. Perhaps they took them away that night. Perhaps they're being tortured at this very moment,' said Susannah.

'Or are already dead,' said someone else.

'Perhaps they revealed something that upset Herod and the soldiers have been sent to teach us all a lesson for sheltering the delinquent family,' said yet another.

The wild rumours fly around without any evidence to stop the speculation.

I don't know what to think. Mari was my friend, she never gave me the slightest hint that she had sympathies with the rebel Zealots or any of the other fanatics who oppose the Roman's rule or that of the Gentile King Herod. But she was mysterious on occasions and would not tell me much about her life before she came to Bethlehem. Then there was that occasion when she said some stupid words about her being a virgin and Joshua being the Messiah. I thought she was joking or pulling my leg.

I didn't take her seriously. Had she been rash enough to make the same comment unguardedly to someone in authority? Perhaps a spy had overheard her joke to another woman in the market or at the well. Perhaps one of our women in the village is a spy for Herod or the Romans, that's a horrifying thought. And if that was the case, why hadn't the soldiers just arrested her and ignored the rest of us? I can't make sense of it.

I mope around the house, these thoughts tangling my mind. I cannot put myself to anything. Nathan has to collect the water, he tells me he was not alone in this, about half a dozen men performed this wifely duty as their women were too weak or injured to undertake their normal role. Many younger girls were pitched into this chore, struggling with water pots overflowing as the weight was too much for their young muscles.

Nathan tells me that I should resume my household chores as these will help me forget at least for a little while, but I cannot do this. I stare at the cooking pots and feel numb. I go through the act of preparing a meal for Ben and then realise the futility of my actions and abandon the cooking fire until it expires and Nathan has to rekindle it. How long will I be like this? How long will Nathan put up with my behaviour before he begins to nag me? Will he stop loving me if I'm miserable all the time and do not provide him with food and clean clothes? Are the other bereaved women better able to recover than I am? When am I going to pluck up courage to tell him I was raped? He hasn't asked me. Perhaps he suspects and dare not in case he learns the truth.

How long will I be like this?

Days.

Weeks.

I lose count, but I suppose in the end the grief becomes a dull nagging ache while I do other things, my mind sometimes coming round to what I'm doing. I become more conscious of my other hurt, my shame. The loss of Benjamin is so acute that my own rape seems to fall to insignificance, but my neighbours do not think this. They know that several of us suffered this humiliation at the hands of the soldiers and while on the one hand they express such sympathy, I get the feel that they are treating us as unclean, as outcasts and they are more sorry for my husband than they are for me. I sense this. Sometimes they lower their voices when they are talking to Nathan and I can't hear what they are saying. I ask Nathan and he shrugs his shoulders and says it was nothing important. I'll have to tell him soon, or one of the other women will tell him. Perhaps they already have.

Today is very hot - stifling in this small house despite the shade. I have a headache and the shouts and screams of children playing outside make it worse. Apart from the noise aggravating the pain, the playing of children reminds me of what I have lost and it is unbearable. I'm inclined to go out and stop them or at least ask them to be quiet but I do nothing, fearing that they'll mock me or perhaps say something that will reopen all my wounds.

In the end, I can stand it no longer and go to the door of my house, if only to breathe some fresh air. It's late afternoon and the older boys are scrapping in their usually boisterous way. I know them of course, everyone knows everyone here. Most of them are about ten years of age and letting loose their pent-up energy after being cooped up with the rabbi in the synagogue for most of the day. There are one or two older boys, including Joshua bar Abbas, the rather wild son of Matthaeus, another scribe, who is getting a reputation for bullying some of the smaller boys. He is bossing them about now, and if any of them are slow to do what he commands he cuffs them about the ears. He has, or rather, had, two younger brothers, one of whom was a toddler like my Ben, and who was murdered along with the rest. I'm not sure that he was ever the sort to spend much time with the toddler, but the massacre has given a vent for the suppressed anger that seems to be bubbling just under the surface so much of the time and he is muttering a few oaths that really should not reach the ears of the younger children.

He is slinging tiny stones now at the younger boys, I'm not sure if it's still a game or whether he's taking out his anger in this violence, for it won't be long before one of the stones catches a younger child somewhere painful and a howl will pierce the air. Suddenly there is a sharp retort, one of the stones has missed its target and slammed into the wall of my home, not a couple of feet away from my head. The game, if it is that, stops and some of the children slink away, but Josh bar Abbas is no coward and he walks right up to me. I thought for a moment that he was even going to apologise, but he just smirks at me.

'I nearly got you then, didn't I? If I were you, I'd go inside, it's safer there. Best place to be, anyway, for a woman defiled by the Romans. I know, my dad told me you'd been raped and I saw you coming back, your bloody breasts on view to everyone.'

'Joshua, it's not right to speak like that. I had no choice Your family was hurt too, don't you feel sorrow for what happened to your baby brother?'

'It's one less mouth to feed. Oh, I know I shouldn't say that. But he moaned and cried a lot and often kept me awake at night. And it showed us what the Romans are really like. Dad says they pretend to give us protection from criminals and then they show their true colours by doing this. I'll get even with them one day. I won't forget. I'll have my revenge in my own good time.'

'What can you do, Joshua? You're too young to say such things.'

'I'm having my 'bar mitzvah' next month. Dad tells me everything now. He thinks I'm old enough to know. I'll join one of the Zealot bands and kill as many of the scum as I can and those Jewish collaborators who let them do these things. They don't deserve to live.'

'Joshua bar Abbas, you'll come to grief yourself if you speak like this. You'll bring nothing but further sorrow on your own family.'

'I don't care. My father feels the same. He says you can't just lie down and let them walk all over you without standing up for yourself. He's ashamed that we Jews just seem content to let the Romans do whatever they want without any protest or rebellion. He says your husband should be seeking to avenge you, not just talking strong words with the other men and doing nothing.'

'I want Nathan here with me. I don't want him charging off into Jerusalem on some hopeless cause and getting himself arrested or killed.' Then I realise it's a waste of time arguing with this precocious kid. His mind has been twisted by what he hears his father and friends say. I turn my back.

Joshua shrugs and loses interest in both me and the conversation and slouches off. All the other boys have disappeared. If Matthaeus and his friends know I've been raped and even the boy's overheard it, I must tell Nathan myself. I'll do it today, I vow to myself.

As I am about to move back inside the house, I see Nathan coming with a couple of the other men. They are talking animatedly to each other, their arms gesticulating as they speak. Perhaps they have some news. I retreat to my pots, which are simmering gently with the evening meal. Nathan will expect me to be there and he'll tell me soon enough if something of interest or concern has happened.

He sweeps into the room and before he's even slung off his cloak, he mutters brusquely,

'It was your friend Mari's fault. Some of the men have been in Jerusalem and got one of the soldiers to talk. Apparently there was a rumour going round that a miraculous child had been born who would take Herod's throne, and Herod had persuaded the Romans that the prediction was about the expected Messiah who would throw the Romans out. And somehow, the rumour got linked to Mari and Joseph and their son, so apparently Herod gave orders to kill the boy.'

'But why them? Why on earth did anyone think Joshua was going to be the Messiah? It's ridiculous!'

I have never said anything to Nathan about the secret that Mari blurted out to me a few weeks ago. She must have said something unguardedly in the hearing of someone sympathetic to Herod.

'I've no idea, Rachel. I think it's ridiculous too. Joshua was an ordinary toddler. Okay, he seemed very bright for his age, but so what? Other children are bright too.'

'And for that reason they came and killed all our children here? Did the soldiers kill every young boy in Judea?'

'Apparently the prophets predict our village as the likely birthplace of the Messiah and there were rumours about Mari before she came to live here. Herod's advisors must have put two and two together.'

'What rumours about Mari?'

'I don't really know. The soldier was reluctant to say much. Only that Mari's son wasn't really Joseph's. I never got that impression, Joseph always seemed proud of his wife and son. That wasn't the behaviour of someone who suspects his wife of being unfaithful.'

'Did the soldier say what had happened to Mari's family? Have they been arrested? Is that why they disappeared?'

'No, I don't think the men who spoke to the soldier got that out of him. It seems unlikely to me that soldiers would have been sent to our village if they'd already got Joshua and Mari in their clutches. They must have thought they'd still be in Bethlehem and by killing all the boys, ensure they'd got him.'

'In that case, Joseph must have known what was going to happen. That's why they disappeared in such a rush. They'd taken their donkey and some of the things they'd want on a journey. I know because I looked inside their house when they were first missing.' Then I have an afterthought.

'Nathan, remember those exotic looking strangers who visited Joseph's house the night before he and Mari disappeared? They must have said something to cause them to leave their home so quickly. Perhaps they'd heard something in the city and came to warn them.'

'In that case, if they had been tipped off that they were in danger, why didn't they warn all of us?'

That thought is what is gnawing at me. I can't believe that Mari would not have said something to me if she thought I was in danger too. To just go off like that without warning all of us, that seems so cruel, so unlike the Mari I thought I knew.

And I did get round to telling Nathan that night that I'd been raped. I cried and he held me tight.

'I know,' he said. 'I've always known. I knew you'd tell me one day.'

Chapter 11
Nathan

I don't know what to do. We can't carry on like this. Rachel is just not the girl I married any more. She just sits around, in silence. Some days I have to make my own evening meal after a back-breaking day in the field. She even left me to fetch the water on a couple of occasions, although I only went the once, on that first day, when I was one of several men performing that act as our wives were flattened with grief. Doesn't she think that I have to cope with my grief too? The other women who lost their children seem to have recovered, I see them in the street going about their routine duties. I have tried various methods to try to get back the girl I knew. At first I was gentle with her, I suppressed my own anger for her sake, and was all softness and comfort. This just seemed to make her more tearful. Then I tried a firmer approach, chiding her for not carrying out her duties, comparing her with the other women who were getting back to normal. I told her to snap out of it, she would forget Ben if she would concentrate on other things. This just brought an outburst of temper, something I'd never seen from her before, followed by a day of wailing and sobbing that could be heard outside in the street to my embarrassment and shame.

Other men have begun to comment on Rachel's continuing grief and have murmured their sympathy to me, one or two have even uttered criticism, urged me to take control of her and get her to buck her ideas up. I try to hide from them how much I'm having to do, or they would think I'm too soft, they would laugh at my weakness and I would be humiliated. I thought we were getting somewhere the other day. I told her what the men who'd gone to Jerusalem had found out and got her into conversation. She even suggested a link between the strangers who visited Joseph the evening before they disappeared, and for a moment she became animated, then she sank once more into deep contemplation, and has been withdrawn and sullen ever since. She lets me put my arm around her when we lie together, but she is unresponsive, like a log.

I left her this morning still lying on her bedroll. I made my own breakfast and found a stale piece of bread to take with me to stave off hunger until this evening's meal. I guess I'll have to make that too when I return.

I cheer up when I meet Andrew and Jude who tend the neighbouring plot to mine. Andrew's family was not directly affected by the murder of the children although, of course, everyone in the village was incensed and grief stricken by the atrocity. Jude lost his second child who was barely a year old, but his older boy who was just four had evaded the slaughter.

After our usual greetings, Andrew looks at me with knowing eyes.

'How goes it? Any better yet?'

I shrug my shoulders. He knows the situation. His wife, Rebecca, is Rachel's best friend since Mari disappeared, and she has tried in vain to get her to stir out of the house and take an interest in the daily activities and gossip. When Rachel has gone down to the well, I know it was because Rebecca had called for her and virtually dragged her there.

'It's a pity you have no other kids for Rachel to busy herself with,' says Jude, 'Salome was devastated at first as we all were, but looking after Simon occupies her time and gives her someone to focus all her feelings on.'

'My mother isn't helping the situation. She criticises Rachel for moping around and not putting her grief in its proper place and just tells her to hurry up and conceive another son to replace Ben. That just makes matters worse.'

We leave things at that for a while, strip off our cloaks and begin to tend our crops as the sun's heat begins to blanket yet another day, about a month now since the day the soldiers came. We toil all morning to tend and protect the grain we grow to sustain our families. At noon, we pause to have a bite to eat and rest a while.

'Have you heard,' says Jude, 'some of the other village men are meeting tonight. They want to plan some action to revenge themselves on what Herod's soldiers did.'

'What can they do?' says Andrew, 'We're powerless here and they should know it.'

'I've no idea. At least talking about it gets some of their feelings and anger out into the open. That's healthier than brooding on things.' Jude shakes his head.

That I know from my own experience at home. Perhaps I'll go to listen. Better that than another long evening in embarrassed silence.

'I think I'll join them to find out what ideas they've got. Probably nothing practicable, but anything is better than letting them get away with it and doing absolutely nothing.'

I surprise myself by uttering this intention. I had not sought before to join any of the other men who frequently gathered to discuss the aftermath of the massacre. I had always hurried home to Rachel, to see if she had changed, had prepared the meal and then all too often, had to undertake the evening chores myself.

There is no meal prepared. The ingredients are all there, but the fire is dead. Rachel is sitting on the bedroll staring into space. I feel my anger surfacing, but realise it is useless. Tonight I have other things to do, I have no time for recriminations and dealing with the aftermath. I'll have to manage with a hunk of bread to assuage my hunger for the moment. Rachel will just have to rouse herself if she intends to eat. Perhaps being forced to fend for herself will jerk her out of her stupor.

'I'm going out. If you want anything to eat, you'll have to kindle the stove and prepare the meal yourself. I don't know what time I'll be back, but I'll expect more than a piece of bread.'

This has stirred her a little. She looks at me with startled eyes, then they brim over with tears which run slowly down her cheeks. She says nothing, but that look hurts me. Can I withstand it, will I give in and stay at home? I must go. Something must change, otherwise we shall never progress. I must be brutal to be kind.

I say a little more sympathetically, 'I have to go out. The men are meeting to discuss what actions we can take to avenge the massacre. Herod must not and cannot be allowed to get away with such a crime without some retribution, at least he must be made aware of the evil he has brought about.'

Still she says nothing, the tears glisten on her cheeks.

'When I'm gone, try to prepare a decent meal for yourself. You need to build up your strength, you're wasting away with so much grief. It is not healthy for you to give yourself over to mourning all your waking days.'

I bend down and clasp her round her shoulders. I give her a squeeze and then, before she can say anything, or I can hesitate, I'm gone.

We meet in the whitewashed synagogue in the centre of the village, now a place of uncomfortable memories for us since we men were herded there while Herod's soldiers did their worst. In God's house we should feel strength and power - instead we are reminded now of our powerlessness. Zacchaeus and Joel, priest and rabbi, are already there, but I'm the only other man from the village as yet, I'm early in my anxiety to leave home before I'm inveigled by guilt into staying with Rachel. Both religious men know my situation and sympathise. Zacchaeus just tells me to trust Jehovah, but Joel is more practical and tells me that his wife has offered to spend some time with Rachel, helping her with her daily chores and giving her company so that she does not fritter away the day dwelling on her misery.

The other men are drifting into the building in twos and threes, some already arguing. About a couple of dozen of us have come, most still dirty from the labour of the fields or herding our animals. We squat on the mosaic floor of the inner courtyard and the chatter continues until Rabbi Joel lifts up a hand to signal the commencement of our proceedings.

'Friends, you all know why we are here. What is your advice? Have you any ideas on actions we can take without causing even worse to befall us?' Joel is businesslike and straight to the point as usual, a good person to take charge of what could easily become a very disjointed and confusing discussion getting nowhere.

At first there is silence while we all look at each other. Joel's blunt challenge to us has stopped the several conversations dead. Then my friend and neighbour, Jude, calls out, 'Herod can't get away with it. He must see our anger, feel it.'

Other voices join in, expressing similar views, but Joel holds up his hand once again to stem the flow of words, for he perceives that they are getting carried away with emotion without any practical options being offered.

'Men of Bethlehem, what you say is from your hearts, that I understand, but such words will not achieve your goal. Have any of you any specific suggestions of action that you can take?'

Andrew, Rebecca's husband, a mature and thoughtful person who over the years has earned the respect of many in the village, suggests quietly, 'We could send a deputation to the High Priest in Jerusalem and seek his support to make a complaint to Herod.'

'What good will that do?' Matthaeus is a scribe, but one who knows full well that his education gives him an edge over other men that he is not slow to exploit. 'You'll be lucky to get the High Priest to listen to you, let alone challenge the king and put his own authority and position at risk. He knows where his interests lie, and it'll not be through angering Herod.'

'What about a complaint to the Roman Governor? Herod would have to take notice of him.'

'Do you think the Romans care? Do you think they're unaware of the actions of Herod's guards? They make it their business to know everything that's going on. They must be aware of the stories of the massacre which are awash in

Jerusalem. The Romans just want Herod to keep the lid on things, to control events and maintain the peace. They'll not welcome anything that weakens his effectiveness.'

Argument continues between the men on these lines for sometime. I listen but add little. I'm in sympathy with Andrew's suggestion of making a formal complaint, but I can see the counter-arguments. Apart from anything else, it's now nearly six weeks since the infant murders, a bit tardy for making such a complaint. I can just see now the reaction of the High Priest. 'You've waited this long before making a formal accusation? You're too late. Go home, you'll never get any of Herod's guards to admit to the substance of your complaint so long after the alleged offence.' This response, nay excuse, would satisfy his own conscience of saying nothing and thus condoning Herod's actions to defend his throne from being usurped by a two year old child.

A couple of men, however, James the village potter and Joshua, a herdsman, are fired up for revenge of a more active kind. Matthaeus, the scribe, and father of the wayward twelve year old bully who terrorises the smaller children on occasions, is all for joining a group of nationalist fanatics in the north he calls the 'siccarii', who are patriotic rebels who from time to time ambush a Herodian or Roman patrol, or kidnap and ransom one of the Jewish collaborators with the occupying power.

'What good will that do? They don't dare to come near Jerusalem. They stay in the Galilean hills where they can depend on village support, far enough away from the capital where they would soon be outnumbered, captured and executed. And how would joining their operations voice our anger at Herod for what he's done? We need to do something that focuses his mind on our grievances.'

Despite that point, Mordecai, a tradesman who originally came from a village beyond the east bank of the Jordan to get work in the capital, and still has connections there, indicates that he wishes to speak.

'If you wish, I can make contact with a group of men who call themselves 'Zealots' operating on the far side of the Jordan river. They have been known to come as far south as Jericho. But it'll take a few weeks to get a message to them and receive their reply. What do you want? Do some of you wish to join them, or do you just want to acquaint them with Herod's atrocity and leave them to take action on your behalf?'

Zacchaeus and Joel look a little concerned at the direction that the debate has taken, they clearly do not wish for the synagogue and the religious authorities to become tainted with such rebellious considerations for fear of the consequences and the risk of diminishing the little power and independence that they have been allowed to weald on behalf of the Roman and Herodian authorities. When a suggestion is made to Mordecai that perhaps a clandestine meeting could be arranged between a couple of local men and the Zealot band to explore options, Zacchaeus is quick to argue that such a meeting should not take place in the synagogue, nor indeed, anywhere else in the village, as in any case this would be too dangerous for the Zealots themselves. What he means of course is that it would be too risky for himself and the other synagogue rabbis and scribes.

The meeting is closed without any decision to raise a complaint formally with either the Herodian or Roman authorities, but two or three of the men, including Matthaeus, slip away with Mordecai. I'm not sure what will become of it. I feel frustrated and return home. To my surprise Rachel has got the fire going and a hot meal is simmering. She doesn't ask me where I've been or anything, but she hands me a meal and we eat together something she has prepared for the first time since Benjamin was killed.

Afterwards when we've cleared away the remains, I look at Rachel and wonder if tonight perhaps she'll be ready to receive me. We lay down together and I reach out my arm and hold her. Emboldened, I slip my hands under her shift and feel her breasts. At once she recoils from my touch. I lay still as

Rachel turns away from me. Tears are flowing softly onto the bedroll.

I am still in two minds. I thought that tonight might have been different. I find it hard to think of sex with Rachel without recalling that she has been raped. I know that some of my neighbours refuse to have intercourse with their wives once they have suffered the shame and indignity of rape. This seems unfair in the extreme, yet I find it unsettling to consider the resumption of normal sexual relations. How could it now be normal? However, at present there seems to be no possibility of such relations, normal or not. Rachel is clearly not ready yet.

Then, the next morning, she is sick. My concern is now for her wellbeing. Each subsequent morning she is unwell and I tend to her before leaving for the fields. She surprises me by being more her old self when I return at the end of the day. Tonight is special. She actually smiles and after the meal we lie down together and gradually, slowly, gently, we make love. When we awake, I'm still clasping her body to me, wrapping myself around her naked limbs. I am lying here feeling that at last my Rachel is restored to me. We can move on.

Then, suddenly, she is awake, and jerks herself away from my arms. She struggles to stand and before she can find her shift and reach the door, she retches and stumbles to the corner of the room where she is violently sick. It hits me then, the realisation that Rachel is pregnant again. Then, even as my heart lifts, the horror rises in my gullet. She cannot be bearing my child. She is pregnant by the rapist soldier.

Chapter 12
Rachel, BC 5

Ruth is suckling at my breast. She is just a week old. She is so small, so vulnerable and yet each time I look at her a feeling of revulsion overpowers me. She has dark hair and brown eyes, just like Nathan's, no-one will know for certain that she's not Nathan's child, but I know and Nathan does too, that she is the child of my child's murderer.

Nathan has tried very hard not to let his feelings about the child show. He has protected me, he has said nothing to anyone about my shame, not even to our parents. His mother was overjoyed when he told her that I was pregnant again, she predicted another grandson to replace the one she'd lost and carry on the male line of the household. She was bitterly disappointed when a girl was born, she was scarcely civil to me, although Nathan remonstrated with her. I shudder to think what she would say if she knew my child was not her son's. His father was more understanding, but was clearly disappointed.

I said nothing either to my own parents about the origin of the child growing within me and they were pleased for me and thankful for the restoration to health and activity of the daughter they had known. They congratulate Nathan on bringing me out of my grief and fathering another child, even though it was a girl. Nathan bit his tongue and said nothing.

Rebecca attended me as well as my mother when my time came. She has been a good friend to me, as has Miriam, wife of the rabbi, Joel. Throughout my pregnancy I have had their support. I don't think they suspected that the child was not Nathan's although they do know I was raped by one of Herod's soldiers as were several other women and girls that night. All of us were dishevelled and bloodstained after our children's murder. Who knew then and cared which of us had been additionally defiled? Some of the women made their distress very public, they cried out and accused the soldiers in their anguish, they wailed in the street, their shame and humiliation was only too obvious. I was deadened by my experience, shocked into silence. I thought I'd confided in no-one except my husband, but someone knew, and the rumour had reached Matthaeus' son, or else why did he taunt me, or did he just guess?

So everyone appears to be happy for me, they see the child at my breast and my husband at my side and I try to show that I am happy too, but it is a sham. She is the result of a great crime, a hideous act. How can I look at her and love her? What does Nathan really think each time he looks at her, at us? Does he see my rapist, does he imagine him violating me even as he's just ripped the life from my only son? There is something guarded about Nathan's joy, he handles the baby carefully as though he fears to drop her. He wills himself to embrace the child.

We called her 'Ruth'. I don't know why, there is no 'Ruth' in my family or Nathan's. It was as though we were acknowledging her to be a stranger in our home. Nathan's mother kept asking him why we had chosen this name and not the name of one of her sisters or cousins as was normal.

And so, Ruth, we have got to get used to each other, you and I. I must learn to love you, because the mess of your conception was not your fault. You try your best to be lovable. You search for my eyes and I try to look back into yours, although sometimes I flinch and look the other way. You stare so intently, sometimes I think you are accusing me. You are pulling at my breasts now, you are a greedy child and I am sore. When you cry at night and wake me because you are hungry, then I feel resentment, not the maternal love that I ought to experience. I know it's wrong to feel like this, but I can't help it. Forgive me, little one, I'll try my best. Nathan will acknowledge you as his own. I pray that no-one will ever tell you that your real father murdered your half-brother. I pray that I shall never betray you in this way, however angry or upset I may be with you.

Ruth is satisfied at last. She relaxes and slips from my aching nipple and I hold her and try to sing to her. Her eyes close and I feel her warmth against my skin. I could put her in the cradle that used to hold Benjamin, but I deliberately hold her in my arms to try to compensate for my lack of natural love for her. She is relying on me. She has no-one else to care for her. I cannot, I must not, let her down, but it will be tough.

Nathan has had to work especially hard these last few months. A number of the men from the village have gone away. They went mysteriously one night, without any public farewell. Nathan tells me that they have gone to join a Zealot group to take revenge against Herod and his soldiers, but that I must not speak of this to anyone. The absence of these men puts extra burdens on the remaining male adults and youths. Several have left families behind that need support and sustenance. We are honour bound to help them, share what we have. So Nathan spends longer in the fields, tilling and planting the land of other families as well as our own.

We have this particular additional duty and responsibility for Jude's family, for he has deserted his wife, Salome, and his four year old son, Simon. And unbeknown to Jude, his wife is pregnant, a child conceived before Jude left with the other village men. I have to be the comforter now, because Salome was distraught when her man left with the others. She remonstrated with him, tried to get him to see his responsibility for her and his remaining child, but his anger at the loss of the younger boy was too great and he was persuaded to go in search of revenge. Salome is doubly vulnerable now, burdened also by the knowledge of the little one within her and desperate to know how they will survive. Her own father died many years ago, and her husband's family can be of little assistance as they are nearly destitute - Jude's father is crippled with arthritis and cannot labour in Jude's field, which was going to waste until Nathan stepped in and offered help.

Our well is just outside the village down one of the rocky slopes where such water as falls is likely to sink into softer soil, and a couple of streams form when it rains. It is a bit tricky to get there without slipping on the rocks, especially when we return back with our laden water-pots. It is the first time since the birth of Ruth that I have been down to the well myself to fetch water - both Rebecca and Miriam have done this duty for me this past week. I'm a little nervous as the other women will all want to see my baby and there's bound to be speculation over whether she's Nathan's or the result of the rape. I ponder whether I should go later when the sun is high and when no-one else will be about, but that is what outcasts and women who are ostracised will do, and in the mind of the other village women, that would only confirm my child as an object of shame.

It is now time, therefore, to go. I secure Ruth in the shawl and tie it round my body so that my arms are free to check any slip. Then I can hold the large water jar, especially on the return trip when it is heavy. My situation is not unique, four of us have had babies in the last few days. There will be much gossip in any case, and speculation about our children's fathers because they all know that conception would have been about the time of the massacre and violations. We shall all be under pressure to admit that our children are bastards, they don't mean to hurt us, they will express sympathy, but in their hearts they will not accept our children and treat us as unclean and to be pitied.

There are over a dozen of the women already there waiting their turn to draw water. I see immediately that Ripah, Miriam and Susannah also have tiny bundles in their arms. The other women all have toddlers trailing round their feet, these children are running around playing together without restraint, rushing back and clinging to their mothers' legs if they need reassurance.

Everyone turns to look at me as I arrive.

'Rachel, let's have a look at her! Look at her dark eyes. Is she like your husband, Nathan?'

See, they are already probing, testing me!

'Yes, of course, Nathan's mother is convinced that she's the image of him when he was a baby. Well, with one obvious exception, of course,' I add as some of them burst out laughing.

'Well, you do wonder when you think of the time of conception, four of you at once, it can't be coincidence, can it?'

'I'm sure she's Nathan's, I really am,' I say as convincingly as I can, feeling that my lie must be transparent to them.

'How can you be so sure?'

'I just have this feeling and Nathan is convinced, he has no reason to doubt,' I lie again.

A group of the women huddle round me and I pull back the shawl to reveal Ruth's face. She wakes and opens her brown eyes and stares at the faces peering so inquisitively at her. They note her dark hair. It is not inconceivable that she's Nathan's. They give me the benefit of the doubt. I'm not sure how many of these women, anyway, know that I was raped. I have not consciously confided in anyone other than my husband that I was violated by a soldier, although as I've mentioned before, Matthaeus' son tried to taunt me. I still don't know if he really knew through some unguarded word of mine that spread rumour until it reached his ears, or whether he was just guessing, looking for some snub in the manner typical of that obnoxious boy.

After the first flurry of interest in Ruth, speculation and gossip centres on the other new-born babies present. This is not Miriam's first child, her new son already has a sister and an older brother who just escaped the massacre as he was then three years old. She is a feisty woman, loud and outspoken compared with most other village women, and she is not shy of admitting that she had been raped and there was the possibility that the child was that of the rapist. However, in her next breath, she says that her man, Barthaeus, a gruff giant of a man and no fool, took her immediately afterwards, in order to ensure no-one could ever be certain of its parenthood if a child was conceived. In any case, the boy does not look unlike his father, her husband is quite satisfied to call him his own and act accordingly, so she holds her head high and seems to defy any of the women present to cast any further slur. I think, she's a strong character, she'll get away with it, even if the child was a soldier's she'd not let gossip and the opinion of others get to her.

Neither Ripah nor Susannah can cope with the speculation as well as Miriam. Ripah is very guarded. One of the women, Martha I think it was, challenged Ripah very directly, observing that her baby bore little resemblance to her husband. I'm glad that the attention has gone away from me and Ruth until I see Ripah suddenly burst into tears. She is sobbing her heart out, unable for a while to get out any words of explanation. Then it all comes tumbling out. She admits that her child is the consequence of her violation and her husband has refused to accept the child, what's more, he's threatened to divorce her.

The mood of the women changes violently, her tears have worked their effect and they commiserate with her, they are angry with her husband Thaddeus.

'What will you do? Will you oppose him?'

'What can I do? Of course I don't want to lose him. But I've no children of his own to hold him. I'm not like Susannah or Miriam who both have older children for whom their husbands have responsibility.'

Susannah joins in the general comforting of Ripah, saying nothing about her own situation. Her own violation is no secret, nor the fact that her child is probably that of one of the soldiers too, but the women have not pursued their curiosity about that fact any further because they are too preoccupied with supporting Ripah who is still sobbing.

The hauling up of water has ceased while the gossip about our children has been the sole source of interest. Other women, not affected by our predicament, contemplate aloud what their own husbands would do, were they in the place of Ripah or Susannah. Some of the women present must have been close to a similar situation for rumour has it that over a dozen rapes took place that dreadful morning, although only four of us have born children as a possible outcome. And some of those present now certainly lost children in the killings.

As we at length get round to filling our water-pots and make our way unsteadily up the rocky path, I'm joined by Susannah, who peers afresh at my Ruth and confides in me.

'Lucky you! At least your husband does not doubt his own child. Even if mine understands and does not blame me, I can feel his shame that the boy is not his own.' As she says this, she is pulling back the cloth to show the face of her sleeping baby boy. 'He would have been so proud that I'd delivered him a son at last after the two daughters.'

'Yes, I'm fortunate, I suppose.'

I was going to add more, but I'm frightened I'll give away that my situation is similar to hers. The other women may sound sympathetic but the children spawned by the soldiers will always be objects of curiosity, they'll be pointed at in the village, they will be called 'bastards' behind closed doors, if later there is mischief caused by children in the village, they'll be blamed. Bad blood will out, they'll say, and that cloud of suspicion and prejudice will always be there.

I will not have that for my child. I may find it hard to love her, but I'll protect her, that I will promise. I'll not have her labelled a 'bastard'.

Chapter 13
Nathan, BC 4

Thank God Jude is home. We heard a commotion last night, after dark. There were shouts and screams, our hackles rose once again, before we realised they were exclamations of joy, not panic or fear. I went round at once to find out what had happened and discovered Jude and Salome grinning at each other like newly-weds, and Simon jumping up and down in excitement. I made as if to leave them at once, to let them have some privacy, but Jude stopped me and made me stay to have a homecoming drink with them. He looked more rugged than I expected, well I should have guessed that he'd be coarsened for sleeping rough so long. His beard was unkempt and his clothes were dirty and torn, but that was not bothering Salome at the moment. We'd scarcely started to celebrate when Jude began to thank me over and over again for keeping his field from growing wild, for helping his family grow their crops. His gratitude was almost embarrassing, it was so effusive.

Matthaeus and Saul are home as well. I guess there are some thankful hearts in those homes also.

'What about James and Joshua? Are they not home as well?'

'That's a long story, I'll tell you tomorrow.'

'There's nothing wrong, is there? They've not been injured or captured?'

'No, nothing like that. They're alright as far as I know, but they left us to go north to Galilee.'

Jude emptied his earthenware goblet and looked at Salome and then stared. He had just become aware that Salome was pregnant, it was very obvious, he needed to say no more. She'd not even had a chance to tell him before I intruded on them.

'Jude, I'll be going now. There are things you need to talk about with each other. You can tell me all about your experiences tomorrow.'

'I know Matthaeus has told a number of men in the village that we'll meet at the synagogue in the morning. I'm sure Saul will join us and I'll certainly be there. At least Saul has no clinging wife to stop him coming.' He said this light-heartedly enough for it not to be any kind of rebuke.

I went back home and told Rachel all I had learned. 'About time too,' she offered, 'that poor woman has been worried sick, especially since she knew another child was on the way. At least he'll stay home now and be present for the birth, then he'll see his duty holds him here.'

We assemble in the morning in the synagogue's outer courtyard. The return of the three men is now common knowledge and the flagged space open to the sky is heaving with a crowd of Bethlehem's menfolk, a few standing, but most squatting on the ground. They all assume that Matthaeus or Jude will give a full account of their adventures since leaving the village some five months previously. Zacchaeus and Joel are present too, although they mingle with the crowd and do not take the lead or stand conspicuously. They are being cautious, they fear even now that Herod's informers may have infiltrated the village and will do nothing to jeopardise their own reputation or that of their beloved synagogue by appearing to greet possible known sympathisers of the nationalist fanatics.

Jude is the first to speak to us.

'Brothers, thanks for your welcome and interest. When we left you a few months back we first met up with the contact Mordecai had given us, no names, you'll understand why. He led us to the other side of Jerusalem, to the Jericho road, where a group of nationalists were operating from one of the wadis leading down to the Jordan. Initially they treated us with some suspicion, although when they heard of our experience here at Herod's hands, we were accepted.'

Matthaeus, already looking much more groomed than Jude, as befits our waspish scribe, interrupts.

'At first we thought we'd found the right outlet for our revenge. The rebels would watch the travellers on the road and a couple of times they ambushed men they knew to be collaborators with the Romans, Sadducees, whom they robbed and beat up, before sending them, limping, on their way. Then they attacked and robbed a priest. We were horrified that a leader from our Temple in Jerusalem should be treated in this way. The rebels argued that the Temple priests were in cahoots with the Romans, that they were part of the established authority that found a way of working with the enemy that was mutually convenient. Anyone who made life easier for the Romans was therefore a target for robbery or even assassination. This was not in our minds at all, we wanted action directed against Herod and the army that kept him in power.'

There is an upswell of murmured assent and the crowd stirs, then settles to listen further.

Matthaeus continues, 'One day we spied a small contingent of soldiers coming up the pass. We thought, at last, the opportunity we've been waiting for. But the Zealots - that's what they called themselves - wouldn't act. Too many, they said, too risky. They're armed and even if we catch them by surprise, we'll lose men. And then the remnant of the soldiers will advise the Romans and all hell will let loose in the hills here. We'll be hunted down until all of us are captured and crucified. So we had to watch them pass, while we skulked like cowards behind our rocky outcrops, just six of Herod's guards there were, and they looked so relaxed, so easy it would have been to have surprised them.'

Saul, the son of Judah, a young man not yet betrothed, decides to say his piece, taking advantage of Matthaeus pausing for breath.

'This caused a rift in our relations with the Zealots. We began to think of them as bandits, just after the loot of anyone who looked wealthy enough. They saw us as dangerous foolhardy nationalist extremists bent on suicidal missions. We stayed on a few more weeks, but when we were involved in the ambush of a couple of wealthy Pharisees and one of them got killed in the skirmish as he fought back, we'd had enough.'

Jude now has his say again. 'The leader of the group took us aside one day and told us if political revenge was our sole motive, we should form up with the so-called 'siccarii' who were operating in Herod's stronghold in the north. There, apparently, the rebels harry the Herodian soldiers at every turn, although they pay the penalty when the Roman garrison at Caesarea is brought into the action. But it's wild country up there, hideouts are plentiful, villagers are said to be sympathetic and often risk the wrath of the Romans.' Jude pauses for breath and is about to continue when Matthaeus interrupts once more.

'So Joshua and James decided that they would seek out such a band in Galilee. One of the Jericho group promised to lead any of us that so wished to a contact in the north - I think they were only too glad to be rid of us. They left one night and it was made pretty plain to the rest of us that our continued presence was unwelcome. So we've come back, at least for the time being. Joshua and James promised to return to Bethlehem once they'd had some experience of the 'siccarii' and witnessed at first hand their effectiveness as a tool against Herod. We said we'd await them here and might join them at a later date if their report is positive.'

Andrew then says what has been in the minds of many of us.

'What about your families here? You've all got children as well as wives. Your fields are lying fallow and your trades are being neglected, or they would be if we hadn't stepped into your shoes.'

'Brothers, we thank you for looking after our families' welfare. We knew we could trust you to do that. If we are to get revenge on that scheming tyrant, we have to make sacrifices. We were sure of your support - through your actions enabling us to fight, you are joining our campaign.'

'I'm not sure all your wives see it like that.'

'They will when we are able to show them how we've avenged their losses and violations.'

I'm very doubtful about this. Perhaps the women will be glad enough to have their husbands back and will say nothing to disturb that pleasure. Perhaps the men will see only what they want to see, and still revelling in their experiences, will not pick up the body language of their women. We shall see. I'm sure Jude, for one, will not leave us again. Now he knows Salome is pregnant and the child will be born within the next few weeks, he'll not let her down, I'm sure he'll see it that way.

We drift back to our labour. I go to tend Jude's field as it seems only right to allow him a few more hours back with his family before he resumes his duties.

*   *   *

Life in the village slowly returns to normal. Ruth is now three months old and Rachel seems to be coping, although I know she finds her a constant reminder of that wretched day. I try to be as supportive as I can, at least no-one mentions the fact that she might not be mine. It is common knowledge in the village that there are at least three children who are the product of the rapes. Initially there was some hostility and shaming, then the mothers received constant pity and commiseration which must, I think, have been even worse for them. I'll shield Rachel from all this, if it's the last thing I'll do.

Salome's baby daughter was born last week. She's named her Naomi after our ancestor who returned home from exile to her native land, part in celebration of Jude's homecoming, but I think as some, perhaps unconscious, recognition of the return to a semblance of normality in our village after the last few months' trauma. Salome is clearly more relaxed as she believes her husband will not leave her again now. Jude is a little disappointed, I think, I get the feeling that he was anticipating another son, perhaps in some measure to stand in for his murdered child. He doesn't say as much, but I just sense something is still missing.

It will be the Passover Festival next week and there's speculation that Joshua and James will try to return at this special time. Their wives are making preparations, they are optimists. I'm dubious, Galilee is a long way away, at least four days' journey. Rachel has been collecting the ingredients for the Passover meal and we plan to make our way with others from the village to the Temple in Jerusalem for the main ceremony.

When we assemble for the pilgrimage journey, I'm astonished to see Joshua and James among our number. Apparently they returned late last night especially for the festival, fulfilling the faith of their families. They are now mixing with us, telling us excitedly of the life they have been leading with the 'siccarii', the nationalist group they have been linked with. Apparently they call themselves by the name of 'Zealots' also. They are saying that they have joined one of the bands which is operating in the Golan hills to the east of Genneseret, the large Galilean inland sea, and that they've been involved in a couple of actions against Herod's soldiers, although they seem a little vague about the outcome. Their enthusiasm seems infectious, both of them are trying to persuade Matthaeus and the others who went initially to Jericho to join them in the north. When the women hear the drift of the conversations, they are horrified. They believed that their men had come back for good, not to return taking others with them.

Salome has been left at home with the new baby and Simon, it is too soon for her to venture the walk into Jerusalem and the crowds they will encounter there. If she were to hear them arguing with Jude and realise that he'd not rejected the argument straight away, she'd be furious. I take Jude aside and caution him against considering returning with Joshua and James, and he promises me he'll think carefully about it, but I can see, to my surprise, that he's tempted.

When the Passover period is behind us, the arguments rage in the village every day. Joshua and James have found out that some of the women raped by Herod's men have given birth to babies, and this has only increased their determination to take up the fight once more.

This morning I met Matthaeus, with Joshua, his son, walking to the synagogue. After our usual greetings, I asked him what his plans were, how soon he intended to leave us again.

'We go tomorrow, Nathan. You should come with us. You have young Benjamin to avenge, I'd have thought you would have been one of the first to join us.'

'Rachel needs me here. She has a new baby to care for and she needs my support. And some of us have to care for the families left behind.'

'I respect your point of view even if I don't agree with it. Some of us have to carry the fight on. At least give me your blessing.'

'That I gladly do. And moreover, you have this young man here,' I say, 'to look after your wife and other son. Joshua here must be of age by now.'

And that is when the boy breaks in and says in no uncertain fashion that he is joining his father. I'm certain that Matthaeus will quickly dampen the boy's ardour, but I'm astounded when he seems to encourage him.

'The boy is of age as you say,' says Matthaeus, 'he seeks revenge too - his younger brother was slaughtered with the rest and he is not lacking in physique or the requisite skills. What he doesn't know, he'll soon learn.'

The boy picks up some stones and slings them at birds with his catapult, to demonstrate his aggression and expertise.

'See, I'm like the boy David fighting Goliath,' he boasts. 'Jehovah will be with us, we'll kill the scum and avenge our brothers.'

There is no doubt that Joshua has the spirit and physique, in fact many of us have been concerned for some time that he is too aggressive with the other boys, too boisterous in his playing and some mothers complain that he'll cause serious injury to another child soon. Perhaps I should be glad that he is leaving us, yet I cannot really accept Matthaeus' encouragement to the boy as he has only just reached his majority. Thirteen is too young for roughing it with experienced rebels twice his age.

I'm still thinking about Joshua and Matthaeus' decision to let him join the Zealots. Is it really the father's decision or is he too influenced by the boy's bravado? Many in the village have wished for years that Matthaeus would take a stronger line with him, but people have been afraid to speak out because Matthaeus is a scribe, an educated man, who will always find a slick answer to any hint of scepticism or inferred criticism.

I tell Rachel of the conversation I've just had with Matthaeus and the fact that he's allowing his son to join him in Galilee. Her first reaction is good riddance to the boy, she's never liked him, although she agrees with me that Matthaeus is foolhardy to let the boy go. Then she looks at me with those soulful dark eyes of hers, and puts her hands on both my shoulders, staring me in the face.

'Nathan, my husband, I want you to make a promise to me. Don't ever leave me, don't you ever decide to join the other men in their vengeance. I need you here to support me. Will you promise me that?'

She has caught me off guard, it is not that I have ever thought seriously of joining the other men, but I'm hesitant at declaring myself so unambiguously, especially as many of us are still arguing about the issues and I have tried to remain rational and balanced. But Rachel persists, I cannot fudge this direct demand being made of me, I have to declare my intention or face a wife who will always be uncertain, untrusting. I make up my mind, for Rachel is here in front of me, and she needs me, I can see that.

'Yes, Rachel, my love, I promise that I will not leave you to join a rebel group. I will stay here and support you and our daughter, Ruth.'

Somehow it seems right to include Ruth in the promise. If I cannot leave to avenge my firstborn, then somehow I need to make a promise to the child I have adopted, at least in my own mind. I need to own her in my heart as well.

Rachel hears me out and breathes a sigh of relief. Then she hugs me. As we are still clasped together, suddenly a cry comes from the cradle. Little Ruth is awake and hungry, although in my mind she is crying out to be included in the centre of our family. I break away from Rachel and pick the child up. She stops her crying and looks at me as if she understands. I hand her to Rachel and put my arms around them both.

She is ours. 'Forget her origin, Rachel. God has placed her in our care. We must not let her down.'

She looks at the child, then at me, and tears are rolling down her cheeks.

'Yes, Nathan, I will try, you know I will.'

We both acknowledge the feelings we have had about the girl, our doubts, our misgivings, our feelings of betrayal by this child, and we solemnly declare to each other that she shall be our own, that she will be as valued as any future child of ours.

'You will be a better father, Nathan, than that brute of a soldier would have been. I pray that she finds in you a father who teaches her mercy and forgiveness, so that she grows up to make us both proud.'

'So be it. Love her, Rachel, cuddle her in your arms, let her eyes feast upon yours, smile at her, do not weep. Do not let the sadness of her creation be reflected in your eyes when you look at her. Together we'll overcome the past, and face with her the future.'

Matthaeus was as good as his word. He joined Joshua and James and took his son Joshua with him. Saul went as well and a couple of men who had not joined the first time. And to my great surprise and Salome's great anger, Jude went too. I cannot fathom that man, I thought he'd reasoned it out that his place was here, the defence of his family by supporting them was his best response to Herod's deeds, but the man is not rational. He lets James and Joshua sway his emotions too much, they incite his quickness to anger, and play down his feelings of loyalty to his wife, they make him think it would be cowardly and shaming to refuse to go a second time. So once more I'm sweating to plant Jude's crops for him and seeking to mollify a seething Salome. Rachel spends time with her and their new baby girl. It is at least more company for her and the grief and anger of others takes her out of her own remaining feelings of distress, she is too busy trying to coax Salome and young Simon who misses his father dreadfully.

Just as our family happiness seems to be returning at last, there is a scandal that threatens to destroy another family. James, one of the sheep farmers in the village, and who has been away in Galilee again the past few weeks, has a young wife, Rhoda, who also lost her firstborn in the massacre. The girl, for she is little more than that, was already near a breakdown from that loss, but has found the departure of her husband too much to bear. Her mother has tried to comfort her, but rumour has it that another has taken advantage of the distress of the girl and offered a little too much sympathy. A youth, Clodis, has been looking after James' sheep and has been seen going to and from Rhoda's house with great frequency, and tongues were already wagging, before it became obvious that Rhoda was carrying a child.

When challenged, she broke down and confessed her shame. She could do little else for James had been in Galilee for his first stay there when the baby must have been conceived. Here was a major problem, because James was once more in the north and hard to contact. The girl was confined to her mother's home, while the men of the village argued over her fate with the rabbis. The youth, Clodis, was interrogated, and under such pressure, eventually admitted his guilt. He was flogged and expelled from Bethlehem. Rhoda was meanwhile showing, she must have been at least five months pregnant. Her initial attempts to argue that James was the father were ridiculed and some men were for stoning her to death as could be justified under the law. Others tempered their condemnation of her with a little mercy, arguing that the murder of her son, followed by the desertion of her husband, albeit with good cause, was too much for the girl to bear and she should be treated with some sympathy.

I was of this latter school of thought. I'd argued this strongly at the debate in the synagogue and the rabbis, although normally the first to uphold the law, were, I believe, more in sympathy with my point of view. In any case, they argued, we are more sophisticated than this, we must apply the law but temper justice with mercy. We are not like some barbarians in rural villages who throw rocks first and think afterwards.

The problem, however, was what action we should take in the absence of the husband. Should we turn the girl and her baby, when born, out of the village? Should he divorce her by proxy? We resolved to try to get a message to the man and summon him urgently back to Bethlehem. Meanwhile Rhoda was to remain in the home of her mother and not show her face in the village until her husband returned and decided her fate.

That action was put into effect, but it was a good three months later before James eventually returned home, after having been found the other side of the Jordan river. By then Rhoda was approaching the time for delivery of the child. James was naturally furious and was initially inclined to condemn the girl to the punishment our law allows. But several of us prevailed upon him to temper his outrage and in the end he agreed that he would just divorce the girl and abandon her and the baby to the protection of the mother, whose whole family would now be shamed. Once the legalities had been conducted by the priest, James returned to Galilee, metaphorically shaking the dust of Bethlehem from his feet. His anger would be taken out on Herod's soldiers, or that was his intent. We heard that a few days after his departure a baby girl had been born to Rhoda.

I am in the village square this morning when I hear the shocking news. Rhoda has murdered the baby and killed herself. Apparently, since the birth, the girl had been weeping continuously and would not feed the child properly. The baby had therefore cried incessantly and when Rhoda's mother had tried to instil some sense into the girl, she had just grabbed the baby and left the house. They had let her go, assuming she'd return when she came to her senses, but she'd stayed out all night and her father and brother only searched for her in the morning. They apparently found the baby first, strangled, lifeless, on a rocky outcrop at the edge of the village. Then they found her body at the foot of the crag, she'd thrown herself off the edge and had died before they got to the scene.

Sounds of grief are echoing from Rhoda's mother's house and a group of women are gathered outside participating in her distress, because they can be seen to sympathise with her mother now the shamed girl is dead. I come across them as I'm making my way home to Rachel. I feel the embarrassed guilt of the village. We have hounded that poor girl to her fate. Some will try to justify their actions and the attitude of the crowd, but in the end we cannot deny our part in the tragedy.

When I tell Rachel what has happened, she bursts into tears, even though Rhoda was not close to her.

'That poor girl, she can't have been more than fifteen, left alone to cope with the grief of losing her firstborn, and then vulnerable to the attentions of that rascal, Clodis.'

'I think it's a tragedy too. Many will condemn her, but we are too quick to criticise, she was ostracised by the other women and no-one tried to stop them.'

'Perhaps I should have said something, befriended her, visited her at her mother's home.'

'Don't blame yourself, Rachel, she was not a particular friend of yours, why should you have been the one to show her kindness?'

'Well, someone should have done.'

'There'll be many feeling guilty now. Too late unfortunately. Some will still condemn, call her a murderess and good riddance.'

'I'll visit her mother. When the wailing is over and she's buried, then I'll show her mother that we do not all hold her shame as reason to ignore the rest of the family. They need us specially now.'

'You're a good woman, Rachel.'

I look at her and am glad that the woman I married has such feelings and is not hard like some of the older self-righteous wives. The person who should have her death on his conscience is James. His decision to join the siccarii always seemed a dubious one to me, experience has shown it to be disastrous. What sort of revenge is this on Herod? All he has achieved is death and disgrace in his own family. Paying back violence with violence, whatever it says in the scriptures read by the rabbis, it doesn't make sense. It just seems to breed further violence.

There is an argument on whether it is necessary to tell James what has transpired. After all, he divorced the girl, it could be maintained that he had no further interest in her fate. What would the news of her death and that of the baby achieve? Would it give him a guilty conscience? If so, what was the point of that? Should we not let him continue his war of justice against Herod unprompted by doubts?

Then weeks later fresh news reaches us. Herod is dead. The tyrant, that brute, has finally succumbed. They say his last days were spent in torment, great physical pain that drove him out of his mind. So justice was being administered by the Lord, not by mere mortals after all. We should send a messenger to James and Joshua and the others who went back with them. Perhaps they'll come home now, their vengeance completed, no need for further action.

'No need,' says Mordecai when the suggestion is put to him. 'They'll find out soon enough. The intelligence systems of the siccarii will soon discover the truth. They find out the movements of Herod's troops easily enough, they'll soon discover that Herod himself is dead. Then they'll be home, you'll see.'

Salome and the other wives speak optimistically about their men's return, they believe it is over, the horror of the last few months has been finally laid to rest. They are waiting in anticipation.

Part 2

Pharaoh's Children

'And when he was cast out, Pharaoh's daughter took him up, and nourished him for her own son.'
(Acts, chapter 7, verse 21)

'When Israel was a child, then I loved him, and called my son out of Egypt'
(Hosea, chapter 11, verse 1)

'And was there until the death of Herod: that it might be fulfilled which was spoken of the Lord by the prophet, saying 'Out of Egypt have I called my son.'
(Matthew chapter 2, verse 15)

Chapter 14
Joseph, BC 6

'Mari,' I said, 'I'm worried.'

Mari had been settling Joshua after the disturbance of our visitors. It was a quite extraordinary occurrence and our minds were still reeling. These men from Babylon or somewhere east of that, they said – I didn't understand everything and I might have misunderstood – just suddenly appeared out of nowhere as we were finishing our meal. I thought they'd got the wrong house at first but they were insistent that they'd come to see our son, so we had to let them in and I was most embarrassed that we had just eaten and had little we could offer them. They insisted that they had come to bring us gifts, not the opposite and produced the most extravagant offerings. I was really scared that something was wrong, especially when we learned they had come straight from Herod's palace in Jerusalem. And when I saw what they had brought – that really shocked me – I'd never seen such riches.

Mari to my surprise didn't seem in the least put out by their visit. It was almost as if she'd expected them. She'd gone to fetch Joshua without any hesitation and shown the boy off to them with pride. The men, there were five of them – two older and three younger men, perhaps their sons - crowded round and praised the boy and told Mari that they'd divined from their astrological calculations that he was to be a great king. I don't believe in all that mystical stuff myself, I don't see how we can be influenced by all those stars and planets but the rumour is that Herod and his advisers pay great heed to it. In which case it doesn't seem to have done him much good because everyone says he's ill and losing his influence and is becoming crazy about his children and their threats to his throne.

Anyway I was assuming we'd have to find room to accommodate our visitors and they were clearly people used to luxuries that we could not possibly offer. I was all for sending for the rabbi from our synagogue to see if he could help us, when the men said that they had servants - they'd remained outside the village so as not to create a crush in the small house. They were therefore not staying but had to get back to Herod's palace as he and his courtiers were keen to honour the prince also. That's when I panicked. If Herod could murder his own sons because he feared that they were plotting to overthrow him, what could he not do to a peasant family who were rumoured to have a claim on the throne, however ridiculous that might be?

I implored them not to go back to Herod, but they said they had promised and that the king had been most courteous and had expressed great interest in their pilgrimage and quest. That worried me even more and I pleaded with them not to tell Herod or any of his court who we were or where we lived. I risked telling them what I knew to be common knowledge about the tyrant and recounted how he'd had his own sons, Alexander and Aristobulus, executed for treason as he'd feared they were trying to take his crown. They were clearly unsettled by this and discussed it in their own language so I've no idea whether they have taken my pleas to heart or whether they have returned to the king, in which case I fear our lives might be in danger.

All this went right over Mari's head. 'I told you Joshua is very special. God has protected me from the very beginning and the visit of these rich and powerful men just proves that God has planned great things for him.'

When I expressed concern at what Herod might do if he believed what these men were saying, Mari, bless her, just said that God will protect us just as he's done for over three years now. She looked so lovely as she cradled the boy and offered to hand him to the men to hold, but the men looked in awe and even bent as though they were bowing before him.

And then they just went, as suddenly as they came. All that way just for an hour or so, it seemed extraordinary and incredible. You'd have thought they'd want to stay for several days – perhaps they found our house full of smells they are unused to, with all the wood and dust mingling with the odour of the donkey and the chickens, and just wanted to get back to the comfort of rooms that the court would surely have made available for them.

I was curious and asked how they had travelled as they didn't look as though they'd walked from Jerusalem, and they replied that they'd left the camels with their handlers well before the village and arrived on foot as they did not want to cause a disturbance or get the attention of everyone in the village. Their visit was to pay their personal respects to the boy, not to cause us the embarrassment of having everyone crowding in and making our lives impossible. I was certainly grateful for their thoughtfulness on this matter and hopefully their visit has gone unnoticed as everyone was in from the fields and eating their evening meals before settling for the night when they entered the village. I doubt if anyone was in the street to see them.

And so I repeated to Mari after they'd gone, 'I'm worried.' Mari looked so surprised at me. She does not hear the tales of the king and his goings on that I hear when I'm with the men, or when we hear news from the rabbis on the Sabbath. These things don't interest the women. I doubt if they gossip over such matters round the well, they talk about their children and who is getting married and who is ill and problems with their husband's families and all the latest scandal. I haven't bothered Mari with news of politics in Jerusalem because I've never thought that she'd be interested in the slightest. Perhaps I should have done, because Mari does not now comprehend the danger we might be in.

I try to tell her the risks we now face, especially if the strangers return to Herod as they said they'd been commanded to do. It would only take them a couple hours, less even, to get back to the city and therefore they'd be reporting what they'd found to Herod tomorrow morning. Herod could send his soldiers to find and arrest us as early as the middle of the next day. I have a decision that has to be made now. I leave Mari with Joshua for a while and go into my workshop to think. We can stay here and take the risk that the visitors will heed my pleas and not go back to Herod; or that they do but Herod thinks it's all too improbable and takes no action. Or we can escape before Herod's soldiers are sent for us, in which case we can either go back to Mari's people in Galilee or join the other refugees that take the coast road to Egypt as I hear is common practice these days as Jews find themselves in trouble from the Romans or the Herodian authorities.

The more I think about it, the more agitated I become. We have so little time to make such a life-changing decision. The temptation is to stay here and rely on Mari's profound faith that God will look after us whatever happens. But perhaps it is God prompting my mind now to protect my family by fleeing this dangerous place. She'll think I'm mad to uproot us just from fear, but I can't help it. I'm convinced that Herod will seek us out – why else would he tell the strangers to return to him and report where we are so he can honour the prince? I know it's absurd, we have no claim on the throne whatsoever, but from what I hear Herod will act if there's the slightest chance of a rival to his crown. We can deny this until the day we die, but his guards will torture us until we confess anything that they want. I can't risk it. We must be out of here before daybreak and well away before Herod's soldiers are sent to arrest us. We must spend the next hour sorting out what we need to take with us – please God, let this be the right decision.

Now for the really difficult bit. Mari is going to take this very hard. I return to our main living room and find Mari already lying on her bedroll and nearly asleep. I must arouse her quickly and get her thinking about the food we'll need for ourselves and Joshua. I shake her roughly by the shoulder.

'Mari, Mari, we've got to get up. We can't stay here any longer!'

Mari stirs and looks at me with shocked eyes.

'Why, Joseph? It's not that bad, is it? Has something else happened?'

'They'll come for us, I know they will. We can't wait. They may even come today. We've got to leave before it gets light.'

'But I thought you asked those men not to go back to Herod.'

'I can't trust them. Herod's spies have probably been following them and know who and where we are. I'm not going to risk your life or Joshua's.'

'But he's only a baby. What threat could he possibly be?'

'Well you convinced me and Eli in Nazareth that he would be the expected Messiah. It won't take much to persuade a vicious tyrant like Herod not to take a risk. He won't bother about the life of one inconspicuous family from an outlying village. We've no-one of influence to speak for us.'

'Trust God, Joseph. I did when everyone was threatening me with death and God saved me.'

'Suppose God is saving us now by telling us to flee?'

'Do you really think he is, Joseph? Really?'

'I believe so. I've been thinking and praying this last hour or so and I've become more and more convinced we have to go.'

'But where to, Joseph? Back to Nazareth? Our family can hide us there.'

'You know as well as I do that Herod's soldiers are even more active in Galilee than here in Jerusalem. At least here they are garrisoned in the city. In Galilee they are everywhere on patrol because of the rebel groups. It's still Herod's land and he has spies there in every village. I don't think we can risk Nazareth although I know you'd like to go back and be with your mother and sisters.'

'Where then, Joseph? Where else can we go?'

Before I can answer, she suddenly bursts into tears. It's all too sudden, all too much for her. I realise that she's still confused, she was nearly asleep and my decision has come like a bolt from the blue. She's had no time to get her mind round the issue I've been tussling with this last hour or so. I put my arms around her and dry her tears and hold her until she's pulled herself together. When I think she's listening again, I say something that I know will really shake her.

'We could go to Egypt. At least we'd be out of Herod's jurisdiction and protected by Roman law.'

'But Egypt! That's a foreign country. We don't even know the language. How could we live there?'

'Many Jews live in Egypt. Lots have gone there because the harvests are better and many who have fallen foul of Herod have fled there. I'm told that most of the cities have a Jewish population so we could live among them and I could find work.'

'It's a huge decision, Joseph. Do we have to decide tonight or can we wait and think about it in the morning? We could ask Rebecca's opinion or Jude or Andrew to see what they think.'

'We can't share this, Mari. We mustn't breathe a word. If we go, no-one must know why or where we've gone so that if soldiers come looking they can genuinely answer that they don't know. They'll try to guess where we've gone and probably assume that we've returned to Nazareth to your family. That'll give us a head start if we've gone in the opposite direction.'

'Do you really think that's the only choice for us? Are you sure?'

There is a long silence. I decide not to rush her, despite my increasing conviction that every minute is precious and we must be away as soon as possible. Minutes pass. I must bite my tongue and let her wrestle with the momentous decision before us. At length she speaks very slowly and carefully as though she herself has come to the decision.

'I'll not try to dissuade you. Perhaps God is looking after us this way after all.'

'I think so, Mari. I wish I had your confidence and certainty sometimes, but every moment that passes makes me more convinced that this is the right, indeed, the only thing to do.'

Again there is a long silence. I can see her screwing up her brow in deep thought. She gives a sudden sigh, shakes herself as though she is brushing off the implications of this life-shattering and momentous decision and becomes suddenly very practical as though she'd been resolved on this course of action for days.

'Then what shall we need? What do I need to pack? How much can we carry?'

I breathe a sigh of relief. I was fearful that I'd have to spend a long time - time that I fear we haven't got - persuading her. A fear perhaps that she'd refuse absolutely to go. What would I do then? I become practical too.

'We can take the donkey. I'll kill the chickens and you pack them - we'll need fresh meat. Don't pluck them now, we haven't time. Get a set of spare clothes for all of us - just one change of clothes. We'll have to eat mainly grain and fruit we can pick on the journey. One cooking pot and one water jar - no more. We need to set a good pace so we mustn't overload the beast.'

'What about the things you've been making in your workshop? Is everything finished?'

'No, that's very unfortunate. I feel bad about that. But it can't be helped. We can't warn them or they will guess where we've gone and will be a risk to our safety. That reminds me, I'll need to take my tools to be able to earn some money wherever we finish up.'

I'd nearly forgotten that. I go into my workshop and look round. I gather my tools together and look at the unfinished work promised to my neighbours. I feel guilty about letting them down, although to be honest they'll get nearly-finished articles for nothing. To be fair to Mari, now she has accepted my decision, she doesn't argue any more but hurries about her work and is busy harnessing the packs on the donkey before I'm ready. She is just about to go to fetch Joshua from his cradle, when she points to the gifts the astrologers had brought.

'We can't leave those things, not after they brought them all that way for Joshua.'

'Perhaps we should take them to sell in case we need food or other essentials.'

'Joseph, no! They belong to Joshua, not us! We can't sell them.'

'If we take them all the way, there's a danger we'll get robbed. Things of such obvious value will be a great temptation to people we meet on the way, let alone outlawed thieves.'

'So let's hide them here, ready for our return. Somewhere really safe. Should you bury them? No-one knows they're here.'

I start looking around for somewhere safe to put them. There are nooks and crannies in my workshop, but perhaps some of my customers will root about searching for the things I'm still making for them and look for my tools. I can't risk them finding these things – they'll be too much of a temptation. I think Mari's idea of burying them is probably best. I find an old cloth to wrap the caskets in and dig in the yard where the chickens normally scratch about. When I've dug deep enough, I lay the cloth inside and cover it up with earth and batten the soil down as hard as I can to try not to show too obviously that the earth has been disturbed. I'd better slaughter a couple of chickens for our journey too – to take all of them will be foolish – the meat will rot before we can finish them. We'll just have to eat off the land. I'll take the money we have to buy food when we can. I'm sure our neighbours will take the remaining chickens when they realise that we're not coming back. I chase the chickens round the yard and catch and tweak the heads of a couple and wrap them ready for Mari to pack with the other food she is gathering. There are four eggs as well so I collect those and wrap them carefully although they'll probably crack with the movement of the donkey.

I suppose it must be less than an hour since I woke Mari up and here we are ready to leave our home for another life. It's all been so sudden. I realise that I'm in shock as well. I've been so intent on persuading Mari of the need to leave that I haven't really taken in the impact of my decision until we are ready to go. I'm the one who is now dithering, double-checking everything, fearful that in our rush, I might have forgotten something that might give ourselves away, or not packed something that will be vital to our survival.

And now Mari is waiting for me, though she's let Joshua sleep right up until we're ready to go. I nod to her and she picks the boy up and he doesn't stir. I put all we've prepared into the saddle packs on the donkey's back and we slip as silently as we can out of the house and into the street. At least the child's asleep and hasn't woken and cried to alert the neighbours, but I'm petrified that the donkey will bray as I get him under way, but apart from a quiet snort, the animal picks its way out of the yard and we set foot on the street, Mari carrying the sleeping child, with me leading the beast. But which way shall we go? In all the hurry of our preparations I'd given that little thought. Which way is Egypt? Which way shall we go ...?

Chapter 15
Mari

I don't know what to think. In fact, I'm still half asleep and all my attention is concentrated on holding Joshua tight and trying not to wake him. The events of the last few hours are as if a whirlwind has hit us. One minute, there we were in our domestic routine. After all the fuss and excitement of Joshua's birth, the last year or so had seemed somehow an anti-climax. In one way I'd been keen to take Joshua and Joseph back to Nazareth and have a proper wedding. But of course I was ill after Joshua was born and in no fit state to go anywhere. So Joseph had just got us to his own house and let me and the baby rest after that astonishing night and had sought the help of a neighbour to tend to me. And then he'd unpacked all his tools and tidied up his workshop, and before we'd realised it, he had a string of customers all wanting him to make something for them, because there'd been no carpenter in the village since old Simon had died, a man Joseph had assisted when he'd learned the trade. So even after I'd recovered we put off going home and I got to know the village life and was fully occupied in getting used to looking after Joshua – it was all new and exciting then.

And I'd made good friends, Rachel and Rebecca and the other women of the village were welcoming and helpful, so we'd stayed although Joseph assured me that we could go home to Nazareth once he'd made enough money to look after us all properly and not have to rely on Eli's charity. And then I'd really taken to Rachel, her little boy was nearly the same age as Joshua and they got on so well together, it was a joy to see. Sometimes I missed them all at home and felt homesick – Rebecca would be twelve now and Salome eleven. I still think of them as little girls – I can't believe they might even be betrothed for all I know. I'm sure my mother would somehow get a message to me if something important like that happened. Joseph had said that they might be coming to Jerusalem for the Passover three months ago, but there was no news from them. Joseph had promised me that we would journey to Ein-Karem sometime to see my cousin Elizabeth and see how her son John was doing – he'd be over two – but now it won't happen. I don't know when we shall see my folks again. We're off to the great unknown and in the hands of God again. Despite my fear and confusion at what has happened, I can't suppress that glimmer of excitement that is stirring within me again.

It was only the other night that I prayed to God for a sign to confirm all the promises he'd made to me when Joshua was conceived. I know I'm too impatient and the role of being a mother and home-maker spending my time just with the other village women was becoming boring – no, that's unfair. I must be patient I thought, Joseph is good to me, I have a wonderful child. I must not expect all life to be lived in a state of excitement. And now all this! Those splendidly robed men coming all this way to worship my son – worship, they said. What a peculiar way to put it! It's as if they thought he was a god! And they looked pretty important people themselves, they must be for them to have been received in the king's palace. It all fell into place though. Just as we had visitors the night Joshua was born saying he was special, so these rich men said the same. It must be true.

And now this! Just as I'm getting used to these sheiks' visits and making sense of it, Joseph has decided we must leave and become refugees fleeing to another country. I thought at first that we ought to stay, God would protect us against Herod and protect our child. But Joseph sees it differently and I must trust him too. It's frightening and exciting at the same time. I'm sure God is looking after us and preparing some great new step for us to take. I wonder what it will lead to?

We've left our home. I look back at it silhouetted in the moonlight. I wonder when I shall see it again. It's a good job the moon is nearly full tonight, it'll help us see where we are going. I mustn't trip on the rough stones and let Joshua fall. We've headed out of the village to where the paths divide and we've stopped. I hope Joseph knows which way to go.

'Which way Joseph?'

'I'm just wondering. We could go towards Jerusalem and pick up the road to the coast from the gate outside the city. That would be easiest but it will take us nearer possible danger and I want to be as far as possible away from Jerusalem before Herod hears anything about us and sends his soldiers to find us. I know this track to the west takes us through the village of Emmaus but I don't know where it goes after that. If we go beyond that village and then take the first road north, hopefully that will bring us to the Roman highway, then we can make good time and mingle with other travellers because that road will probably be busy.'

I nod at him and am happy to follow his suggestion. I've not been out of Bethlehem since our arrival here on our way from Jerusalem itself, so I haven't the faintest idea where we are going, but the track is clear at first and we make our way with reasonable speed until we reach the next village after an hour or so. Joshua, thank heavens, is still fast asleep and Joseph asks if I want to mount the donkey, but it's easier not to disturb the child if I walk. The village is dark and still. I can hear an occasional wild dog bark and I see the shapes of sheep grazing as we pass, then we are the other side of the village and the moon disappears behind a cloud. It is much harder now and we slow right down. Suddenly we seem to have reached a criss-crossing of tracks and Joseph is undecided which one we must choose. He doesn't admit his uncertainty to me but I can tell he doesn't know. I'm a bit afraid now, but I mustn't let him see it.

I thought he'd take the path going to the north like he said he would, but after a long pause we continue westwards and move slowly in the darkness. Joshua is getting heavy in my arms, but I must keep on though it is difficult not seeing properly where I put my feet and I'm afraid of turning my ankle over and finding it impossible to walk. Joseph senses that I'm dragging a little and takes Joshua from me while I take the reins of the donkey and lead it to follow Joseph. We get to another village equally silent and deserted and can't find a track out. It seems to peter out at the end of a row of cottages and we find just fields of crops and sheep beyond. We seem to have come to a dead end.

'I'm sorry, Mari, I seem to have got it wrong. I wanted to get as far west as possible before looking for the Roman road, but it doesn't look as if we can go any further. We'll have to go back to where the tracks crossed and strike out to the north.'

I hoped that it would be alright and we'd not find another dead end – perhaps we'd have to wait for daylight and cut across the fields until we found another track.

'Are you alright?'

'Yes, Joseph. I can take Joshua back if you like, I've had a rest.'

As he hands the child to me, the boy stirs and suddenly begins to whimper. I try to shush him at first, making soothing noises, but he begins to cry and I have to ask Joseph to stop while I comfort him and offer him my breast to calm him for a few minutes. There is beginning to be a glow in the eastern sky and I get the feeling that Joseph is worried that we are not further on our way. Joshua accepts the darkness and does not seem to realise we are no longer at home and begins to slumber again, so we continue on our way with Joseph now leading the donkey once more while I follow carrying Joshua.

The track leads us over a gentle hill and then we are dropping down into a valley, and in the dim light I think I can make out movement. I think it must be the main road to the coast that Joseph has talked of. My husband has said nothing, but he is striding out more confidently now and after another half hour or so, we find we are approaching a major highway and it is getting light. When we are about a league away from the road running from east to west Joseph halts and puts his arm on my shoulder. We are standing by a small bush, which gives us some cover.

'Let's stay here a while and take a rest,' he says and takes Joshua from me, handing me the reins of the donkey. 'Let's both sit down for a while – we must have been walking for over three hours and I don't want you to get too tired for we've a long way to go today.'

I think he really wants to observe the traffic on the road to check that it's safe before we join it. At this point Joshua decides to wake up and struggles to get out of his father's arms.

'Let him go, Joseph,' I call out, 'let him run around while we've stopped. We'll have to carry him when we're on that road and he'll get fed up then and want to walk.'

I can see that Joseph is watching the road intently and we can see the silhouettes of figures moving slowly on the horizon. People are moving in both directions despite the early hour, though the majority seem to be going towards Jerusalem with their animals – I guess that they are going to the early morning market in the city. Although Joseph doesn't say it, I can see that he is worried about the possible movement of soldiers and has his eyes skinned to make sure none are in sight before he indicates that we are ready to be on the move again. I'm sure his concerns are needless at this hour. The strangers will only have been back in Jerusalem for a couple of hours and I doubt if the king is ready to receive visitors until mid morning so we can go a fair way yet without having to worry too much.

At last Joseph decides we can go on, and I pick the protesting Joshua up and we make it to the highway. At once our pace picks up as our sure-footed beast feels the even paving stones under its feet, and as the sun appears behind and casts long shadows that go before us, we pass a steady stream of travellers shielding their eyes from the red glowing ball which shines right into their faces. We plod on and after a while we halt to let a couple of hurrying men past pulling their cloaks tight round them to keep out the morning chill. I hadn't noticed the freshness until then. All our work to get under way had made me hot and carrying Joshua and clasping him to my body had kept me more than warm enough. In fact I found the temperature refreshing and knew that later in the morning we'd find the temperature rising until we suffered under the full glare of the midday sun. Joshua is getting wriggly now and squirming to get down. I promise that he can ride on the donkey if he will sit still and he beams at me and squeals in delight as I place him on the donkey's back, his legs splayed wide apart. I hold him and take the reins from Joseph so that I can control the pace of the animal.

Although we are making reasonable progress, several groups overtake us and pause a moment to greet us and ask us where we are going. We can't say we don't know, so Joseph just says 'to the coast'. I know he doesn't know the name of any towns there so he has to be vague. One prosperous looking man was curious and asked us where we'd come from and I could see my husband hesitate. Then he answered, 'from Bethany,' which is a small town on the other side of Jerusalem where some distant relations of Joseph live. He told me afterwards that he chose to say 'Bethany' because he'd been there and could answer questions in case the man knew it. He explained to me that we should not mention Bethlehem at all in case Herod's men started making enquiries for us. After that we repeated our story several times and although one travelling family accompanied us for some distance, no-one seemed to know much about Bethany which was a good thing!

The road passes through a number of villages and there are market stalls selling produce beside the road. Joseph buys some figs and dates at one of the villages where we stop for a rest and draw water for our beast to drink as well as quenching our own thirst. As long as we let Joshua ride the donkey he seems content enough, but as the sun draws to its highest in the sky above, he begins to yawn and I fear he'll slip from the animal's back. Joseph keeps glancing back and suddenly I see his facial muscles tighten and he quickly draws our animal to the side of the road and into a grove of olive trees growing there. 'Get down,' he shouts to me and I pull Joshua off the donkey, sit down on the scrubby grass and bare my breast to allow Joshua to begin to feed, looking as natural as I can while Joseph puts his back to the road as if to shield me.

'It's a band of soldiers,' he whispers to me. 'They're marching in formation. Don't look at them.'

I can't help it and give a quick glance as I hear the crunch of their boots on the rough ground. I see enough to gauge that they are Romans, not Herod's guards whom Joseph fears most. They don't give us as much as a glance and we wait until they are specks on the horizon before continuing our westward trail. As I lift Joshua back onto the donkey's back, I realise that his undergarment is wet and I ought to change him before we go any further. This could become a problem I think and I ask Joseph to stop if he sees any clean water so I can wash the soiled cloth and if possible, lay it on the donkey's hind quarters to dry before the sun loses its strength. Once Joshua is comfortable I decide to carry him for a while in the hope that he will sleep and after several false alarms when he rouses himself just as I think he is going off, he finally falls into a deep slumber. It isn't long before my arms begin to ache and I find myself willing him to wake so I can let him ride the donkey once again.

The sun rises high in the heavens and the heat gets to everyone. Joshua begins to whine and the pace of the donkey slackens noticeably. We plod on – we dare not stop. We eat some of the figs as we travel and stop briefly at a village well we encounter to quench our raging thirst. I take the opportunity to feed Joshua at this point and we continue with no further alarms other than the heat – everyone normally shelters at this hour but we feel we've got to keep on the move. The further west we go, the sparser grows the traffic and I begin to feel nervous when the road begins to climb some rolling hills and then cut through them down to the open countryside beyond. I feel so exposed and worried that we could easily become the targets of robbers, with no-one in sight to hear any calls of distress. But no-one comes and I begin to breathe more easily as the road descends from the barren hills to the fertile plain and I can see men toiling in the fields.

At last the sun begins to sink and Joseph says that we must soon find lodgings for the night. Suddenly we can see another major road ahead – I can glimpse men and beasts moving slowly along the horizon. We join it and head south because Joseph is sure this is the way towards the country of Egypt, but we are a little puzzled as we can see no sign of the coast and Joseph is sure he'd heard that the main north-south Roman highway hugs the coastline most of the way to Egypt. We continue south for a few leagues now passing groups of people I guess to be merchants and just before the sun sinks we come across what seems to be an important road junction. Our road continues southwards, but another road, which looks equally impressive, veers off to the right in a westerly direction. We stop and Joseph looks unsure. Should we continue in our present direction or will this new road take us to the coast and the main route to Egypt? Can we take the risk of displaying our ignorance by asking one of the passing groups of men who would doubtless ply us with questions and remember us if Herod's soldiers were in pursuit?

Joseph points to the signs of a village in the distance on the road south and he suggests that we continue to that point and find an inn where we can stay the night and seek advice from other lodgers there. It is a small town, not much more than a village – a bit bigger than my native Nazareth but smaller than Bethlehem. There is, to our relief, an inn there and Joseph goes to barter with the owner to ensure accommodation for all of us for the one night. He comes over to me while I hold both Joshua and the reins of the donkey.

'There's room for us but the owner is asking a high price and I'm not happy at letting so much of our savings go this soon on our journey. I've suggested that we could pay in kind

– with the two chickens and the eggs. After all, it's not going to be easy to cook them on the road and the landlord is willing to take them in complete payment for our stay.'

'What are we going to eat tomorrow?'

'We'll buy some fruit and bread in the village first thing. The chickens will soon be unsafe to eat, they'll go bad in the heat and make us ill. We can't risk giving them to Joshua. The innkeeper's wife will serve them as the evening meal for her guests and her own family.'

I agree reluctantly. I'd thought the flesh of the chickens would sustain us better for our journey and I'm reluctant to part with them, but in the event we have meat for the evening meal once we have tethered the beast in the courtyard at the back of the inn and have unpacked sufficient for the night. We are made welcome and the owner's wife is fascinated with Joshua who begins to show off to the new audience and amazes the woman with the words he knows and his obvious understanding of them.

'My!' she exclaims, 'You've a clever little bugger there! I've never seen a child as young as he obviously is, who knows so many words. How old is he?'

'Just eighteen months. Yes, we're pleased with him.'

'He's your first?'

'Yes.'

'Of course, you're still a wee young thing yourself! Get a good fill of this meal – you'll need that ready for your next. I'm sure that won't be long coming.'

I look at Joseph and we both blush. Despite her outspoken familiarity, the woman is a kind soul and lets me put the clothes I've rinsed by the well beside her fire to dry. But she is curious.

'Where are you off to, then? Are you another family off seeking your fortune in the south? If you're thinking of Egypt, I'm not sure you'll find it as easy as some people say. We've had returning travellers staying here and some of them have talked about the prejudice and rejection they received instead of a welcome.'

Joseph sees the opportunity here to ask for the route to that country without specifically answering her question.

'Is this the route that travellers to and from Egypt usually take? Do many stop here overnight?'

'Oh, we get quite a few, although we're not on the direct route. You probably saw the route via the coast just before you got to our village. But many come out of their way to stay with us as we look after them and they feel safe here. They know we are fair and won't rob them. You can't trust all the innkeepers on this route. Some are unscrupulous cheats.'

Joseph nods as though she's confirming what he already knows.

'If you're going on via the coast road, I'll give you the name of a trustworthy dwelling lodge where several of my regulars have stayed and recommend. It's in Ashkelon, just about a further day's journey, right on the coast. You'll meet the main route to Egypt there – it's well guarded, you'll not meet any trouble on that road. That's at least one advantage that the Romans have brought. They won't tolerate the thieves that used to operate in these parts before they came. There are regular patrols from the garrison in Ashkelon, manned by both Roman and Herod's troops.'

This is both reassuring and alarming at the same time. Will news of our flight already have reached Herod's ears? Could he already have got a messenger through to the garrison there to arrest us when we arrive tomorrow? It's certainly possible, because a swift messenger on horseback could arrive while we sleep. We shall need to be very wary tomorrow morning. There is little we can do about it tonight. I try not to show my concern although I catch Joseph's eye and I can see he shares my thoughts. However, Joshua needs me and I spend the next hour feeding and cleaning him after our dusty journey and getting him down to sleep on the bedroll I have folded to try to stop him turning over and off the cloth on to the earthen floor. Joseph meanwhile has obtained some fodder for our animal and is busy securing our more valuable possessions in a bag he places on our bedroll as a pillow, despite the assurances given by our landlady.

It's a strange night. I listen to all the unaccustomed noises from the inn, constant movements, animals braying, I'm sure I heard a camel and a horse. When I heard that animal all my senses became alert and I strained to hear any voices, fearing it might be a soldier. But I heard little and just succeeded in waking myself right up and took ages to get back off to sleep despite the weariness of my limbs. And just when I did get to sleep Joshua cried out and woke us both up. I lay there hoping it was but a momentary disturbance, but the next thing I knew was that Joshua had climbed off his bed and had come trotting over to me, bleary-eyed but with a mischievous grin on his face that I felt was quite inappropriate at that hour. I let him squeeze himself between the two of us and in the end we all fell asleep squashed together, and only awoke as the first cock crowed and the rays of dawn slanted across the sky we could glimpse through the opening in our tiny room.

We are able to buy some fresh bread and grapes from the innkeeper's wife now – she's been up early and has already got in provisions for the day's expected meals. She pumps us for a bit more information about our journey and the circumstances that have caused it, and Joseph reiterates his story that we are poor people from Bethany intent on a better life in Egypt. The woman shakes her head as if to warn us that we are on a fool's errand, but she teases the boy and keeps making him laugh and puts a few dates extra in our bag which we have not paid for as I think she feels sorry for us. We've not seen much of the innkeeper, but he helps Joseph load up and secure our bags to the donkey's saddle and bids us 'godspeed' on our journey, wherever that might take us.

We breathe a sigh of relief as we leave the village that no soldiers have come looking for us and retrace our steps back to the junction of the roads and steer our patient beast westwards once more, knowing for the first time that our immediate destination is the city of Ashkelon. Joshua has insisted on riding on the donkey and is holding its neck by its rough mane making braying noises imitating the noise that the donkey made as we harnessed it this morning. The road continues to be of a good standard, paved with large even blocks for most of the way, although it becomes little more than a rough track at one point where it climbs a small hill in quite a steep little stretch. On the other side the road soon returns to its proper paved state and our animal makes good time with Joshua now making 'geeing' noises as if he is riding a horse – heaven knows where he got that idea from.

Anyway, we pass midday without incident, stop to rest in the hottest part of the day by a group of olive trees that provide a little shade and where another family of travellers also is resting. I want Joshua to sleep for a while, but the other family have a couple of children, girls of about four and six years of age and Joshua wants to join in their games. The children play up to him and make him so excited that sleep is out of the question. When we restart I'm much more relaxed and my previous worries are beginning to disappear. It must be about an hour before sundown, when we reach a crossroads with what is obviously the highway from the north to Egypt. Joseph looks worried and I ask him what the matter is.

'Do we go into Ashkelon and risk being seen and questioned by Herod's soldiers garrisoned there or do we turn south immediately and try to find an inn off this highway?'

'How much of a risk do you think it is to go into Ashkelon? I'm tired and Joshua hasn't slept at all today and he didn't have that much sleep last night. Isn't that the city we can see on the skyline?'

'You're probably right about that. It looks as though it has walls, which means it must be Ashkelon. We could be there before sundown. But we'll have to go through the main gate, which is sure to have guards, and may get some close questioning on where we've come from and where we're going and the reason for our journey. It won't be so easy to convince them that we are ordinary travellers moving south for a better life. It's a big risk.'

'Joseph, if we go south on this road and we don't find rest soon, we shall be very conspicuous with a crying child and an easy prey if there are robbers taking advantage of darkness. Is it safe to go without being part of a larger party after dark?'

Joseph thought for a long time before turning the donkey's head towards the city of Ashkelon.

'You're right, Mari. We must seek rest. We'll trust God that he will protect us once more.'

Chapter 16
Mari

We were stopped at the gate to the city. My heart was in my mouth. A soldier and a customs official made Joseph unpack all our belongings and the official said we'd have to pay two silver shekels tax. I didn't know we had to pay to enter a city in our own country – after all, everything we bought had a tax on it. Joseph argued. I'm sure he suspected that the official and soldier were taking advantage of us – they must have thought we were ignorant peasants and when they found our money, thought they were on to a good thing and insisted on a 5% tax on everything we were taking into the city. Joseph bargained with them and eventually they accepted 2% which made me think they weren't entitled to anything, but we were nervous of them discovering who we were and detaining us for questioning by Herod's soldiers who were said to be garrisoned in the city.

Eventually they let us pass through the imposing gateway and once inside we were immediately surrounded by a gaggle of scruffily dressed young men who revealed themselves to be touts for various inns and lodging houses, all of which were promised to us as cheap and top class quality. We tried to brush them off, but they followed us as we moved forward and Joshua began to howl, frightened at their pestering of us. We therefore made the best of it and allowed ourselves to be guided by the most insistent of them to 'his' inn, a dwelling which looked no different to the others crowded together in a smelly area of the city. The lane was filthy with refuse and animal dung, but we were too tired and frightened to object and at least we were given a small room and promised a meal once we had unpacked and I'd fed Joshua, changed his soiled clothes and settled him in the wooden cot that the innkeeper brought in for us.

The meal was pretty basic, but at least there was plenty of bread so we did not retire hungry. The wine was too acidic for me and of poor quality, but I forced myself to gulp down sufficient as we'd not had much to drink during the day. I was worried how much we'd be charged for the night, especially as we'd already had to give money to our guide who'd brought us here. I heard Joseph bartering with the innkeeper as his wife was clearing the pots away and I gathered that Joseph was relieved that the cost was not exorbitant. At last we were on our own and Joshua was well away – he was so still that I worried at first that something was wrong, but I lay my ear on his chest and felt his gentle breathing.

The relief of at least being in a shelter and now two full days away from Bethlehem allowed us to relax and I was comforted when Joseph cuddled up to me and we lay silently for an hour or more, just man and wife together. For a few minutes we forgot the cares of the day and ceased our worrying about the morrow; then, before I was hardly aware of sleeping, dawn was breaking and I could hear Joshua stirring. Joseph wanted to get us on our way early – he had discussed our route with the innkeeper the previous night and had been told that the city of Gaza was on the main highway to the south, about twenty Roman miles away. As I had no idea of what that meant, Joseph explained that it would be a good day's journey for us. He'd also confirmed our suspicions that the customs official had no right to charge us tax for entering the city – there was a tax included in our tariff for the night's stay. We were warned not to yield to any such demands on leaving the city and to resist any attempt to charge us when we got to Gaza. However, we were also warned that we'd have to pay at the border town as we entered Egypt and that we should keep sufficient cash for that purpose or we'd find ourselves turned back.

I noticed that we'd passed some vegetable sellers as we were being led to our lodgings and I could smell bread-making over the powerful stench of a refuse strewn stream that trickled nearby. We stopped to buy sufficient bread for our day's journey and also grapes, figs and milk. I worried about how much cash we had left but Joseph assured me that we'd be alright until we got to Egypt but he'd need to find work as soon as possible after our arrival there. We managed to pass through the city gate without being molested this time, joining a couple of merchants and slipping through while they were arguing with a different customs officer. I think we were not bothered this time because, compared with the merchants, we obviously had little to offer and were not worth stopping when there were potentially richer pickings to be had.

We joined the highway heading south, Joshua already mounted happily on our donkey, as the sun rose to our left. The lad seems content, it's all a big adventure for him. He doesn't appear to miss Benjamin yet. Perhaps when the novelty has worn off, he will be homesick and fretful. There's a lot of traffic on the road, mainly merchant trains heading in both directions, their camels and donkeys heavily laden. Within the first hour we've already passed a couple of military platoons but they've paid no heed to us and I'm beginning to believe that we're not being sought by Herod's men after all.

The road is good and flat and we make excellent progress during the morning. There is a slight breeze from the west off the sea, which is not actually in sight, but the innkeeper said it was always only a few leagues distant. I feel safe here, there are lots of people about, the visibility is good and I can see a long distance in each direction. We pass a few villages and we refill our waterskins. I think we must be at least half-way to our night's destination before the sun is at its zenith.

We stop under a fig tree and rest a while in its shade when the heat becomes oppressive and I let Joshua run around and stretch his legs. He is excited to be let loose and dashes around aimlessly at first, then he nuzzles up to the donkey and I have to prise him away lest the animal kick out and injure him. I carry him to the other side of the tree where he finds amusement poking the scratchy grass and watching the insects scurry away. I'm reminded of the time when, as a girl, I used to go to my favourite fig tree and watch the insects while I let my uncle's sheep and goats graze. I have a guilty conscience then, for that's where I always used to talk to God, and I realise since we left Bethlehem that I've really neglected him. I've said a few panicky prayers when I worried we were in danger, but I haven't spent time talking to him as I did every day before we fled from Herod. So when I'm sure Joshua is safe, I sit cross-legged and begin to share my thoughts with God because I know he listens to me.

'Look at Joshua,' I say to him under my breath, 'isn't he a fine boy? You've promised that he'll be our Messiah. Keep him safe, please, dear God, keep all of us safe. We've set off into the great unknown, the big adventure. Thank you for holding us in your arms so far. Thank you that Joseph is so strong, that he knows what to do.'

Then I'm quiet because I think I can hear God talking, whispering through the branches of the tree above me. He just seems to be saying 'Trust me like you did when you were bearing Joshua.' I stare at the boy moving so gracefully through the shadows cast by the branches. It is as if he is dancing.

'Oh dear, God, I've neglected you in all the rush to get away. I've hardly had time to stop and think. I feel very guilty about it, God, because I'm sure you're still thinking and caring for us. Please keep on looking after Joshua and Joseph and me, as we travel to this new land. Help us to see your plan, show us the way, give us the strength.'

I've allowed myself to get all keyed up and worried when I should have trusted God just as I did when I was in Nazareth. I breathe out and let myself go all limp. I try to relax. I close my eyes, then open them again, lie back and stare at the blue sky that is seeping through the tracery of the tree above me.

Once more I just watch and I'm satisfied with this. My worries are ebbing away. My thoughts go to Nazareth and I wonder what Rebecca and Salome are doing now? Are they thinking of me and Joshua? Do they pray for us every night as I try to do for them? And little Benjamin will be joining the other boys at school now. Does Rabbi Joel search him out as he helped me? Is he special too? Thinking of my young brother reminds me of my next-door neighbour, Rachel's child. In many ways he's like I remember my brother, and it's not just that they share the same name. I wonder if Bethlehem Benjamin is missing Joshua? It seems a pity that they'll be parted for so long, they were so good together. And Rachel, what has she made of our disappearance? It was such a shame we couldn't confide in them. I really wanted to tell her why we were leaving in such a hurry, but Joseph said that telling them could put them in danger too, so I had to abide by his advice.

My eyes are feeling heavy and I have to force myself to stay alert to watch over Joshua, then I hear my husband calling me. I push myself up and chase after the boy. Typical, he thinks it's all part of a big game and runs off so that I have to lift my tunic and run after him. Then he trips over a tree root and begins to bawl, puckering up his little face so that I have to laugh! He isn't really hurt, I soon check on that, he is more surprised than anything. So I pick him up and sit him back on the donkey and we are ready to go again.

We've been going a good hour since our rest and Joseph hasn't said a word all that time. This is unlike my husband. I know he is not given to unnecessary talk – I'm the chatterbox – but he is not usually silent for so long. I've been concentrating on keeping Joshua amused. Perhaps he's feeling hurt that I'm giving him so little attention.

'Joseph, is anything the matter? You're looking worried, is something wrong? Have I said or done something you don't like?'

'No, Mari, it's nothing to do with you. Well, perhaps it is, but it's not your fault. I've just been thinking of the momentous thing we've just done. Suppose all this flight was unnecessary. Have I uprooted you and Josh from everyone and everything you knew for no reason? Why should I think Herod would care about people like us? He's probably not given the astrologers another thought and we could now have been safe at home, you chatting with Rachel and Rebecca while the children play together. And me finishing off the implements I'd promised to our neighbours and getting well paid for it, so that you and our son could be well looked after. We could have accumulated enough savings to fund us back in Nazareth while I rebuilt my business there.'

'Nonsense, Joseph. You mustn't blame yourself like this. We took this decision together. Who knows what might have happened if we'd stayed? For all you know, we might have been dead by now.'

'That seems unreal. All I know is that I've committed you to an unknown and possibly risky future and I don't know if it was justified.'

'That's because we're out of danger and Bethlehem seems so far away. If we were back there, you said that we could still be very vulnerable.'

'You talk as if it's all plain sailing now. You've no idea what difficulties lie ahead of us. We've no idea where we're going to sleep tonight. We don't know how long our money will last. We don't know if we'll be allowed into Egypt. We don't know if I can find work there to keep us. We don't even know if the road is safe to our destination. We don't actually know where our destination is.'

'We've trusted God this far. I was often in a far more dangerous situation back in Nazareth and I trusted God against all the odds and it worked out. Why shouldn't he support us now?'

'I envy you your faith, Mari, I really do. I believe in our destiny but at times I find it difficult and I get assailed by doubts.'

'Look at the boy. Everything that has happened to us is because God promised me that he would be the Messiah. If this is wrong, if I've made it all up, would we have got this far? I'd have probably been stoned to death – that would have happened if you'd not intervened and you believed God was guiding you then.'

Joseph nods and perhaps would have said more, but the donkey suddenly stumbles on a loose paving stone and I have to grab Joshua quickly before he falls. The sudden activity jolts us out of our reflective moods and I lift the child down and let him run beside us for a little way until he struggles to keep up, whereupon I decide to carry him for a while. Joshua starts to pull faces at me, then he reaches up and starts to stick his fingers up my nostrils and giggles. I retaliate by pinching his cheeks and blowing in his ear and every time I stop, he just shouts 'more, more' or 'again, again' and I oblige him. It's actually very difficult to carry on a serious and problematic conversation when you're being mauled by a child, even if it's just in fun and Joseph says no more, but steers us onwards towards Gaza and evening.

We have no more scares – the road continues to be busy and no-one questions us or doubts our intentions. We are just one of many families seeking a better life in the more prosperous country of Egypt. We could, I suppose, have tried to link with another family going south, but Joseph was hesitant to make that commitment in case it revealed more about us than was safe. As we draw near to Gaza in the early evening, just before dusk, we both tense up a little and I know Joseph is getting ready to argue with the tax officials at the main gate, but they scarcely acknowledge us and wave us through. They are far more intent on stopping a merchant who obviously is transporting much produce, a much more profitable source of revenue than we are.

I suppose if I hadn't been so preoccupied with Joshua I'd have marvelled more at the fine buildings around me. A lot of the biggest public buildings looked new, Joseph said later that it looked as though they'd been constructed by the Romans. I wouldn't know, but Joseph said he recognised the style from the work he'd been involved in at Sepphoris. All I wanted was to find somewhere to rest and clean Joshua up – he was beginning to stink a little with a mixture of donkey smell mingling with his own odour. I realise now just how tired I was feeling and I'd have willingly gone with the first youth who volunteered to take us to an inn, but strangely we were left alone here. I suppose there were too many obviously prosperous merchants around taking priority – we were by now looking a little dirty and bedraggled and produced little interest from the young men out to earn a few tips from the lodging houses in the city. We had to ask directions to the quarter where most of the inns were to be found and we enquired at three places before we found someone ready to take us in. It soon became pretty obvious that our host was interested in more lucrative guests than we were and we only got enough attention to take us to the smallest room in the house and be quoted a price before he left us in the hands of a servant girl to help us unload the donkey and tether it in the yard with beasts of the other guests.

Although the innkeeper was brusque – almost rude – neither Joseph nor I were bothered at this lack of attention. The more anonymous we were, the safer we felt. I had to admit that the attention of the innkeepers' wives at our previous two lodgings, whilst it was good-hearted and cheerful, filled me with some concern in case subsequently Herod's soldiers came looking for us – they wouldn't fail to remember us and which way we'd departed. Anyway, I felt there was no such danger of that here. We joined in the evening meal among a crowd of other men - a couple had their womenfolk with them. I had been able to wash and change Joshua and feed him and gave a small coin to a young girl – probably the daughter of one of the servants – to keep watch over him until our meal was over.

Joshua was fast asleep when we returned and the girl scampered off. I thought that a really good night's sleep lay in store for us, but I'm awoken by Joshua crying when it's still pitch dark. I light a candle and go to him and am shocked to find that he is so hot, bathed in sweat. I bring the light to his face and see it's flushed and burning to my touch. I wake Joseph and he senses my alarm at once and fetches water with which to bathe the child. I at once assume that we must have drunk some bad water on our journey, although Joseph and I seem alright. His little stomach is not so used to the differences in the well water and has not yet built up resistance to the many infections that children in particular suffer from. I nurse him for the next couple of hours, bathing him regularly until Joseph stirs again and offers to take over from me so I can get some sleep. But I just toss and turn, I am too worried.

When dawn breaks we are both bothered as to whether it is wise to continue with Joshua still showing the signs of fever. Many children, especially those so young, often succumb to such ailments and I feel we should stay at the inn in case we need to call a physician. Joseph assures me that we have enough money left to pay for such help if we really require it and then suddenly the fever leaves him, as quickly as it had come and he's sitting up chirruping away, albeit a little pasty-faced. Should we stay a little longer in case the sickness returns? I'm in two minds, but when Joshua attacks the bread we're served for breakfast as if he's ravenous and guzzles afterwards at my breast without the slightest sign of nausea, I agree with my husband that we should continue our journey, which he says ought to take us to the border post by the end of the day.

So we continue our journey nearing the border of our own country. I begin to feel nervous. What will we find in a strange land? Will we find a home? Will Joseph be able to find work to look after us? Will we be accepted there? Will I find friends? I'm sure Joshua will not notice the difference. He'll adjust, find other children to play with. But will he be healthy there? Will there be strange diseases we haven't encountered before to afflict us. All day, whilst these thoughts are constantly coming to mind, I'm watching Joshua closely to catch any signs that the fever might be returning. I keep picking him off the donkey to carry him, but in truth I'm checking to see that he is not unnaturally hot. It's difficult to tell in reality as we are all sweating profusely from the rays, which burn us fiercely from the midday sun right overhead and from which, on this part of our journey, there is very little respite. There are hardly any trees, just barren scrub and sparse bushes on the sandy boulder strewn earth beside the highway. The heat reflects from the giant paving slabs polished by the hooves of animals bringing sacks of wheat and flax from the south and returning with olives, honey and wine from our native soil.

Towards sundown Joshua suddenly flags and falls asleep in my arms. I feel his skin – it's a little clammy to touch and I worry that the fever is returning. His breathing is even and relaxed, however, he's not wheezing or gasping which are the danger signs. I used to talk to Rachel a lot about such matters as neither of us had much experience ourselves. Of course, we had illnesses in Nazareth and I remembered some things my mother said, but both of us used to seek Rebecca's advice as she'd brought up three children successfully.

I can see the ramparts of a town in the distance and Joseph says that this will be a place the Romans call Raphia, the last city on our land before the country of Egypt begins. It used to be a totally foreign place, but after the Romans came to this part of the world they established many similar features building baths and amphitheatres and gymnasiums – I'd noticed them in both Ashkelon and Gaza but had been too preoccupied with our own concerns to have taken much notice. As we draw closer I can see a crowd of people and animals around the city wall and gateway and wonder what is happening. Then I see that they are seeking permission from the uniformed guards to enter the gateway and we join the throng to wait our turn. A few Roman soldiers hang around looking for signs of trouble in the crowd and Joseph warns me that we might be here for a long time. I sit on the dusty bank and lay Joshua across my lap and hold the reins of the donkey while Joseph goes to find out what is happening. It's not good news.

'I asked some merchants near the front. They said they'd been waiting since the middle of the day. There'd been a hold-up whilst two military convoys took precedence, then there had been a long gap when no-one had passed through in either direction and the queue had only begun to advance in the last couple of hours. Meanwhile apparently a backlog of traffic has built up. It's very frustrating.'

'Is this the border into Egypt? Is that why there's this congestion?'

'I don't think so. I believe the city is in our country and that the border is on the far side. We shall have to deal with the customs officials there.'

'How long must we wait then?'

'I don't know. We will have to be patient.'

I'm not very good at being patient. It's never been my strong point. My family always accused me of stirring things up unnecessarily. If there's a problem or something unpleasant to face I'd rather confront it and get it over with. Joseph is the patient one. He's more placid than me. Perhaps it's a skill he's had to learn to make all the implements he does. I've seen him spending hours smoothing down the wood he uses, removing the splinters, a perfectionist.

Night falls rapidly and we hardly seem to have made any progress towards the gate. Many in the crowd are grumbling and complaining that their animals need fodder. I feel like saying that we do too. Most of the people around me are speaking Greek – Joseph can understand quite a lot and can speak a bit as he'd learned it during his years in Jerusalem where it was as common as our language. I'm afraid I know nothing of it – no-one spoke anything else in our village. Perhaps I shan't understand anything when we get to Egypt and I'll be completely reliant on Joseph. I'm sure Joshua will soon pick it up and I'll be the one who struggles.

We must have been waiting for over two hours now. Joshua wakes up and I've have to feed him, sitting here at the roadside, like other women in the crowd. It's going to be a lot longer yet and the temperature is dropping rapidly. I wind my shawl round Joshua to try to keep him warm – I can't afford to let him get cold now and make his fever worse. Joseph has put his arms around me and when he feels me shiver he takes off his cloak and draws it over my shoulders. I snuggle against him. Occasionally the crowd moves closer to the gate and we have to move too or we would lose our place and be delayed even longer. Suddenly there's shouting from the front of the crowd and I see a few stones being thrown. A rumour goes round the crowd that the gate has been shut for the night and that we will all have to wait to the morning to gain entrance. A couple of Roman soldiers appear and wave their lances threateningly and then it seems that the gates were only closed temporarily while the soldiers on guard changed duties and a new set took their place.

I'm so tired – I just want to lay down where I am and let my eyes close, but I daren't. Joshua is suddenly wide awake and toddling off exploring, finding the animals and making eyes at strangers, especially a couple of middle-aged women who encourage him. I'm sure the delay is because of several groups of merchants with laden beasts – the officials are making them unpack everything and they are searching the produce diligently. All night we wait. I'm now desperate for sleep but I can't relax. It's cold now and I've got Joshua snug against my body. I don't think there's any danger but it's so tedious. When at last we are called forward and the sun is already showing its red glow above the horizon, the soldier on duty takes just one look at us and waves us straight through. All that waiting and finally in the blink of an eye we stagger into the rough lane on the other side of the wall.

Joseph had intended us to make our way into Egypt this morning but there's no way any of us are fit to continue our journey until we've had some rest. But all the first inns we find are full. Everyone else has had the same idea – all are looking for lodgings to rest the day. I'm swooning with exhaustion now. Joshua is crying, he's hungry. I've no solid food for him. One innkeeper takes pity on us and allows us to rest in the shade of his house until a room is vacated which he says will be later, in the morning. I can't drag myself any farther so we take advantage of this offer and Joseph leaves me to go in search of bread and dates to feed us both.

When he gets back, I'm too tired to eat. I give Joshua some bread and some figs which he scoffs, he is clearly better despite our restless night. He alone of us manages some sleep, lying with his full weight in my arms. I feel sore as morning approaches, my arms ache, my breasts feel tender. His dead weight during the night has had its effect and – because of the shortage of solid food for him – he's had to make do with prolonged sucking from me and I guess that's why I can feel them. He's got strong teeth now and probably bit me there although I didn't notice it at the time.

Joseph takes Joshua from me and I fall asleep where I'm sitting despite the discomfort and movement of people around me. When I stir, Joseph tells me that the innkeeper has just said that a room is ready for us and he helps me to my feet. I feel dizzy – I'm not properly awake yet, and Joseph carries Joshua and our bags, while I follow as best I can. When we have made ourselves as comfortable as possible, I try to see what I can do with the food that Joseph's bought, but in the end we just eat bread and grapes and dates. Luckily Joshua is ready for a sleep and as soon as he's breathing softly, I kiss him gently on the forehead and fall onto the bed roll and am asleep in minutes. When I wake up, it's already dark. I must have slept all day. Joseph has been kind enough to leave me be, he's looked after Joshua and some bread and grapes are beside me. I'm really very fortunate in my husband – there are not many men who would treat their wives with such consideration.

I gradually come round and we eat a meal together. Joseph says that he has arranged for us to stay until the next morning, then we must move on and should consider ourselves out of any danger from Herod for we will at last be out of his jurisdiction. It seems as though I'm hardly awake before we're settling for the night. Joshua comes and wants to bounce on me – I think he believes I'm his donkey. I encourage him until he falls across my face and starts jumping up and down on my breasts. I yelp and push him off, it really is painful there. I give him another kiss and move him down my body so that he doesn't take fright at my expression of pain and let him sit for a while. I tell him a story which keeps his attention for a few minutes then say it's time for him to sleep and to my surprise he doesn't object. When I'm sure he's asleep, Joseph comes to me and we huddle in each others arms and fall asleep entwined together.

Slowly my eyes are adjusting to the faint glow that is seeping into our room from an opening outside our door, which has swung ajar. I feel peculiar. At first I think it is because of the irregular patterns of sleep that I've had, my body has not adapted to a new rhythm. Then I'm aware of nausea. I lie still for a few minutes trying to fight it, then I can feel the bile rising in my throat and I can stay on my bed no longer. I rise up rapidly and stagger through the door and just make it to the lane in front of the inn where I am sick. I prop myself against the front wall and take a few deep breaths. My first thought is that I've contracted a fever through contact with Joshua, then a disturbing idea comes to me. Could I be pregnant again?

I cast my mind back to those days in Nazareth over two years ago when I first revealed to my family and Eli that I was bearing a child. I remember the churned stomach and nausea I experienced then, although some of it I put down to nervousness at the magnitude of what I'd done and fear at its possible consequences. But the morning sickness I'd suffered for several weeks was real enough and I recognise the symptoms now. A few days ago I'd have rejoiced at the thought of bearing Joseph a child that is really his own – a son perhaps that he knows is his. He's been splendid about Joshua and treated him just as a father would care for any child of his own, but I do wonder sometimes whether he harbours any doubts and whether he can dismiss from his mind any thought that perhaps after all I might have been unfaithful to him.

But now? When we are homeless and refugees fleeing to a strange country? When the future is so uncertain? I decide to keep my sickness from Joseph for the time being if I can – he has enough to worry about without the additional burden of concern about my possible condition. Can I disguise it enough though? He'll soon spot my sickness each morning and guess the reason, even assuming I don't have to reveal the extent of my symptoms. For I recognise now the soreness of my breasts as another of the signs. In just one swift hour I've gone from a confused feeling of unease to a sure knowledge that I'm bearing a second child – who, I realise, will be probably born a foreigner in Egypt. I'll be alright, I'm two years older, I'm fifteen now, so I don't need to fear the physical birth, except that the circumstances are so uncertain. We might be anywhere when the baby's time comes. Will there be help at hand? Will there be other women to confide in, women who are friendly or will I be alone? It would have been good to wait until we were settled in Egypt perhaps, but it is not to be. I'll tell Joseph soon, but perhaps I'll wait until we're safely in Egypt and have found somewhere secure to stay.

I stay outside in the cool morning air until I am sufficiently recovered. There are a few people already about, men taking produce to the market stalls, women with large water pots making their way to the nearest well. They ignore me until one of the servants from the inn returns with a full urn of water and asks if I am alright – it must be obvious that I look unwell. I say automatically that I am, then, as she hesitates, I add that I will be fine in a few moments, that I was too hot inside and just needed a bit of fresh air. She looks at me quizzically, but I say no more and the woman just shrugs and goes about her business. If it is that obvious to a casual observer, I realise that Joseph will see at once that something is wrong and I'll have to own up to the truth or brazen it out, insisting that nothing is untoward. I decide that I must if necessary be frank with him even if it causes him to worry on my behalf.

However, when I finally go back to our room he does not question where I've been. Perhaps he has only just woken – there was only a glimmer of light when I ran outside and I didn't stop to look if he was stirring. Anyway, we're in heavy shadow and perhaps my pale complexion is not obvious in here. I check that Joshua is still sleeping and we both wash and dress for the day with hardly a word spoken. It is clear that Joseph is now impatient to be on our way, so I pick Joshua up and rouse him slowly bringing him to my breast before offering him some bread. As he sucks I wince for his urgent mouth grasps my nipple and the tenderness of that area is now very evident to me. But still Joseph notices nothing unusual and he busies himself packing our bags and fastening them on the donkey after feeding the animal with fodder that the innkeeper has provided. He is ready and waiting for me. I'm sure he wants to get us to the border point, the southern gate of the city, before too many other folk are on the move. He does not want a repetition of our experience when we arrived.

I still feel a little rough but I'm preoccupied with holding Joshua on the beast's back and gradually the feeling of nausea subsides. We spend several minutes walking through the empty lanes and we pass a number of imposing looking buildings. At other times I might have been more curious about their identity – the only one that is obvious is some sort of arena, an amphitheatre or sports gymnasium I guess. These are becoming more common in any city where the Romans are in any numbers, although I haven't the remotest idea what they do there. The edifice looks very new, with shining white stone and marble. But it's empty – well, of course it would be at this hour of the morning.

So we come to the south gate and find a number of soldiers hanging about there looking bored, for there's no queue at all. Two customs officials come bounding towards us and now I feel very nervous as if we're doing something wrong. Joseph squeezes my wrist and tries to reassure me that it'll be alright, we've nothing to fear now.

'Your name and business?'

The first man to speak is brusque and businesslike.

'My name is Joseph of the house of David and this is Mariam, my wife and my son, Joshua. We're travelling to Egypt.'

'I can see that. You wouldn't be at this gate otherwise!'

Joseph is silent, not offering any further information.

'Where are you travelling to?'

Joseph hesitates. We don't know where we are going. Joseph has mentioned a city called Alexandria to me because he's heard some of the merchants we've met talk about a Jewish settlement there.

'Alexandria. Eventually,' he adds when the official looks at him quizzically.

'What is your trade?'

'I'm an experienced carpenter.'

'Where are you from?'

I can see Joseph is now reluctant to say Bethlehem in case an order from Herod to find and stop us has been communicated to this outpost. He sticks to his earlier story.

'Bethany, a village the far side of Jerusalem.'

'And what is the purpose of your journey to Alexandria?'

'I need to find work there. There is insufficient need for my trade in Bethany.'

'Do you need to travel that far to find work? Surely there's building work going on in Jerusalem for you to find enough to do there.'

'I find it difficult to obtain work there. There are many carpenters in Jerusalem and I'm not well connected there. It is difficult to make a good enough living to support my wife and son.'

'How long do you intend to stay in Alexandria?'

'If I can find enough work there in the Jewish community, I might settle my family there permanently.'

'I have orders to limit numbers entering Egypt. Too many tradespeople are seeking their fortune there. It is not as easy as you think. I'm not convinced that your skills are in demand there. You'll have to convince me that I should allow you to go through on the limited quota I've orders to admit.' The official then turns to talk in a language I can't understand to the other official. I now realise that the one questioning us is a Jew, but the other is an Egyptian.

Joseph seems to feel it necessary to add some special pleading.

'We have a particular problem, sir. There is jealousy and bad feeling. My wife and child have been threatened and I need to get them to greater safety and a new life.' This is as much as he dare say without revealing the source of the threat. The Jewish customs officer grunts and says something else to the Egyptian who just shrugs his shoulders.

The Jew now turns to Joseph again and orders him to unpack our bags and lay everything on the ground. I am now getting really worked up and fear that we'll be turned back and either have to find a dwelling in Gaza or Ashkelon or even risk going back to Bethlehem. We could probably disappear and keep hidden in one of the cities. To stop in one of the villages we've passed through would cause more comment and we'd be easier to find if Herod's soldiers come looking for us.

The two officials are now turning over everything from our bags as Joseph unties them from the donkey's back. Nothing is spared from their gaze. They find our cash and count it. They are particularly interested in Joseph's tools and spend along time examining each piece. Joseph bends to me and whispers that he thinks they are angling for a bribe to let us through. Joshua is getting bored and is trotting over to stare at one of the Roman soldiers. I thought the man might be amused at Joshua's antics, but the soldier bad temperedly shoos the boy away and the lad is frightened and runs back to me crying.

At length the Jewish official says that we might be allowed through if we pay the appropriate taxes on the articles we have with us. He names a price, which horrifies me, it is half of the shekels we've saved to set up home again. Then I realise that they know how much money we are carrying, they've already counted it and know what we can afford to gain entry. Joseph shakes his head to me and mutters that we have little choice if we want to cross the border. He is obviously annoyed but is trying not to show it for fear that we can still be turned back or that they might even find an excuse to increase their tax demand. I feel so powerless. These men are just greedy, they are taking advantage of us. Perhaps we should have waited and come later, attaching ourselves to a group of merchants. Perhaps then they would have found someone else from whom to extract a bigger bribe. Joseph in the end, with much shaking of the head, gives in and pays them what they have demanded. They are the worst sort of collaborators with the Romans, enriching themselves at the expense of their countrymen. Anyway, the officials finally give the nod to one of the soldiers, who opens the gate and beckons us to go through.

We are there. We are in Egypt.

Chapter 17
Mari

It is with obvious relief that we progress steadily on the road away from Raphia until it is but a speck on the horizon behind us. Our spirits are lifted, we feel free despite the uncertainties ahead of us. For the first few miles, the landscape is unchanging. Then the road veers westwards, the sun now on our backs and the landscape becomes even more barren. There is little respite from the sun in this treeless landscape and we soon feel the need to halt and rest.

It is at this point I decide to tell Joseph about my sickness earlier this morning and the conclusion I'd drawn from this. We are sitting at the verge of the road on a small raised bank and I am nursing Joshua, feeding him with grapes and getting him to spit out the pips.

'Joseph, I've got some news I need to share with you.'

He is already crouching next to me and puts his arm round my shoulder and looks me straight in the eyes.

'What is it, Mari?'

'Did you see that I felt unwell this morning? I was very sick – I think perhaps you were still asleep.'

He looks alarmed and thinks I'm going to tell him that I fear some serious illness.

I realise that he was not present during the early stages of my pregnancy with Joshua and it dawns on me that he probably has no idea that morning sickness is a symptom of the early stages of child bearing.

'There's nothing wrong, Joseph. It's good news, at least I think it is. We're going to have another child, and it's yours, it really is this time.'

He looks shocked. It's been a bit sudden and he obviously had no inkling or premonition of the news I've just imparted. He's stunned. He says nothing for a while and then the arm around my shoulder tightens and he gives me a squeeze.

'Mari, that's wonderful news. I had no idea, really. When did you first know?'

'Only this morning. When I was sick I thought that I'd developed the same fever as Joshua had, then I remembered my experience when I first knew he was on the way. I was sceptical at first, but there are other symptoms which I'd dismissed but when you put them all together ...'

'So you're sure then?'

'As sure as I can be.'

'When's the child due?'

'I don't know exactly. These signs usually start in the first six to eight weeks of pregnancy, so it'll be at least another seven months, well into the winter.'

'I promise I'll have us in a proper home by then, before the rainy season starts. They tell me that lasts for two to three months in Egypt when their great river called the Nile floods. Nearly all the merchants I've talked to coming out of Egypt mention the great river and the fertile land around it. Perhaps we shall find land there where we can settle and care for both our children.'

'It's not very good timing, is it Joseph? It would have been better to have settled properly in the new country before being faced with a young baby.'

'Well, it's probably better now than before we left Bethlehem. Just think of the journey we've already had. How would you have coped with a tiny baby as well as Joshua? At least we've time to get a home before you're delivered. You must be careful though. We can take it easily, there's no need to rush now we're out of Herod's reach. You must tell me when you need to rest.'

We watch Joshua eating. I wonder if he'll understand anything if I tell him. I really don't know what goes on in his little mind. He seems so forward for his age. He needs a playmate anyway, but it'll be a long time before a young brother will be ready to be company for him. Perhaps he'll help me look after the new child. I know how much I enjoyed mothering Salome and Rebecca and mother used to say that I helped her from a very early age. But I was a girl. Is it different for a boy? Can I teach him to care for a younger child or will he be impatient with such things? Will Joseph encourage me to let him help or will he insist on training him in more manly pursuits?

We sit for a long time. Joseph is trying to get used to what I've just told him. I catch a glimpse of a frown, which flits across his face and I know, despite what he says, that he is worried about how we'll cope here and now I've given him this extra burden to be anxious about. Our thoughts are eventually interrupted by Joshua who has finished the grapes and bread I gave him and is now threatening to run after a family with a couple of donkeys who've just passed us. He is making braying noises – he just loves animals so I chase after him and sit him astride our donkey as Joseph packs our food bag and straps it back on the beast.

We lumber on into the heat of the day. The road stretches straight before us shimmering in the heat. Figures in the distance flicker in the haze. We can't be far from the sea, but there is no breeze until, after a hard day, towards evening a wind off the sea springs up and we are a little refreshed. Joshua has begun to be a bit fractious - I tried to get him to sleep as we kept on the move but he was too interested in everything, the animals and people we passed on the road and would not let his eyes shut. I've no idea how long it will take us to reach somewhere we can stay and Joseph can find work. Our money is getting low now and whilst we can find enough for simple lodgings for a couple more days, I was a bit alarmed to hear merchants tell Joseph that the nearest large city is more than a week away and I doubt if we can travel at the speed they maintain. In fact tonight we finish our day early. As I said, Joshua is very tired and when we come across a village beside the highway we decide to look for lodgings at once and settle early.

Next day we arise early and get on our way before the sun rises in order to cover as much ground as possible before the heat becomes overpowering. I suggested this to Joseph as we must rest long enough to let Joshua sleep today. We're hardly on the road, however, before my nausea forces me to stop and we halt for half an hour until I'm able to continue, albeit very slowly. Joseph carries Joshua for a while and he makes me lie on the donkey, straddling our few possessions. I lean forward and cling to the beast's neck and close my eyes trying not to let the jolting cause me to be sick again. Eventually the nausea passes but the sun is now already high in the sky and we are in for another scorching day without respite from any shade. There is not one solitary tree in our vision. The road veers again to the right - the first turn for many miles - and now extends to the horizon in the straight line towards the west, the sun on our backs. To our left is nothing but barren land, sand dunes are beginning to appear and the landscape is pure desert. Joseph tells me that this must be the wilderness where our ancestors spent many years after fleeing from the Egyptian army. They spent forty years there, it is said. I hope it does not take us too long to get to a more fertile area. Otherwise I shall be asking God to provide us with manna and quails too!

There are a few villages on the right of the highway where occasionally we see signs of an effort to cultivate a few plots round the primitive shacks. If the villages are all as poor as the ones we are passing now, we'll find it difficult to find somewhere to stay, for none of these villages has any building substantial enough to act as an inn. When hunger calls us to halt, we stop despite the lack of shelter, and eat some of the food we bought as we left this morning. I try to shade Joshua with my body and eventually he falls asleep, but I get very weary and am nearly overcome by the heat as I have nowhere to hide from the sun. Joseph is getting agitated I can see, for Joshua is having a very long sleep and my husband wants us to move on and make more progress.

Eventually we lay Joshua on the donkey but as soon as we move off he opens his eyes and forces himself to take an interest in everything around him. Joseph had hoped to continue our journey until nightfall but when we come across a bigger village which has an inn, we determine to take advantage of it. It can't be more than mid afternoon as the sun has only just begun to drop but it is now full in our face making us squint against the glare and dust and this makes us even more tired. By stopping early we find we are fortunate in obtaining a bed as later that evening we hear several travellers being turned away as the accommodation is already overflowing. I heard Joseph talking to other lodgers referring to the village as Rhinocoruna - at least that's what I think they said. I've never heard of it. Joseph wasn't sure whether it was the name of the village or the area. However, one of the merchants told Joseph that we'd at least a further week's journey before arriving at the next town of any consequence.

Joseph therefore said to me that evening that we ought to use some of our remaining cash to buy a small tent as we are unlikely to be able to pay for lodgings much longer and we need to keep money back for the purchase of food as our first priority. Whilst I rest and let Joshua suckle, Joseph talks to the innkeeper and is directed to a tentmaker in the village who sells him a very small tent - the largest we can afford. It's just enough for the two of us to squeeze in and get some rest as long as Joshua is curled up with us. It'll be hot but we'll be so weary each evening that it probably doesn't matter. At least now we're not so dependent on finding accommodation although we must be careful to settle each night where it is safe and not in an isolated spot where we might be in danger of robbers.

As we leave the village the following morning, the road descends into a dry wadi where clearly in the rainy season the water gushes out to the sea. At present, however, we have no difficulty crossing as only sand blows onto the road from high dunes. In places there are miniature cliffs of crumbling sand on either side of the dried-up watercourse.

And so each day seems very like the last. We get up early. I'm ill for a while - it seems to vary. Some mornings it's not so bad. One day I was so sick that we couldn't begin our journey until the middle of the morning when the heat was already excessive. The scenery doesn't change. The road remains straight as a die. The land to our left bakes in the midday sun. To our right the land is flat and we can imagine the sea on our horizon although we can't see it. Sometimes in the evening as the wind gets up, we sense we can smell the freshness and the salt in the air. Each day seems a repeat of the last. 'How long?' I ask Joseph. He doesn't know. Merchants and other travellers overtake us because we are moving slowly now. We take long rests. Occasionally someone speaks to us but it is rarely in a language I can understand. Joseph, I think, knows more than he is telling me about the distance we still have to travel.

Then, after what seems like an age - perhaps ten days or more, I have lost count - we begin to see cultivated land. Joseph looks hard at the earth and it is less sandy and there are irrigated ditches presumably dug by the Egyptian farmers as they are straight and clearly man made. As we progress further into Egypt, the countryside is becoming greener by the hour. A number of date palms cluster beside the road and are dotted around fields of grain and flax, the latter making beautiful blankets of pale blue, shimmering in the sun, the five petalled flowers open and indicating that the harvest will soon begin. Our spirits lift stimulated by the sight and the news that we have shared, for my sickness miraculously seems to have waned. The coming of another child now seems a good omen and not the cause of more anxiety which first I feared.

Through conversations with passing travellers I've gathered that the first Egyptian city that we shall reach is called Pelusium which is situated by the banks of one of the branches of a mighty river called the Nile, a river revered by our ancestors when they were first guests of the patriarch,

Joseph, then slaves of the Pharaohs until Moses led our nation to freedom. The Nile, I muse, that river upon which our nation's saviour was cast as a baby, and from which he was rescued by the Pharaoh's daughter. The thought occurs to me that little Joshua, sitting there so innocently on our donkey, has been promised to me as our country's new saviour, the Messiah, and I can't help but see how fitting it is that he too should be rescued from a king's threat of death by growing up in freedom in Egypt. As we journey on, these thoughts fill my mind and make the distance short or so it seems and my legs less weary. In no time we reach a village straggling along the highway, populated by farming folk whose prosperous fields we have been traversing. We find an inn for a change and Joseph manages to make himself understood remembering sufficient of the Greek language he'd learned as a boy in Bethlehem and Jerusalem. We sleep well this night. We are in a new nation. I think I shall be happy here.

The new day dawns and we are up early and feed well before packing and securing our belongings on the donkey. By giving ourselves a good start, Joseph says, we should reach Pelusium before nightfall.

'Where are we going?' I say to my husband. 'Are we going to settle in Pelusium or do we need to travel further?'

'I don't know yet,' he replies. 'It depends whether I can find work there. Also whether we can find a Jewish settlement in which we will feel at home. I'm told the largest Egyptian cities have a Jewish area where many from our nation have settled, some for many generations.'

He doesn't tell me then that the innkeeper has warned him to try to stay as far as possible with other groups as there are known to be thieves waylaying lone travellers on the way to the city and that the city is notorious for the number of criminals operating there. It apparently has improved since the Romans arrived although they have not yet eradicated the problem entirely.

All goes well at first. We make good speed across the flat well watered landscape and pass plenty of other travellers on the road. We rest from the hottest part of the day under some date palms with a couple of other families although they are going in the opposite direction. Just before we leave the security of that location, we are joined by two young men who speak to Joseph in Greek. They look respectable and we trust them, foolishly as it turns out. They apparently told Joseph that the road splits just before the city and that there are several crossings of the river. The Romans charge a tax, they tell us, to use the bridge on the main highway, but there are other routes using a local ferryman, which are cheaper and lead straight to the Jewish part of the city. Joseph apparently queried the ability of a ferry to take our animal but they assure us that it will not be a problem. We are ignorant of the circumstances in which that assurance is literally true.

So, for better or worse, we take the left hand fork onto a sandy track while the city is just visible on the skyline. Almost immediately the track itself splits further and we bear left, to the south, again and come across a muddy stream, barely more than a trickle in places, which one of the young men tells us is just a branch of the Ostia Pelusiacum, the main river being another few leagues hence. We continue south along its bank beside tall reeds, papyrus, one of the young men tells me, until sandbanks block the river's passage and it is constricted to a few feet through which we can easily wade. I climb onto the beast and hold Joshua tight against my lap and Joseph removes his sandals and hitches up his tunic and our guides splash along beside us in great humour. Their laughter is infectious and calms any nerves we may have felt in accompanying them off the main highway. The track turns westwards then and brings us eventually to the banks of a broad river, which has wide muddy shores on both sides, with masses of papyrus growing as tall as I am. I'm surprised that the ramparts of the city are now almost invisible to the north –

I'd expected that our route would have taken us to at least the outskirts of the city.

There is another surprise then when we turn and follow the pathway leading southwards along the bank away from Pelusium and I begin to get uneasy. Joseph has said something to the men, obviously querying our route, but they have apparently assured him that we are on the right route. We ride for a further half an hour or so. It is beginning to get dark and there is no sign of habitation on the far bank, just fields of grain and the occasional palm tree. The buildings of Pelusium have disappeared over the horizon.

'Soon,' one of the young men says in my language, seeing my apprehension. 'Soon we'll be at the crossing point. See!' He points to a small boat I can just see in the distance moored on our bank, and surrounded by a group of silhouettes against the setting sun. As we get closer, I notice that the boat is really small and I can't imagine how it will take a donkey as well as us and our guides. Although the river looks shallow in places, with sandbanks in the middle of the river, it is wide and there are obvious channels where it would clearly be too deep to go on foot.

Joseph is getting anxious, I can see that. He keeps asking the men questions and getting assurances that he is clearly beginning to disbelieve. He doesn't say anything to alarm me, but that's unnecessary. I'm extremely nervous and have a bad feeling about the group of men ahead. I sit tight and hold Joshua tightly against me. I wish we'd stayed on the main highway and paid the tax, but it is too late to do that now. We are committed and have to trust the young men we are with. I'm reassured when our guides recognise the group and call out a greeting. We draw up to the side of the river by the boat – it's certainly too small to carry a donkey. Perhaps we will use the ferry and they know a route across the river where it is safe for the animal to tread.

The men begin to unpack our bags and I assume that this is what is going to happen, then everything becomes a nightmare. We are surrounded by the group and looking at them in the dimming light, I see malevolence in their eyes. A couple of them have brought out knives from their robes and are cutting the ropes holding our packs instead of untying them and are slashing at our meagre belongings. They tip out our pots and clothes and precious tent and throw them in a heap on the mudbank and then find Joseph's tools and handle them carefully and grin. Then, while my mind is still reeling, one man has his knife at Joseph's throat and is threatening him. Joseph is pleading with them – he later told me that he was protesting at the robbery and saying how little cash we had with us. Then a couple of the men pull me off the donkey's back and wrest Joshua from my arms. I scream and feel a man's rough hands clasped over my mouth. I watch in horror as the knife is held against the shrieking boy's neck and Joseph is forced to strip and hand over the remnants of our cash we had brought with us. They leave him in his undergarments, then strip my precious shawl from me that my mother made for my wedding. I would normally have been distraught at the loss of that precious garment, but my immediate fears are for the life of my son and my own honour for I am afraid that they are going to rape me.

Then as suddenly as they set about us, they pile with our belongings into the boat and begin to row to the other shore. The two guides, obviously in cahoots with them, having steered us into their clutches, make off with our donkey back along the way we'd come, leaving us dazed and helpless, sitting on the muddy bank of the inhospitable murky river. Joshua is still screaming, petrified and I fling my arms around him mingling his tears with mine. Joseph is looking helpless, his head buried in his hands, sprawled on the ground. The heat of the day is disappearing rapidly as the sun drops over the horizon and we are cold and frightened, with no food, no money, nowhere to sleep and lost, several miles from the safety of the city.

Joseph keeps murmuring that he is so sorry, it's all his fault, he should have believed the warnings of the innkeeper. This is the first time I've heard of this and I really don't know what he is talking about. He is crying. I can't handle this. I rely on my husband's support and strength. I sit up and think. I've still my darling Joshua, unhurt, although badly frightened. I've not been violated. I'm thankful for that at least. The child in my womb is still secure. But how do we face the future? What do we do now?

Chapter 18
Joseph

I've tried apologising, but it seems so lame. Mari just looks at me. I don't know what she is thinking. Perhaps she is just stunned. Joshua has stopped screaming and I take him gently from Mari's arms and he whimpers with an occasional choking sob against my breast. I help Mari to her feet. She shakes the mud and sand from her tunic. Her long dark hair, now untrammelled, glistens softly in the pale moonlight, for in the last few minutes darkness has fallen. I look at the turgid river reflecting the moon dimly. It is barely moving between its mudflats. We have no money, no food, only the clothes on our back. All my tools have gone. How shall I earn money to keep us? Inside I'm panicking but I try not to show this to Mari.

The temperature has already noticeably dropped since the sun sank below the horizon and I realise that unless we can find shelter, we are going to get very cold. Instinctively I put my arms around Mari and give her a hug. But in truth, what comfort can I offer? It is all my fault. I should have listened to the warnings I was given by the innkeeper. But the two men we met when we rested in the heat of the day were so plausible. They seemed so friendly. I know now how naïve we were. Everything was going so well, we were so exhilarated with the lushness and prosperity we saw, Mari's news of another child on the way, the nearness of a large city where I could probably find work, and then this.

Now what shall we do? We need to get out of this place as fast as we can in case the thieves return. I don't trust them. At the moment, whilst we've lost all our possessions we still have each other. Mari could so easily have been raped and they could yet return and violate her and abduct our son. I've no means of protecting them except for my bare fists and what is that against a gang of half a dozen armed with knives? Mari is weeping silently now. Tears are rolling slowly down her face and I taste them as I kiss her gently on the cheek. But what solace can I give? I mutter some meaningless words that are meant to convey comfort and hope, but they are just sounds. I apologise yet again.

'Joseph, don't torture yourself,' she says laying her hand on my bare arm. 'It was not your fault. How could you know that those men were leading us into a trap?'

She doesn't know of the warning I was given by the innkeeper and so foolishly ignored. When I say nothing, she adds:

'We just have to trust God now. Perhaps we had taken him for granted. He's showing us that we must trust him and trust him absolutely. I was in a more desperate state than this when I was pregnant with Joshua and faced the wrath of the rabbis in the synagogue. God looked after me then. He will look after us now.'

I wish I had her faith, her unwitting trust. I know God has been good to us and I believe the signs we've had that Joshua is special and will eventually be great. But I'm assailed by doubts in stressed times like this. Why can't I be more positive like Mari? Anyway, I must not stay here dithering. We must move on and see if we can find some sort of shelter. We must go north towards the city.

I carry Joshua and we make our way quite quickly as we are now unencumbered although we stumble from time to time as we try to follow the rough path beside the river. I have no real idea where this track will take us, except that the city is obviously to our north, so we must eventually find it if we stick to the river. When we reach the city I've no idea what will happen. Will we be allowed in? Do they turn destitutes away? Will they think we are beggars? We have nothing to pay either legitimate taxes or bribes. When I think about it, I realise that we are in effect now beggars. How else will we sustain ourselves? I keep all this to myself as we move wordlessly along the track. At least the pathway seems as though it will lead somewhere. It does not peter out but skirts the fields of corn and flax. We stop to get our breath at one point and I explore some of the flax plants and can feel the seed pods, but they don't look edible. Then I remember someone telling me that children eat the roots of the papyrus plant and there's a forest of the stuff along the river bank. I give Joshua back to Mari – the lad had fallen asleep in my arms – and I go foraging, grubbing the straggly roots from the water in case they are all we can find to eat. With a bit of luck we will find some date palms and perhaps we'll find some that are ripe and fallen that we can collect.

I see that Joshua has stirred and Mari indicates that we should wait a while for Joshua to feed. At least the boy won't starve as long as Mari's milk flow holds up. He drinks long and noisily and then falls straight back to sleep on Mari's shoulder as she seeks to wind him. At least he is not old enough to be aware of our predicament. We get up and continue on our way. I have no idea how far we have to go – clearly the villains diverted us well to the south of the city. We have to choose whether to walk through the night and arrive at the city gates exhausted and in darkness or whether to rest in the open and come to the city at dawn, when we can properly appraise our situation. At least we'll keep going for the moment. I hope to get us within sight of the city gates before we stop. It'll be cold overnight. Walking gives us a little warmth.

Eventually, a couple of hours later, I think I can make out the beginnings of the city wall the other side of the river and about half a mile in front of us. It must be well after midnight now and there are a cluster of palm trees beside our path just ahead. We stop and I scrabble about in the darkness to see if I can discover any dates, but I can find none. However, this seems as good a place to rest as anywhere and we lay down, huddling together for warmth with Joshua fast asleep squeezed between us. I think Mari has drifted off, I can hear her soft breathing, but I lie fretfully, cold and wide awake as the events of the last few hours torture my brain. Time and time again I curse my stupidity. I want to keep turning over in my restlessness, but I'm fearful of disturbing Mari and the boy, so I lie there staring at the stars. Finally I come to my senses and use my watchfulness to pray to God, asking for his protection. I must have drifted off then into a shallow sleep. When I wake I'm aware of disturbing and uneasy thoughts, dreams near the surface of consciousness, then open my eyes and see a pale dawn breaking, the sun not yet over the horizon.

Both the others are asleep and I disentangle myself from them and start tramping around under the trees looking for fallen dates. I find a few and brush off the sand and dust from them and am tempted to eat them for I can feel a gnawing hunger. But I resist – we must share every little thing we have. I try one of the papyrus roots instead - it doesn't seem very appetising but at least it's something. If we chew the stems at least it will provide us with some sweet sustenance.

I return and find Mari and Joshua still fast asleep. It is cold, there is a slight mist creeping up from the river. I'm astonished that they can appear to sleep so peacefully. I sit and watch them. Joshua will be twenty months old soon. I put a finger into his dark curls and feel the softness. His big brown eyes are tightly closed. I lay my hand against his cheek. It is cool. Mari has cuddled his chubby body in the folds of her skirt and her bare arm is slung protectively around him. He is special, of course he is special. He is our first born son. Well, Mari's, I suppose. But most of the time I think of him as mine. He is in my care, my protection. Some protection, I think. If God has given him to us to look after for a special reason, then I've failed. He is so vulnerable lying there, with just our love to ward off the violence of the world that we've experienced. But is he so special? He looks like any other healthy Jewish boy of his age.

Then I stare at my Mari. Her long dark hair is flowing over the sandy soil, her head is turned towards the child and there is the trace of a faint smile on her lips. As she lies there so defenceless, so trusting in her slumber, I'm reminded of her when we first cohabited on our way to Jerusalem and Bethlehem. She was so young then. She's settled down a little now - her responsibility for Joshua has matured her and she is not quite as impulsive as she used to be. She has filled out and grown a little taller, but her face is still unlined and, without the stolen shawl and wedding necklace she looks like the virgin lass of our betrothal ceremony. Despite my trepidation, in that moment my heart fills with the overwhelming love I experienced on that first night together, away from the intrusive attentions of Eli and his family. I'm tempted in this moment to disturb her sleep and part her flimsy clothes and take her there beneath the translucent sky, but I hang back, it seems inappropriate in our dire situation.

As if to confirm my hesitation, she suddenly awakes, sits up and goes white. She gasps for air for a moment and looks wildly about her, taking in the reality of our situation. She hurriedly untwines Joshua from her folds and staggers to her feet and rushes to one of the trees off the track and I hear her cough twice, then she is sick. There is a low moan and she is sick once more, then she retches once and I see her staggering back wiping her mouth. All my thoughts of a romantic tussle with the girl subside in the instant and my stirrings of lust are replaced by the practicalities of dealing with Joshua who has woken up as his mother cast him aside in her urgency to cope with the nausea welling up within her. Mari goes down to the edge of the river and wipes her face in the murky water while I jiggle Joshua up and down to calm his crying, his slumber so rudely interrupted. When Mari returns, she smiles weakly at me and nods. It is her morning sickness again, nothing more. It is a little more acute today. Perhaps the experience of the last twelve hours has disturbed her system and accentuated the severity of the symptoms of early pregnancy. Perhaps her lack of food has not helped. I let her rest awhile as I feed Joshua a couple of dates I picked up earlier, then, as the sun casts an orange glow over the cornfield behind us I indicate that we should be on the move.

'No, Joseph, wait a while. I need to feed Joshua.' She puts the child to her breast and I feed her a couple of dates to chew while I scrape back the sand and dirt from the papyrus roots I had picked earlier. It seems nondescript but harmless. I doubt if it'll still the pangs of hunger that I'm feeling. While Mari is feeding the child I go in search of more dates and find a bunch on a low lying palm that I can just reach and pull off as many as I can grasp in the hope that they'll keep us going until we get to the city.

When we start to walk towards the walls of Pelusium that we can just discern picked out by the dawn rays, Joshua insists on walking with us, holding his mother's finger only. She is bent towards him, an uncomfortable posture to keep up for any length of time, but Joshua is in no mood to be picked up, so I try to take over, but he will need to let go of his mother first. She indicates to me that it's alright, let the boy have some exercise. She persuades him after a while to change hands and leans in the opposite direction as if to uncurl her body.

We plod on at Joshua's pace for a mile or so until his tiny legs begin to weary and he allows me to hoist him on my shoulders. The city's ramparts still seem a long way off, but now we're able to stride out and Mari's colour has returned. Suddenly the river seems populated, there are boats stacked with timber and other merchandise going upstream. The river itself seems fuller and deeper here and there are boats of varying sizes moored on the opposite bank and a couple of boatyards where small vessels seem to be under construction. If only I had my tools, I think, that is work I could do.

We are now level with the southernmost rampart of the city and imposing it is. The walls are set back from the river which acts as a further defence for the townspeople and the shoreline between walls and river is crowded with industrial activity intermingled with the primitive dwelling tents of families huddled round smoking fires. The stench from all this human and animal presence hits us on the other side of the now widening river and the muddy banks are full of squatting children and adults defecating publicly without shame or seeming embarrassment. Mari looks at me and pulls a face and Joshua looks curiously at the hive of activity. As we round a wide bend in the river, a bridge comes into view and we assume that we are reaching the Roman highway at last, a point where we should have arrived before sunset last night had I stuck to the advice I'd been given.

We are now facing another test. Will we get past the sentries and customs officers at the gate? After all this way, will we be turned back? If so, what should we do? It hardly bears thinking about. And yet I can think of no strategy to help us on our way. Do we throw ourselves on the pity of the city's guardians, telling them the truth about what we have been through? Will they reject us as ignorant refugees, one more set of homeless wastrels to clog up the obviously overcrowded city streets? They'll see at once that they'll have no chance of extracting any money from us either as a tax or bribe. But what other option have we? I can think of no other plausible story that could possibly convince anyone charged with restricting entry to the city. Should we try and slip through with a crowd of other travellers? How vigilant are they?

Before I've resolved anything in my mind, our track has turned into a stinking narrow thoroughfare surrounded by a maze of hovels, populated by outcasts, men with misshapen facial growths and stunted arms, and I recognise we're passing through a leper colony. Filthy children are running naked in the mud beside the river, women peer at us behind veiled faces with blatant curiosity. If we are rejected at the gateway, will we be sentenced to reside in this den of outcast humanity? I look at the innocence of my young wife and shudder at the thought of a fate that could await her here. And Joshua? How could we ever return to our own country and expect Joshua to be accepted as the promised Messiah, if it were discovered that he had lived among such paupers?

I look at Mari and expect to see her hiding her face from such pathetic and obscene sights, but am astonished to see tears glistening in her eyes. I've been too wrapped up in my own thoughts to have noticed. What's wrong? What have I missed?

'Mari, my dear, what's the matter? Are you still feeling sick? Have we been going too fast for you?'

At first she says nothing but just waves her arms in the direction of a gnarled old woman clinging to the skeletal body of a tiny child. Her eyes brim with tears once more.

'It's awful! We've got nothing to give to these poor people. How could they live like this? Does no-one care for them?'

'Mari, they've contagious diseases. They can't be allowed into a crowded city without causing an epidemic. It's sad but there's nothing we can do about it. It's just like in our own towns, we have to exclude such diseased persons from our villages too.'

'I think that's cruel too. But at least they're given food and old clothes and our villages are clean, not like this dreadful place. It's nothing but a slum of the worst kind.'

Trust Mari to be thinking of these poor creatures rather than our own predicament. I hurry her through the narrow muddy pathway aware that her signs of distress have been observed and that any moment we will become the object of importuning hands clamouring for alms. We have nothing to give and I fear we shall be molested if they think they can get something from us. Despite our lack of possessions, even our remaining clothes will mark us as people of greater substance and they will not believe we have as little as them. Joshua has seen the children and he is struggling on my shoulder – he wants to get down and play with them. I suppose it is the natural reaction of a child who has not yet learned the barriers that we erect as we grow older, learning from our bitter experience. I hold him tight until our track widens and we find a few poor stalls selling bread and dates and some shabby clothes scattered alongside. Joshua sees the bread and he's gesticulating that he wants some, but we can't even afford a hunk of the cheapest loaf. I give the boy one of the dates I've picked earlier and hope it will satisfy him.

Our track finally becomes a wide open market space alongside the main highway with myriad stalls and beasts of burden everywhere – donkeys, camels, even a couple of horses. Joshua is excited now, his eyes opening wide in wonder at the frantic scene before him. I realise that we can watch here without it becoming obvious, there are too many people milling around for anyone to take any notice of us. It crosses my mind that perhaps we can enter the imposing city gateway in front of us in a crowd of other travellers, but as I watch I observe that the crowds are thinning out as they near the walls and officials there, protected by soldiers, are sorting out those who would enter into orderly queues. We watch for many minutes. Mari realises why we are waiting.

'What are we going to do now, Joseph? Do we join the crowd at the wall and hope they'll let us through?'

'I don't know. I've been trying to see if I can discern the system the customs officials are using. It looks as though those with animals and merchandise are separated and queue to go through the main arch, but their progress is slow and I suspect they are having the value of their goods assessed. Other travellers are making their way through the side gates. Perhaps there is no hindrance for people without obvious taxable belongings or perhaps they are just residents of the city being allowed back in. I don't know whether we should risk joining that group of people and trusting to good fortune.'

I am just wondering whether we should take the plunge, when a large caravan of traders arrives in the assembly area with their animals. They look like Jewish merchants to me and they stop to water their beasts and check over their baggage and secure some items, which seem to have slipped. A couple of the men stop alongside us and look at us with some curiosity. They must recognise that we are Jews but they will puzzle why Mari is not veiled and why I seem to be missing my outer garment. Their curiosity ultimately gets the better of them, and one of the men speaks to me.

'You're a Jew too? Is that your wife and son? Why is she not wearing a veil? It's not right, you'll risk being misunderstood here. Or is she your daughter?'

I try to explain our misfortune, including the theft of my wife's symbols of marriage. The man then seems to warm to me and listens carefully while I tell him the outline of our travels, although I say nothing about our reasons for leaving Bethlehem. He obviously assumes I've come here to try my luck in the hope of a better life for my family. He draws over a couple of his colleagues and speaks to them rapidly about our situation. I can catch the odd word - they are speaking in Greek - and gather that he is attempting to persuade the other merchants to absorb us into their party to get through the entry point to the city.

'Bring your wife and child over here. We're prepared to say that you are members of our group to get you through the customs check-point. We're on our way to Alexandria to the large Jewish community there. If asked, just say that you're accompanying us to visit your relatives there.'

I thank him profusely and call Mari over and tell her what has been offered to us. She beams at the man and he smiles at her and the child, then says to me,

'Just as far as inside the city, then you're on your own. There are Jews here. I strongly advise you to find them - I'll point you in their direction once we're through the gate. And I've asked one of the lads with us to find you an outer garment and a shawl for your wife to cover herself to avoid any misunderstandings.'

I thank him again and say that I'll give him the garments back as soon as we're in the city as I have no money to pay for them. He indicates with a hand movement that that is of no consequence, they are only cheap cloth and we can keep them, but that is the limit to their assistance. We then mingle with the group and Mari accepts the pale blue simple cloth to cover her head with gratitude. The lad exchanges a few Aramaic words with her and chucks Joshua under the chin, then he's back retying the sacks of cloth on a camel's back talking to one of the merchants in Greek again, but far enough away for me to be unable to discern what he is saying.

We don't quite know what to do, waiting with these strangers for our turn at the entry gate. Are they expecting us to tell them more about our reasons for coming here? Should we tell them the truth as we should be safe in another country? Then again, I guess Herod's spies will be everywhere and I'm sure it's not beyond the reach of that tyrant to have us illegally abducted or even killed here in Egypt if he's that sure that we might be a threat to him. I therefore choose discretion, thinking the least said the better. I offer no conversation and the merchants soon cease their inquisitive looks at us and concentrate on sorting their goods out ready for the negotiations with the Pelusium officials.

We finally get through into the city in the early afternoon. One of the merchants, realising we have no food and no wherewithal to buy any, purchases some bread and grapes and gives them to Mari, who is feeding Joshua at the same time, just before we are beckoned forward by one of the soldiers at the gate. After all our fears and conjectures, the crossing proves easy and uneventful. There are prolonged negotiations of the value of the various rolls and bags of merchandise and the merchants are forced to open up some of the baggage for scrutiny. A sum of money is paid with much shaking of the head and grumbling by our benefactors, then the huge door is pushed open and our party stirs itself and proceeds into the shadows of its walls and the narrow street that is filled by our animals and the crowding roadside vendors. We continue with the merchant group for a few leagues, then the merchant who befriended us calls me over and points to a narrow street on our left which is descending gently back towards the river.

'You'll find a Jewish community down there. And if you go all the way to the river, you might find some casual employment – the docks are down there and when a ship is in there is frequent need of labour to load the grain for Rome and the Italian provinces. I wish you and your wife 'good fortune'.'

I put my hand on Mari's shoulder and we watched the camels, donkeys and their masters continue to the west. We could see the roadway widening and glimpse tall imposing buildings in the distance. But our destiny is here down this dirty little alleyway on the left. I wonder what lies in store for us. I gently lead Mari and Joshua down into the unknown ...

Chapter 19
Mari

What are we going to do now? We are in the city but the generous merchants have moved on and we are back to relying on our own non-existent resources. The houses here look small and shabby and get worse as we drop down towards the river. There are a few faces peering from the window openings, but they display no welcome, just a sullen scowl or appearance of indifference. Where can we stay? I thought perhaps if it was a Jewish settlement there might be a synagogue and we could ask a rabbi there for advice or even shelter, but I can see no sign of one, only poor dwelling places mostly devoid of people. I'm feeling tired, I want to sit and rest as the sun is scorching down and the dust is choking me. But there are no trees, there is nowhere to sit.

After walking for about a quarter of an hour, the brick and mud built houses peter out and there are tents and open hearths with assortments of pots and pans simmering on open fires, the stench from the smoking ashes mixing with the foul smell of garbage and human excrement. Within sight there is much industrial activity and we run out of road into a general hive of activity, metal and wood construction, a fearful din of banging and scraping and the tortured screech of metal against metal. There are fires burning in strange brick stoves, Joseph says they are kilns where glass is melted and shaped and there are piles of newly made bricks everywhere. The walls of the city are dirty and foul here and there are gaps through to the shoreline, with a few soldiers lolling nonchalantly about looking bored and disgusted at the obvious poverty around them.

I'm feeling low again after the hopes raised by the attention and help of the merchants and I wish that they had stayed with us long enough to see us safely to someone of importance in the Jewish community here whom we could ask for advice.

I just don't see anyone around here. The men seem absent – presumably working somewhere and the women are mainly hidden. There are a few young children about, mainly toddlers and dirty young girls watching them, playing in the refuse that's lying around. I look at Joseph and raise my eyebrows at him. Where do we go now? We seem to be at the end of the road if you can call it that – there are just the walls and the shoreline of the river in front of us.

I can see Joseph has no idea what to do either. He shrugs his shoulder at me and tells me to wait here while he disappears through the wall in search of someone from whom to take counsel. Joshua is struggling in my arms. He wants to get down and run around, but if I let him he'll get filthy here, and I can see broken shards of pottery and glass on the ground and I fear he could cut himself dangerously. I can't see Joseph now. I stand here in the baking sun clasping Joshua tightly. We must stand out and seem lost in this environment, but no-one seems to notice us. I feel lonely and homesick now and miss my friends. It's several days now since I've spoken to anyone other than Joshua and my husband and it's been hard because I'm used to chattering to my neighbours, Rachel and Rebecca and the other women and girls in our village. Perhaps it'll be alright when we've found somewhere to stop and I can get to know some women of my own age.

After a while I wander off the track looking for some sign of human activity. I think there are movements in some of the tents and inquisitively I peer into one of the open flaps and see the prone body of a woman evidently asleep. I suddenly realise that perhaps people are sleeping in the hottest part of the day and that is why I can see no movement in what looks as though it is a pretty crowded place. Two children come up to me and point at Joshua and say something but I can't understand what they are saying. I think perhaps they want to play with him, but I'm not sure. They are both naked and tears streak their dirty bodies, flies crawl about their faces. The tiny boy keeps flicking the insects from his eyes but his sister – I assume she is but you can't tell – just stares at us ignoring the swarm of flies around her face and in her tangled hair. They say something again but getting no comprehensible response from us, they lose interest and wander off and begin clawing stones from the barren earth and throwing them at the wall until one of the soldiers rouses himself and chases them away with what I take to be a few muttered oaths.

When the children have disappeared into the darkness of one of the tents, the soldier saunters over to me and obviously asks me a question but I have no idea of what he means. I shrug my shoulders at him and shake my head and he says something again but louder this time. I still don't understand him. He calls his colleague over and I think perhaps that this soldier may be able to speak my language but he merely repeats what sounds like the same words. The two soldiers are now close to me and are staring at me. I begin to feel very uncomfortable. The soldiers are whispering among themselves and grinning and one of them puts his hand on my shoulder. I flinch and step back and the second soldier starts ruffling Joshua's hair and holds out his arms and takes the boy. Joshua lets him, he is fascinated with the man's helmet and starts tugging at it. The man laughs and starts teasing the boy. The first soldier now comes back to me and starts touching me and suddenly puts a hand on my breast and squeezes and puts his other hand on my bottom and pushes forward as if he means to kiss me. I push backwards. I suddenly realise the danger that I'm in. There is no-one else around and these two Roman soldiers have no shame or fears and could rape me and I would have no defence at all.

I'm petrified. The soldiers begin to laugh and one of them tugs at my shawl and pulls it from my head. My long dark hair falls out and he thrusts his hands into my locks and clasps my head and forces his mouth on mine. I can feel his hand now exploring my bare flesh under my tunic. I want to scream for Joseph but nothing comes from my lips. Then suddenly Joshua howls. I don't know what the soldier has done to him that he reacts thus, and the sudden noise causes me to jerk backwards and the soldier releases his grip in surprise. I take advantage of the moment and tear myself from his arms and rush to Joshua and grab him from the other soldier. Both soldiers now start laughing at me and I feel hot and flushed with shame. Just at that moment Joseph appears from the gap in the wall and the two soldiers turn their backs on me and walk back to their posts with exaggerated swagger as if they are still mocking me.

'What was all that about?'

I can't answer Joseph, but burst into tears. My husband puts his arm around me, then lifts the still crying Joshua onto his shoulders. I can't get anything out. I'm shaking with shock and feel sick. I realise that I have a headache, I'm squinting at the sun, I just feel as though I want to crumple up there on the spot. I think Joseph must have guessed at what might have nearly happened and he guides me a little way back from the walls onto the roadway where the simple mud-brick houses begin.

'What happened, Mari? Did they molest you …? Did they rape you?' He asks the last question very hesitantly as if he doesn't want to hear any answer.

'No,' I manage between the sobs that are now shaking me. 'But I thought they were going to.'

'It's alright now, Mari. I'm here. I'll protect you. Don't be afraid.'

But I am. I'm scared at what is happening to us. In the last day and night we've been robbed of everything we own, threatened with a knife and now nearly raped by soldiers. Wouldn't it have been safer to stay at home? Perhaps we're only fleeing our imagination and we could be living peacefully in Bethlehem and I'd be just making my way to draw water with Rachel at this very moment with our two boys hopping and skipping alongside us. I look at the sullen houses, poorly constructed and without obvious sign of life. What have we come to? God, is this what you want for us? Is this your will, your protection? Everything has changed so quickly and I'm losing control of my emotions. Please God, please help us. My prayer is silent but very real.

'Have you found out anything useful?' I eventually mutter to Joseph. There is a long silence and he gives me another hug, which I take as a bad omen.

'We'll be alright, just you see,' he says without much conviction.

'Have you found out anything useful?'

'I found someone who said that I should go down to the jetty a few leagues from that gap in the wall. If I go at sunrise I stand a chance of being hired for the day if a boat has come in that needs loading or unloading. There's no guarantee mind. However, apparently it's the best chance of earning any money.'

'Where can we stay? Can we find shelter for the night?'

'I was told that if I can work for a couple of days, I can get a tent for us.'

'And what can we eat?'

Joseph is silent. I try to look as though he's reassured me, but my face shows everything and I find I'm crying in his arms again. Joshua is looking at me with puzzled eyes. He's not used to seeing his mother crying.

'Come, let's see if we can find somewhere in the shade to rest.'

'What shade?'

'If we can find a space behind those shacks over there,' he says pointing to a row of dilapidated hovels to the south of the street, 'we can at least rest for a while. I'll search for something to protect us from the dust and dirt.'

I look askance at where he is pointing. The ground, where it is not occupied by other destitute families, is stony and refuse strewn. We walk over to what appears to be a small vacant space and Joseph starts to clear away the worst of the rubbish. I stand there with Joshua as if to claim the ground and a few minutes later Joseph returns with a couple of large dead palm leaves which he places on the uneven surface, takes Joshua from me and helps me sit down cross-legged. When we have made ourselves as comfortable as we can, Joseph finds a few sticky dates that he picked up last night and which he's kept in reserve in case we could get no food. I give one to Joshua who chews it and we both take a couple. I watch as my husband carefully puts the remaining couple back into a piece of cloth he'd picked up, dirty and disease ridden I'm sure, but we have little choice.

It is necessary that I clean Joshua's undercloth – he has been smelling for some time now but I've had no chance to attend to him properly. When I get the sodden material off him, I find that it is soiled beyond redemption and I have absolutely nothing I can clean it with and no spare as all our baggage was stolen. I have no option but to discard the foul cloth with the rest of the refuse round us and it's immediately seized on by a swarm of bloated flies. I try to get up, but Joseph bids me stay and he picks it up gingerly by the edge and carries it away from our immediate environs. I look for something to try to clean up the boy's reddening bottom – he'll get sores unless I can remove some of the faeces. I don't want to use my own clothes or we shall soon be reduced to the outcast state of some of those I've seen in this ghastly place. I tear off a couple of fronds from the palm leaf that we're sitting on and remove the worst of the dirt. I'll need to go through the wall down to the river sometime to get water to clean him properly but I daren't go alone as I don't trust those soldiers and I'm worried if Joseph comes with me that we'll lose our place here.

We've been a long time without water now and my throat is parched and rough. We will need to find a well soon. When the women still asleep in their tents need to go for water, I must follow them. At least I can give Joshua some milk to keep him satisfied, although I don't like the idea of baring my breasts here publicly and feeding him in full view. The soldiers are not far away and if they come back while I'm feeding Joshua I know they'll stop and make rude jest of me, if nothing worse. And I don't want them to provoke Joseph into having to defend me, because they might do him some harm. Joshua seems quite happy having his legs completely free although twice I have to stop him from rubbing his hands in the traces of dirt that I was unable to remove completely. I scoop him up and let him nuzzle my breast and he's soon sucking vigorously. I realise I need to drink and take some proper food or soon my milk supply will weaken and even dry up.

Joshua is still drinking avidly when an ill-kempt woman emerges from the nearest tent to us, sees us and immediately starts screaming in words I cannot understand but her gestures make her point all too clearly. She obviously wants us out and she comes right up to me and starts bawling right into my face. Joseph stands up and tries to pull her away and she rounds on him and yells at him also. At first I think she is objecting to my feeding Joshua in public, but Joseph murmurs to me that apparently we've taken the space of some other member of her family who is working somewhere else and will come back to claim his plot shortly. I scramble to my feet and Joshua's mouth slips from my nipple and he cries in surprise. Then as I'm still clutching him to me, I feel something warm and realise he's pissing down my skirt and by the time I turn him away from me, my clothing is soiled with his urine. We retreat bedraggled and embarrassed, Joseph just remembering in time to recover the broken palm leaves, and regroup at the edge of the road, the woman still shouting at us words in coarse Greek which Joseph won't translate for me.

We move off the land adjacent to the street and back towards the wall, then turn along the wall upstream past many families now beginning to stir after their afternoon slumber. Everywhere is occupied. As we pass, we are stared at, but no-one says anything. The looks are one of hostility. We were told that this was a Jewish quarter, but they don't look like Jews at all. They are just a bunch of outcasts, derelicts, paupers and I feel so out of place. Then of course I realise that I am a pauper too. I look at my soiled clothes, the half naked toddler, Joseph's face covered in layers of dust and grime. Why should I look down on these people? I am the same as them. Perhaps they too have had similar experiences, disasters as we have had. I cannot afford to be proud now.

Every patch of ground seems to have some rough piece of cloth or makeshift tent on it. We keep walking trying to ignore the eyes following us. At last we find a space. Joseph puts our palm leaves down and looks around as if expecting someone to appear and drive us off again. We are ignored at first. We are full in the sun – there is no shade here whatsoever. I pull the shawl the merchants gave me over my forehead to shade my eyes and put Joshua down. He has been struggling to get down for some time but I didn't want him to hurt his feet on the rough dirty ground we've been traversing. I glance down at myself. I am filthy. My skirt is soiled and smelly though that is scarcely noticeable in this area, a pungent smell of rotting food coming from the river that is just the other side of the wall for the banks now come right up to the city wall, though at this point we have no access to it.

Joshua is already exploring and I want to hold him back to pick him up from the dirt, but I realise it is hopeless. I cannot keep him a prisoner. He has immediately found another child, half naked like himself and they are disappearing into the entrance of a tent where I can just make out the silhouette of a woman. I want to call to him to stop, but realise that it is best for him to make friends. He will not feel the danger and shame of our situation. The pair are lost to sight inside the tent and Joseph is looking for more cast off materials to augment our primitive carpet, but returns empty handed. He sits beside me and puts his arms round my shoulders. Then he traces the tear stains that are veins across my cheeks and kisses me.

'Mari, it doesn't matter where we are, we still have each other and the lad. We are both dirty and travel-stained, hungry and broke, but I love you. It will get better, I promise that. We'll rest here tonight, the sun will go down soon and it will cool. I'll search for work in the morning. We must get some food. And you need to find out where the nearest source of water is.'

Eventually the woman emerges from the tent opposite with the two infants trailing after her. She is older than me, though it is hard to tell by how much. At least she is smiling and her clothes, though old and ragged, look clean. She smiles at me, which is a relief, and says something, though once again I cannot understand. Joseph says something to her in Greek and she appears to say the same thing again.

'She says she is a Jewish woman, although she's been here since her youth. She is speaking a form of Greek but with a very strong accent which I struggle to understand.'

'Ask her where we can get water.'

Joseph has a further conversation with the woman, with much head shaking and waving of arms to try to make himself understood. I'm impatient to learn what information she is imparting, but I have to wait as she seems to have a lot to say. While they are talking the other child, a small girl perhaps a few months older than Joshua, comes over and looks shyly at me. I hold out my arms to her and at first she runs back to her mother and buries her face in her skirts. The woman says something to her and she sidles back to me and gives me a big smile and puts her fingers on my hair and pulls a few strands from beneath my shawl. Her mother scolds her sharply but I hold up my hand to indicate that I have no objection. After all this time, contact with another soul, especially a child, is welcome.

'She says that we'll have to pay rent for this site. Every bit of land here is owned by scoundrels who exact money from us and if we fail to pay they send thugs in to move us and steal anything we own.'

'Where can we go, Joseph? Is there nowhere we can go without having to pay money?'

'She says that the only empty spaces are right at the end of the city wall where it curves away from the river – there is a gateway there that leads right to the city rubbish tip which no-one wants for fairly obvious reasons. Only the outcasts go there, people with leprosy or other infectious diseases.'

'Do we have to go there? Is there no-one who will help us?'

'She says it might be worth trying to negotiate a loan with the guy who comes to collect the ground rents, especially if I can demonstrate I can get employment at the jetty.'

'Has she said where we can get water?'

'Apparently there's no well in this party of the city. Everyone gets water from the river and has to boil it to make sure it's usable. She says we can use her stove until we can afford our own.'

'But how do we reach the river? There's no way through the walls. Do we have to go right back to where the soldiers were, by the road we came down? That must be half an hour's walk at least each way, more with a heavy jar of water and a young child.' Another thought. 'And how do I fetch water? We have no jar.'

Joseph asks the woman my question and I listen to a stream of incomprehensible sounds.

'She'll loan you her large jar but you'll have to fetch water at a different time to her as she only has one large waterpot. And she can loan you some smaller vessels to store a bit of water. She says most of the women go to the gate by the rubbish tip because it's not so far, although it means putting up with the foul odour. She also says that the water is cleaner there as it's got no commercial activity nearby though some refuse and drains get to the river there. But if you walk a few leagues further south, you can avoid the worst of the pollution.'

'Thank her, Joseph.'

'She says her name is Naomi. Her husband works on the jetty and he'll take me with him tomorrow morning. She has three other children. Boys of eight and ten are working with their father. Her daughter is seven and is scavenging on the tip. Sometimes the girl stays at home to look after her young sister and Naomi works the tip as she can find more of possible value there herself. She's offered to take you there and show you what to look for.'

At that moment the older girl returns. She is wild-eyed and dishevelled and is carrying small sack, which she plonks at the feet of her mother. She is just wearing a small discoloured tunic, bare feet, tangled hair of indiscriminate dirt colour.

'Anna,' the woman says, pointing to her daughter.

I look at the poor girl and am consumed with pity for her. What sort of life is this for a young child? How long have these people been living in this condition? Is there no way out for them? For us? I realise now that if we are here without means, what chance have we of getting away? I thought we were coming to safety. I thought it was to preserve Joshua for the role ordained for him – not to condemn him to a life scavenging on refuse tips like this poor girl. A Messiah from such a place? Our religious leaders will never tolerate or recognise a child with so much stigma attached. I wonder what led this unfortunate family to this life here. Now is not the time to probe though. If we become friends, I'll learn in good time. Now I'm just grateful that at last we have found someone in this city who has not rejected us.

Anna comes up to Joshua and throws her skinny arms around him and lifts him into the air. I want to restrain her as she's so dirty, I want her to clean up first, but Joshua whoops with joy and I'm forced to realise that I must adjust my thinking and just leave it to God. I can't go round mollycoddling the boy any more – not that I've thought I was in the past, but I'd never imagined this. I'll just have to trust God. If it is truly his plan that Joshua is the saviour of our nation long promised to us, then he'll find a way and Joshua will survive. Perhaps Joseph and I have already fulfilled our purpose and we are no longer in the plan. I banish this disturbing thought at once. Joshua needs our support now as never before. I feel so homesick at this moment. As I watch Anna playing with Joshua, I think of my sisters playing with Benjamin in far off Nazareth. They'll be growing up now and I have no news of them. When will I see them again? Will we recreate the close relationships we had or will it all be so different? I'd imagined Salome and Rebecca playing with Joshua as Anna is doing now. I must stop these depressing thoughts and concentrate on the practicalities. I must fetch some water as soon as possible.

Joseph passes on my urgent need to this angel who has come to our rescue.

'She says you can go now. Anna will look after Joshua and her little girl, and she will accompany you to show you the best place to draw water and ensure you don't get lost.'

I smile my thanks to her and she pours water from her biggest jar into some smaller containers. She hands me the earthenware pot and we make our way along the inside of the wall passing the bustle of activity as many women and children are now stirring from their afternoon rest or returning from the activities of searching for some little income to sustain their lives. She obviously knows most of them well and greets them and must be explaining who I am as she waves a hand in my direction as she speaks. We tramp on. I'm tired and feeling a bit sick. I have had virtually nothing to eat and have been out in the burning sun all day with little protection from the heat. But I can't complain to this woman – she's being so good to us. It was not necessary for her to accompany me but I'm relieved that she's with me. I just worry that I might faint and become even more of a burden to her.

We continue in silence. She tried saying something to me at first, but soon was aware that I could not understand her. She just smiles at me from time to time and waves in the general direction we are going. I can see the corner of the city wall now and can make out the small gateway, which apparently leads to the tip and waterfront. The smell is bad and getting worse and I try not to show how much it is upsetting me for Naomi – I must get used to her name – is showing no signs of distress but is marching on as if we have little time to spare. It occurs to me then that she will be returning here on her own account in an hour or so at the time most women go for water. I must not delay her further and I make a real effort to keep up with her although I'm finding every increasing step agony. We finally reach the gate at the edge of the city and the noise of the gulls over the huge rubbish tips is deafening. There are carts hauled by donkeys carrying piles of refuse making their way to the dump from other parts of the city; there must be at least three converging roadways from gateways further to the west.

There is just one soldier guarding the gate, who is looking fed up – I would think this might be a punishment posting in such a place. He ignores us and we now follow a rough track along the bank. The river is wide here and looks a dirty brown. I'm horrified at first that we will have to make do with such polluted water, but as the path nears the river I see that the discoloration is more from the mud and sand than anything else. I make as if to approach the water to draw, but Naomi holds me back and points further upstream. We cross a couple of drainage ditches with filthy muck oozing from the refuse tip and finally leave the dump behind and come to a place where the bank is shallow and the pathway has been hardened by the trampling of feet over many years. Naomi indicates that I should draw water here and I lower the jar into the water facing the flow and lift it out when I think I have as much as I can carry. I hoist the full jar onto my shoulder – Naomi helps me adjust the load to give a better balance – and we start our weary way home. Every step is now torture for me. I must not give up. I grit my teeth and try not to let her see how hard this is for me.

We get back to the city wall and I notice a second soldier has appeared. Presumably he was down by the water when we came through earlier. As we pass he looks the other way and spits at the ground. Is he expressing his disgust at us or is he just clearing his throat from the dust flying in the air? I'm being pestered by insects now, but I need both hands to steady my load, so I have to put up with the bugs which are settling on my face and flitting round my eyes. I keep blinking and blowing. Naomi is saving her breath now and I feel faint. I indicate to her that I can't go on – I need at least a short rest. She looks at me quizzically and I point to my belly. She looks puzzled at first, then her face lights up and she rocks a pretend baby in her arms. I nod and she immediately takes the heavy jar from me and lets me stop until I get my breath back. I don't want to be so much in her debt, but physically I have no choice. I will have to toughen myself up if I am to survive here. I always thought I was a robust girl and I had what many would call a hard life back in the fields of Nazareth, but this is a whole lot different and I'm going to have to get used to it. Perhaps it will get better once I'm able to get something to eat.

When at last we are in sight of Naomi's tent, the three children spot us and come running towards us. Anna arrives first and stops, gasping, then Naomi's three year old who I find out later is called Rebecca like my sister. Finally Joshua toddles up and makes straight for me and flings himself into my arms. I cheer up at this demonstration of affection and Joseph comes to greet us too. We are no sooner back to the spot we have claimed when Naomi brings out a couple of smaller water pots and we fill those and a cooking pot with the water I have drawn. Naomi immediately picks up the empty vessel and sets off with a couple of neighbours back to the water collection point on the river. Perhaps I ought to offer to go with her, or even go in her place, but I'm exhausted and sink to the ground. I guess Joshua is now going to expect me to tell him a story as I often do at this hour, and I'm just thinking that I should stir myself when Anna returns and Joshua immediately trails after her. He's found a friend.

It's dark when Naomi's man returns from his work at the riverside jetty. After he's greeted his wife, Naomi brings him over to us and he takes Joseph aside and they spend a long time in conversation. He finally goes back to his family and Joseph tells me what he's been saying.

'There's a ship due in tomorrow to load grain for Rome. It's a big load and they need extra hands, so Nathaniel – that's Naomi's husband's name – thinks I have a good chance of getting a full day's work. I'm to go with him before daybreak and he'll put in a word for me and persuade the foreman to employ me without the usual bribe, which they call a 'guarantee'. I'll get enough to buy some bread and dates for us and put a down- payment on this plot of land. He says there is a chance that the ship may be docked for a second day which would give me enough for a week's rent on this space and get some cheap clothes for Joshua and me so we can change from our filthy things.'

A few minutes later Naomi comes over with a hunk of bread each and bowls of hot broth. I'm not sure what it's made from and I don't ask. I'm just so grateful for any food and this seems like luxury. Joseph thanks our benefactors profusely and I nod vigorously in agreement. I tear off a small piece of bread and dip it in the soup and give it to Joshua who devours it ravenously.

I think the offer of possible work is good news and we have gone some way to filling our bellies at last. How quickly we change our judgements of what is acceptable. We sleep in the open air that night and ignore the smells, the cold, the hunger. I cover Joshua with my skirt and I only wake up briefly once in the night and cover Joshua up again as best I can. Despite him feeling chilly to the touch, he sleeps right through the night for once. When I awake again, I find Joseph is leaning over me and bidding me farewell, promising to return that evening with food and enough money to pay a first instalment on our piece of squalid land.

'Make sure you are able to tell the rent collector that we will pay. Get Naomi to tell him for you.'

With that advice Joseph slips away into the darkness. I see another shadow, which must be Nathaniel. Now that I'm properly awake I feel that familiar bout of morning sickness rising in my throat and I have to roll Joshua quickly from my skirt to stagger up and be sick away from our immediate space and that of others for we are very crowded. Eyes are watching me. No other family has bothered to engage with us although there is obvious curiosity. I'm clammy and flushed and soon I'm sick again. Joshua wakes up this time and starts crying because he is hungry. I have to make him wait a while until I feel a bit better and by the time he is fed the sun is up and I can already feel its warmth.

I see Naomi giving Anna a piece of bread to take with her and the little girl joins a couple of others about the same age who are despatched on an identical errand. Then Naomi invites me into her tent and offers me goat's milk and some bread. I haven't mentioned, have I, that there are many animals rooting about this untidy area of barren land, mainly goats, but a few chickens also and a couple of pigs although I'm not sure what nationalities here are allowed that meat in their diet. Naomi's family has one goat, which is tethered to the tent pole and from which the family gains milk and cheese. After we have eaten and Joshua and Rebecca join some other young children around the site, I indicate to Naomi that I'd like her to teach me some Greek words. If we are to stay here long, this is essential or I'll have no company but Joshua and my husband and find difficulty in carrying out the most basic jobs of a wife.

I have learnt, I think, the local dialect for bread, grapes, figs, dates, water and wine, also the common words of greeting and farewell, when Naomi spots the thug the owner of the land employs to collect his rent. I get up to go back to my palm carpet, but Naomi restrains me and I gather she will talk to him on our behalf. We watch as the thickset man moves gradually towards us, stopping off at each tent to collect his due. Naomi shakes her head and opens her palm and puts her fingers in the sign of a cross. I'm puzzled at first then I think she's trying to show a 'plus' sign indicating that he charges too much. Gradually he comes towards us and my heart is in my mouth.

He stops where our dead palm leaves are on the ground and picks up one and snaps it in half, then he does the same to the other. He picks up one pot that I filled with water and pours it onto the ground, then he empties the other. Naomi stands up and shouts to him and they enter into conversation which gets more and more heated. They are clearly arguing and suddenly the man cuffs Naomi about the face and spits at her. Then he advances on me and grabs me by the wrist and hauls me to my feet. He yells something to my face – the sense is obvious, he wants us out. It is clear that the offer of money tomorrow has not satisfied him. I panic and burst into tears but instead of softening him, this only enrages the man further and he hits me violently in the face and then punches me in the stomach. He screams at me again and Naomi once more tries to argue with the man only to be knocked to the floor.

'I'll go, I'll go,' I shout pointlessly to the air, for no-one understands me. I stumble out of the tent and look around for Joshua. I can't see him anywhere. I struggle from the grip of this heartless brute but he crushes my arm and drags me onto the path beside the wall and gives me a kick pointing in the direction of the rubbish tip. He keeps repeating the word I heard him yell before – it must be something like 'go' or 'be gone'.

I stagger blindly down the path, still in his vice-like grip, scanning the area for any sign of my son. After he's propelled me a good distance from Naomi's tent, he lets go of my arm and again points me in the direction of the gate to the rubbish dump. I hesitate, still looking for Joshua. I try to tell him but I can find no words or actions to make him understand. I slink away, ready to return as soon as his back is turned. He is now progressing towards the roadway into the city proper and when he is far enough away, I begin to creep back. I can see Naomi looking for the children and eventually she finds them in the tent of another family playing with their toddlers. By the time I've got back to Naomi's tent she has Joshua in her arms. She looks at me in distress. She shakes her head. I thought that once the man had gone that we'd be able to return to our space as long as we moved before he came again, or at least we had money to pay him. Naomi is trying to convey something to me by sign language and in the end I grasp that he'll send another thug to beat us up unless we go immediately. She signals 'back' and then throws mock punches and puts her hands round her throat. I get the message.

Naomi goes back into her tent and comes out with a crust of bread and goes over to pick up one of the pots that the collector has emptied. She fills it from her own water jar and gives it to me and embraces me. Then she points to the path leading to the tip, makes the sign of a gate with her hands and pushes her fingers through it. I grasp that the only place we're allowed is actually outside the city walls where we saw the outcasts and the diseased. I can't think of anything else to do and I fetch Joshua and bid him trot alongside me. He is not worried. It is all a big adventure for him. I look at his grubby little toes and notice bloodstains where he has gashed them on a stone or bit of rubbish. He hasn't noticed.

He looks up at me and grins. I try to look cheerful to avoid alarming him, but inside I'm confused and upset. I'm sure Naomi will tell Joseph what's happened when he returns with her husband tonight and he'll manage to find me even in the dark, but I'm scared for us all. I fear most of all catching one of the many fatal diseases that must abound in neighbourhoods like this, but there is little I can do to protect us. My trudge compares with Joshua's hop, skip and jump and he wanders around investigating other tents and squats and their children, covering twice as much ground as I do. The smell makes me feel sick, but Joshua ignores it. We're getting closer to the edge of the city and the gateway to the path by the river and the rubbish tip. The soldiers on duty there are busy chatting to each other and ignore us – at least that's a relief. Joshua is fascinated by the gulls and large crows that are circling over the refuse making a terrific din, and attempts to chase a couple of the raven birds that are tussling over some disgusting morsel at the edge of the path. I warn him away - I don't trust these birds with such a small child. They look vicious to me.

There is a small town perched precariously along the bank, inhabited by those considered by the citizens of this city to be the dregs of society – those who because of disease or lack of money are cast out to fend for themselves. There are men, women and children here for these men can find no employment. There are old gnarled near corpses, men with hideous physical deformities, men and women whose loss of mental faculties makes them perform obscene gestures as we pass by. Joshua thinks they are funny. He does not yet realise the pathetic nature of the figures prancing at the water's edge, some naked or in tattered rags. We had a few such creatures in Nazareth and Bethlehem, but someone always looked out for them and gave them alms and food. We did not let them starve.

Here no-one seems to care. There is an old woman whose face and fingers have been eaten by the dread leprosy and a young boy already showing the white skin blotches that denote he too is a victim. I forget my own misery when I see these sights. They are much more unfortunate than me. They have no hope, no future. Surely we are not condemned to live like that? Joseph will earn some money then we can escape, but I shall not forget this ever. And although he cannot appreciate it now, I won't let Joshua forget it either.

We keep walking. We must have meandered for nearly half an hour beside the river before the wretched hovels and makeshift dwellings start having gaps between them. The rubbish tip too has dwindled until it only consists of a few remnants blowing in the wind. There are stray dogs prowling amongst the remnants of the rubbish but no-one chases them away. I watch them carefully to see that they don't come near Joshua. Luckily he seems to be wary of them - I was worried that he might chase after them and get bitten. We now have a full view of the river and the path on the other side where we were passing only yesterday morning – it seems like an age already. The path wanders a short distance from the bank now taking a short cut where the river curves in a wide arc.

    The community of the sick and destitute has finally come to an end. I move across onto the barren land on the river side of the path and sit down. I put the bread and pot of water beside me. It is all I have in the world apart from the clothes on my back. We are at the end of the dispossessed, the lowest of the low. We can go no lower. Perhaps we have to learn this before we can become honoured. I must learn to hang on to God's promise. I look at the few strands of brownish grass struggling to survive in this wilderness and remember the times I used to sit under the fig tree blowing seeds from the grasses planting anew. Joshua is fascinated by the river now – I'll have to watch him carefully here or he'll be in the water and quickly out of his depth. We must just wait until Joseph finds us. I watch the red ball of the sun sink over the rubbish tip and think how beautiful it is, shimmering orange and purple even on that revolting mound. The birds wheel dark against the rainbow coloured sky. I must wait and count my blessings.

Chapter 20
Joseph

It's been a heavy day. I'm used to physical work, but not humping sacks of grain for over twelve hours with but a few minutes' break to eat a hunk of bread in the early afternoon. My back aches, but at least I have some money to take back to Mari and get our space secured. The ship is still only half full, so there'll be work tomorrow and if the wages are the same we'll be able to afford to buy some clean cloth as well as food. Nathaniel has been so helpful. He smoothed the way with the overseer this morning and made sure that I got a full day's work in. He told me how much my labour was worth so that I was not cheated. I watched his two sons straining to lift the sacks of grain and marvelled that they managed it – they were strong lads, but I can't accept that it's right for children of that age to do such heavy adult work. I didn't mean to challenge Nathaniel on that point but the remark flew from my lips before I could stop it. Nathaniel didn't take offence but explained that they needed the boys' wages as well as his own to give all the children the nutrition they needed. Despite my tiredness, there's an increasing spring in my step as I near the area where Mari and Joshua will be, close by Nathaniel's tent.

The two lads have run ahead to greet their mother and sisters and play with Joshua before their evening meal. I walk silently with Nathaniel. He hasn't said much all day, but I have gathered that his family came here when he was only a boy, exiled after his father was accused - falsely he said – of cheating an important official in a building contract in Jerusalem. In other words, Nathaniel had said, he didn't give the official the bribe or cut he was expecting. He was hoping to earn enough money eventually to get his family out of this area and into the Jewish quarter where more prosperous folk lived, but there was prejudice against families who'd lived in this slum and he thought they might find it difficult to find somewhere decent and be accepted.

As we get closer to Nathaniel's tent, the older lad comes back and says that Mari and Joshua aren't there – they've been thrown out by the landlord's rent collector. We break into a fast walk, in fact I almost run, but Nathaniel puts a restraining arm on my shoulder.

'We'll find them, don't worry. You can shelter in our tent tonight while we sort the rogue out.'

'That's very generous of you, Nathaniel. Are you sure you've got enough room for us?'

'It'll be a bit of a squeeze, but we'll manage for one night. I'll help you search for them. Let's see what my wife has to say first though.'

Naomi is sitting nursing her youngest when we enter the flap of her tent. She looks up and immediately I notice that tears are welling up in her eyes.

'Joseph, the brute would not accept any promise to pay a rent. We pleaded with him, but he took no notice at all. He made Mari take Joshua out of the rented area altogether and hit me when I tried to remonstrate on their behalf. I went with them. They're outside the city gate, down on the banks of the river on the far side of the outcasts' township. I gave them some water and food.'

'Naomi, we must fetch them back. We can house them tonight until we can sort things out. Joseph has sufficient money now to put a down payment on the rent.'

'Husband, I'm not sure. The man threatened me that he'd be back and would throw us off this land if we tried to support them.'

I can't accept them putting themselves at risk. 'It's alright, Nathaniel, we'll make do somehow until tomorrow. Then I'll find the rent man and negotiate with him.'

'You don't negotiate with scum like that. He will tell you what is acceptable and you pay it or refuse and leave. There's no other way. Come, let us go and fetch Mari and the child now before any harm comes to them.'

'What if that thug comes back tonight?' worries Naomi. I can see her point of view.

'He'll not be back. Not tonight anyway. And in the morning Joseph will be with me at the jetty and here will just be you and Mari and Rebecca and Joshua. Why should he come back anyway? You've just paid him. And if he comes back, what will he find? You've just got a visitor because you're friends. So what?'

'Come, Joseph, let's go and find Mari.'

'Can I come too?' pipes up a voice from the depths of the tent. It's Anna, the seven year old. If she's been scavenging on the tip all day, I'm surprised she has enough energy to want to walk with us.

Nathaniel is about to tell her not to be so silly, when Naomi says, 'She came home in the early afternoon because she was being hounded by some youths and was scared. She's bored and she can keep Joshua amused when you find him.'

So Anna is allowed to accompany us. She holds her father's hand and squeezes between the two of us and grasps my hand too. I think she feels safe between two big men and we set off at a good pace with her putting in a few extra paces to keep up. She is nattering to Nathaniel and I don't catch everything she is saying because her dialect is so strong. I think she's complaining about the threatening behaviour of the boys on the tip this afternoon and the teasing from them that she encountered. Nathaniel in any case is making soothing reassuring noises.

Darkness comes quickly and there is little light as we make our way towards the southernmost city gate. The only light comes from the cooking fires and the occasional flickering candle glowing from some of the tents beside the track. We are now silent and the stench from the refuse dump is getting fouler by the minute. This does not seem to bother either Nathaniel or Anna, they are obviously accustomed to it, but I still find it repellent. The thought of having to spend the night in the open in close proximity to the source of the smell is something I'm glad I'm now going to avoid. We reach the gateway at last and the soldier on duty there looks curiously at us but asks no questions. Then it is pitch black. The moon has not yet cast any real glow and I can only just discern the river flowing to our left, hearing the faint rippling as the water surges against the bank. There is little traffic on the river now. The regular shuttle of barges from the delta wheat fields has ceased until daybreak tomorrow.

As we move carefully between the shacks of the outcasts in the darkness, Nathaniel begins to call Mari. We're not sure how far in she'll be, although Naomi had intimated that they'd progressed beyond most of the dwellings. A faint glow is now apparent from the rubbish tip as it is burning slowly on the far side and this now augments the meagre light. I can trace the outline of the mound and see we are not yet more than halfway along its length. We trudge for a further ten minutes or so and at last we get the sound of a woman's voice in response to our repeated shouts. As soon as she hears this, Anna lets go of our hands and rushes off in the direction of the call. I realise that the girl must know this area blindfold as she spends most of every day in this vicinity.

We stumble over to the river bank where Anna disappeared into the darkness and find the girl hugging Joshua with the boy squealing with delight. Mari pushes herself to her feet when she sees us coming and falls about my neck sobbing. She is cold and I wrap my arms around her and whisper in her ear,

'Don't distress yourself, Nathaniel has offered to share his home with us for the night. You won't have to stay out here.'

'But the man said ...'

'Don't worry, Mari, we'll squash in together tonight and sort things out in daylight tomorrow morning.'

Nathaniel picks up the implements that Naomi had given her and Anna lifts Joshua onto her hip and carries him alongside her father. Joshua is quite content with this, he does not scream for me. Anna, despite her young age and squalid circumstances, seems to have a way with small children – with Joshua at least anyway. I follow still holding Mari tightly and feeling her shiver through her thin cloth. She tries to explain to me what has happened, but I tell her that Nathaniel and Naomi have already told me. When we get back to Naomi, Rebecca and the two boys, we find that the bedrolls have already been pushed together and Naomi has a meal ready for everyone. It's a very simple meal, true, but they were not expecting to have to cater for us as well. When we've finished, Naomi puts her two youngest to bed while Mari feeds Joshua, then he too is laid alongside Rebecca and Anna while the boys are squashed beside their father and me near the exit to the tent so that we do not disturb the others when we rise to go to the jetty.

We get in a full twelve hours' work the following day and I'm happy to receive the hourly rate I'd been promised and realise that I've now enough to pay rent on a space near Nathaniel's tent. A few more days of similar work and I'll be able to purchase a tent as well as a change of clothing for everyone. That night Nathaniel helps me bring back some disused bamboo poles, rope and some oily cloth that had covered the grain and had now been discarded, and we construct a shelter of sorts for ourselves and leave Nathaniel's family to themselves, uttering our repeated and grateful thanks. Anna comes over after cleaning herself – she's apparently escaped attention from the youths who had bothered her the previous day – and she keeps Joshua amused while Mari manages to light a fire and heat a meal for us.

A few days go past and we surprisingly become accustomed to our lowly status and the stench and filth. Some more ships arrive with imports from our country and from islands far away with fruit and honey and I'm able to earn enough to pay the rent, which Nathaniel negotiated for us with the nasty character, who was looking for an excuse to throw us out again. I begin to feel a little more secure and think that if we continue in this way I might be able to save sufficient money to try moving on, perhaps to the big city of Alexandria that Nathaniel says is rumoured to be no more than ten days' further journey and where there is a prosperous Jewish settlement. The grain harvest is beginning to slacken but I hope that the flow of incoming ships will provide sufficient work for me for a further week or two when I calculate that we might make a move. I am a little concerned, however, that my back might give way as I've been feeling sore and stiff, unused to such heavy work. Let's hope I can last a further couple of weeks and then find more appropriate carpentry work in the larger city.

I've been promised employment tomorrow as there is a least a morning's work to complete the current shipment and there's a rumour that a further boat will shortly be calling for some of the last grain harvest. We arrive at the waterfront in good time only to find an angry crowd milling around the foreman's hut demanding work. Apparently the second ship has not yet been sighted and the overseer has played safe by engaging only half the men this morning and has told others to wait. The overseer is a Jew and has been accused of favouring Jews over Greek-speaking Arabs, and the mob is angry and threatening violence. The overseer now finds himself caught between two confrontational groups as some Jews began to hurl abuse at him when he showed signs of caving in to the Arab's demands and standing Jews down who'd already been promised work. The man eventually compromises by taking half the Arabs and half the Jews, but that means I'm excluded, being the most recent Jew to be accepted. I can see that if I protest, the mob could get violent and I could find myself in a riot and arrested by Roman soldiers who would not stand idly by. I am dismissed although Nathaniel is one of the lucky ones and stays. The boys too find no work and we all saunter back to Nathaniel's tent together, frustrated and worried.

I have a talk with Mari this afternoon about what we should do.

'Mari, I think we had enough money now to purchase sufficient provisions for at least three weeks and we have the tent we are using as our home. I've heard men at the dockside talk of the prosperous Jewish settlement in Alexandria and of a synagogue there. Perhaps we should continue our travels westwards and throw ourselves on the mercy of the rabbis there until we find work and a more permanent dwelling.'

'But, Joseph, that means leaving our friends here.'

'We've got to get away from this place. I know you've found friends here, but everywhere is filthy and our prospects, without the promise of further work, are very poor. I fear we'll not be able to sustain our ability to pay the required land rent and then we'll finish up begging food from our friends again who can ill afford it.'

When Nathaniel returns home, he is pessimistic.

'Joseph, more squabbles broke out between Jews and the Greek-speaking Arabs all afternoon and the overseer threatened to dismiss everyone and get the next boat transferred to a different jetty. That calmed the mob temporarily, but I don't think there's much prospect of you getting sufficient regular employment to maintain your family here.'

'Mari, our best chance, while we still have a little money, is to make our way to Alexandria as fast as possible.'

Mari grunts. I think she agrees but she doesn't look very happy about it.

'Nathaniel, why haven't you ever taken the risk, and tried to find your family better accommodation in that city?'

'Don't think I haven't thought long and hard about it. But at least I have a regular income here and I can't put my family in jeopardy. I'll just have to soldier on.'

'Mari and I have to move on, you do understand, don't you? Why don't you come with us?'

'I'm sorry, Joseph. I don't think I dare take the risk. We've got used to our situation here and Naomi won't thank me for throwing what we have away.'

Nathaniel understands my decision and does not try to talk me out of it, although both Naomi and Anna plead with us to stay. Mari is confused as she understands so little that has been spoken in her presence despite her attempts to learn a few key words and phrases from Naomi, but she does not try too hard to argue with me and helps me pack our minimal belongings early the next day. Nathaniel's whole family comes to bid us farewell, with Anna crying as she nearly crushes Joshua in a giant hug despite her wraith-like appearance. Naomi has packed bread and dates for our journey although her store of food is low and presses them on us despite our insistence that they should not be so generous towards us. We part and I thank Nathaniel and Naomi with all my heart and Mari embraces them both and the children. In response to yet another cry from me that I'm unhappy that I cannot repay them for their goodness to us, Nathaniel simply says,

'Joseph, all I ask is that when you are in a position to help another in need, that you remember this and are generous too.'

Despite our short acquaintance, I've grown fond of this huge man and his family and as I watch them in the pale dawn light diminishing in size as they wave farewell to us, I have to admit I shed a tear. Mari makes no pretence at holding back and is weeping, while Joshua traces the tears on her cheeks with uncomprehending eyes. He'd seen more tears from both his parents in the previous few days than in the rest of his little lifetime.

We progress quickly. We leave the worst of the city's stench behind us as we traverse the paved streets and imposing buildings in the centre and find our way without hindrance to the West Gateway on the Roman road to Alexandria, named unsurprisingly the 'Alexandria Gate'. We take it in turns to carry Joshua in order to move fast, although he needs to get down and exercise his legs occasionally. This gives us a chance to try to link with other travellers to avoid any danger of becoming victims of robbers again, but in truth we have now virtually nothing left to steal and I think that is apparent from our state – we ourselves are clean but our few clothes bear the obvious signs of having lived in a dirty slum for several days. We pass along this impressive road, which hugs the coast on our right and borders fertile fields of grain and flax on our left. From time to time we encounter a grove of palm trees under which we can rest awhile in their shade and seek refreshment from a common well. I thought from comments made by other travellers, including the merchants who helped us into Pelusium, that we might make Alexandria in a week or so meaning that we would need to spend just a few days in our tents on the way – at a quiet oasis of palms with a few other similarly poor travellers.

We make good progress during the morning and stop at a village well beside the highway and draw sufficient water to shelter behind a barn and attempt as best we can to wash our outer garments. The sun is already hot so we don the wet clothes knowing that they will dry on our bodies and at least keep us cool for an hour or so. The road is busy and we pass many going in the opposite direction, several mule trains and a group of merchants with a number of heavily laden camels. Joshua watches fascinated and attempts to make the ugly growling noises that the animals utter as they strain their ungainly way eastwards. We can see travellers moving our way too, but we are maintaining a reasonable pace now and few overtake us. We feel safe here, although I keep looking nervously over my shoulder for I can't forget our experience before we reached Pelusium – there's no way I'll trust any strangers now, however friendly they appear to be.

By the middle of the day we're looking out for a suitable place to rest awhile while we eat some of the produce that Nathaniel and Naomi gave us. I can see some palms in the distance and we agree to carry on and seek shade there. We're lucky – it's not just a few trees but a real oasis with a pool of water, although it doesn't look fit for humans to drink. Many other travellers have stopped here however and there are a number of beasts drinking from the water – mainly asses. I look carefully around seeking the company of people who look trustworthy and see a family with two young children and even as I look I catch a few phrases of our own language – they are obviously Jews. We therefore settle down close by them and Joshua is off at once making friends with the older of the two children – a girl of about three, the other child still being scarcely a year old by the look of him.

Despite my resolution not to engage with strangers I exchange glances with the man and Mari brightens at once when she hears her own language and immediately greets the young woman who cannot be that much older than she is. We sit side by side munching our food and I gather that Mari has already established that they are travelling towards Alexandria also and are hoping to settle in the Jewish community there. Mari eventually persuades Joshua to rest and he soon falls asleep and I notice that their youngest is also fast asleep in his mother's arms. Since neither of us is clearly ready to move on, we begin to share experiences. The man introduces himself as Philip and his wife as Dora and we exchange casual information about our journeys so far. I tell them that we have suffered from thieves although I don't go into full details and they look horrified and say that they've felt safe on the main highway with its regular traffic and constant military patrols. Then I find out from them that the story we were told about the heavy tax due to cross the river bridge into Pelusium was pure fiction or at least they saw no signs of such an imposition. It was obviously concocted to persuade us into the clutches of the thieves. I feel sick at heart that I'd allowed myself to be so deceived but there is little I could do about it now, so best to try to put it to the back of my mind.

'Joseph, why are you and your family making this journey?'

'Well, we need to find a better life than the one we could find in Bethany.' I still feel obliged to maintain that cover for our emigration.

This immediately prompts Philip to own up to a similar reason. Apparently he is the younger of three brothers, all skilled carpenters like myself – what a coincidence! However, there was not enough work for the three of them in their village, which was near Ashkelon. I wondered if we had passed through it on our journey earlier. He had tried to find work in Ashkelon itself returning home each night, but there were many carpenters there and they resented a stranger threatening to take some of their business and made it both difficult and unpleasant for him.

'So,' he says, 'in the end we have decided to seek a new life in Alexandria. I've heard from travellers that they need carpenters' skills as the Romans are constructing many new buildings there.'

This is music to my ears. I'm reassured that I've taken to right decision to get out of Pelusium despite the generosity of Nathaniel and Naomi.

'Not only that. There has been tension between myself and Dora's parents ...' Dora nods quite vigorously as he says this. 'Dora is from a Levite family and her parents had been intending to marry her to a fellow Levite and Dora upset them by indicating that she wanted to marry me. That didn't go down well and they accused her of being a rebellious and ungrateful girl.'

'I think we may share some similar experiences, it's as you say, not just for livelihood reasons that cause us to make such a major step ...'

'Yes, it was just the same for us,' interrupts Mari. 'Well, not quite, we had to get out of Bethlehem in a hurry because we were afraid ...'

'Mari, we don't have to tell our new friends all of our problems ...'

Philip looks hard at me.

'Sorry, Philip, I mentioned Bethany only as I'm a bit nervous about sharing our real reasons for leaving Bethlehem so suddenly. Our family has been fearful of having upset the authorities.'

I look hard at Mari hoping she will say no more, and luckily Philip leaves it at that. I don't feel we should say any more at present, after all we've only just met them and although they look innocent enough, you never know, do you?

As we're both going to Alexandria, however, and are looking for similar contacts, we agree that it makes sense for us to travel together. It's heartening to see Mari so animated again. It must be several weeks now since she's really been able to talk to anyone properly apart from Joshua and me, and you can hardly call conversation with Joshua adult however intelligent he is. She is clearly finding a rapport with Dora who can't be much older than she is and they're busy chattering away while Philip and I get some rest. I discover then that they have a donkey which is drinking from the oasis and Philip brings it back and, after checking that I have no beast, offers to put some of my burden, especially the tent, with his own baggage.

We stir ourselves eventually as we need to be on our way once the children have woken up. The young girl, whom I learn is called Martha, has been snuggling with her mother while she has chatted with Mari and once Joshua has opened his eyes, she starts making funny faces at him and the two children are soon chortling away, Joshua now wide awake. We get on our way and although it takes a bit longer waiting to assemble children and beast from two families, the time on the road seems to pass more quickly because of the company. In fact, while we are walking, we say very little to each other but the presence of friendly faces going the same way makes it seem easier and time seems to pass more quickly. As night begins to fall, I find that they too are relying on setting up a tent rather than relying on lodging accommodation, so we look for a suitable site together and set up our tents next to one another. Is this a friendship that will last or is it another of our brief encounters that will disappear under the stresses and strains of the special call we have? Will we ever be confident enough to tell them the truth and if so, will they respect or ridicule us?

Chapter 21
Mari

The men have gone out to have a chat. They are standing in the clear moonlight just out of earshot. I wonder what they are talking about. Dora and I have been busy seeing to our children. We have been sitting together in Dora's tent because it's bigger than ours and both of us are nursing our children while Dora tells stories softly to little Martha who, while listening to her mother, is fixing me with her big brown eyes. Dora's baby boy who is called Simeon – after her father apparently – falls asleep quickly and Joshua, fatigued from all the excitement of today, meeting new friends, soon follows. I make as if to take Joshua back to our tent, but Dora begs me to stay and I hold the little girl and sing to her while the baby is rocked and laid on a cloth rug to keep him off the rough earth. When Dora is unencumbered I move to give Martha back to her, but the girl wriggles on my lap and Dora indicates that it's alright for her to stay. Dora just watches me as I carry on singing and eventually I feel Martha suddenly go floppy and I look down and see her eyes closing. They flutter once or twice, then she is breathing deeply. We wait in silence, then Dora takes her gently from my arms and lays her down next to the prone Simeon.

'You have a real gift, don't you? I've never seen Martha take to anyone like that before. She's usually so shy. She won't even let my mother take charge at bedtime and she is very hesitant about going to Philip's mum at all. How do you do it?'

'I've had plenty of practice. I have two younger sisters and a baby brother and I've looked after them since I was a young girl.'

'I might have guessed. How old are they now? Aren't you missing them by coming all this way to Egypt?'

'The girls would be eleven and twelve by now. My brother Benjamin will be just seven. I haven't seen them since Joseph and I got married and we came to Bethlehem – that's over two years now. I miss them desperately. I find myself wondering every day how they are faring.'

'Where do you come from? Joseph said something about Bethany but from your accent I'd say you come from somewhere further north.'

'You're right. I come from a tiny village called Nazareth in Galilee. I don't expect you've heard of it. It's near a big town called Sepphoris.'

'Joseph doesn't come from there, does he? Is he from Bethany or Bethlehem? How did you meet? Did your parents know him?'

'Bethlehem. He's my mother's distant cousin, my grandmother lived in Jerusalem and my mother was brought up there and only moved to Nazareth when Herod abolished the Sanhedrin and confiscated our family's property.'

'Is that why you're moving away from Bethlehem? Are your family still having problems with King Herod?'

'I suppose you could say that, yes. It's really more of a precaution than real threat.'

'I've heard that Herod is pretty ruthless and has a long memory. Did you think you were in danger? Is that really why you are on the road?'

I suddenly remember Joseph's warning. Does it matter what I say to Dora? She seems so friendly and I can't imagine that either she or her husband would give us away. Surely we're safe here anyway? But I remember Joseph's words and think I've probably said all I should at the moment. Joseph would probably say that I've said too much already.

'I don't know. The problems were a long time ago. I can't think that there's really any danger now.'

We are silent for a while. I can tell she wants to press me for more but is reluctant sensing that I've said all I want to for the moment. If we stay together and become friends, then perhaps one day I'll tell her everything, but we've only just got to meet and it's too soon, too risky. The men come back now anyway and I pick Joshua up and take him back to our own tent. I wonder what Joseph has told Philip. I expect Philip and Dora will exchange information they've got from us and be puzzled and curious if they find we've told different stories. Perhaps I ought to check with Joseph what he's said but I'm reluctant to admit to him how much I've told Dora in case he's displeased with me. So I say nothing and just comment that Dora is a friendly soul and how pleasant it is to chat to another woman in my own language. And I tell him that I sang to Martha and how she fell asleep in my arms. Joseph grins at me and kisses me gently and we cuddle up in the confines of our tent – we can do little else – and I feign sleep before he can ask me any more.

I lie there with my eyes tightly shut and soon I can hear Joseph's deep breathing and I know he is asleep. I roll onto my back and thoughts whir through my mind. It seems miles away from the dirty slum of Pelusium. Then I think of Naomi and Anna, it seems so long into the past, not just a day and night ago. I feel sorry for those two, especially Anna, having to spend all day scavenging amid the refuse and filth. Why doesn't Nathaniel try to take his family away from that hell? What hope for a better life do they have? It seems so unfair. I'm glad now that Joseph encouraged me to leave rather than get used to the squalor there. It would not be fair on Joshua and the little one growing in my belly.

I clasp my stomach and smile to myself. I can't really feel anything yet, but I know he or she is there. I wonder how big he is. There, I'll call it 'he' for now. Will it be best for Joshua to have a little brother or sister? If he's born here will he be an Egyptian? It seems funny to say that! I'm sure we'll find a good Jewish community where he can grow as a proper Jew.

After all, Joshua is called to be the Messiah for the Jews, not for the Egyptians. Therefore one day we'll have to return. I wonder where we'll go. Will it just be back to Bethlehem or even Jerusalem? Or will we get back to Nazareth so I can see my mother and sisters and brother again? How can Joshua be a Messiah in Nazareth? I expect we'll have to stay in Jerusalem itself one day, but not until King Herod's dead. I wonder when that will be? They say he's a sick man, that's why he's so bad tempered. Perhaps we'll be able to go home soon. It's a long way though, I can't face just turning round now and going all the way back. I'm not thinking straight am I? Questions, questions, why can't my mind rest? I think I'm getting muddled and sleepy at last. I wonder what Salome and Rebecca are doing ...

We're on our way together in the morning. Philip tells me about the countryside we're passing. He has obviously been thinking of coming to Egypt for many months and has accumulated much information from travellers from this land passing near his village just a couple of miles from Ashkelon. Very different from us, of course, as we decided to go in such a rush with hardly any time to contemplate what we were doing. He says that this part of Egypt is the most fertile, being irrigated by the mighty river Nile which has split into several rivers in its last few miles to the sea. This area is apparently known as the 'Delta', a Greek word or rather letter, which apparently is the same shape of this area of land where most of the grain from which bread is made is grown. Joseph told me that he spent much of his time at the jetty in Pelusium loading the excess grain for export to the Roman capital city – there are fields where the wheat was grown on both sides of the road although it's nearly all harvested now. There are workers in the fields picking the long stems which are flax and from which Joseph says several products come – I forget what he said. Some fields are in bloom and they look very pretty.

Beside every field there are ditches although most are dry now. Philip says that the farmers dig these to receive water when the annual Nile flood comes. I looked at the earth – it seems quite rich and silty, there is little trace of the light sandy soil we saw earlier. It's all so different from the little plots of land we used to have in Nazareth with a little grain and a few sheep or goats. I've even seen here whole fields of sheep, there must have been hundreds of the animals. The farmers here must be very rich, although some of the tiny villages we pass have dilapidated hovels as homes, so there must be poor people here as well, perhaps working in the fields for the richer farmers and landowners.

I ask Philip what sort of work the Jews do in Alexandria and he says he thinks it's just the same as in Jerusalem. There is a big synagogue and many have employment there as scribes and officials and there are needs for the usual trades, builders and potters and weavers and dyers and carpenters. He tells me that most of the employment opportunities are not in the Jewish quarter but are in the newer part of the city where the Romans are constructing many buildings mirroring their own city of Rome. But apparently the Jews are known as good workmen and are needed, so he is confident of getting a useful income and is sure Joseph will find abundant work too. I'm buoyed by his optimism and look forward to settling there and making a proper home where I can concentrate on bringing up Joshua giving him the care and teaching he will need until he's old enough to go to the synagogue school.

Most of the time, though, I walk with Dora and we chat about all sorts of things. I give her a hand with Martha when she has to see to Simeon and the little girl seems totally at ease with me and wants to hold my hand as we travel, as often as that of her own mother. She talks fluently – non-stop even, although I don't catch everything she says. Dora calls her a chatterbox and says she's never seen her so loquacious before. It must be my influence. I tell her I was known for my chattering when I was a girl too. My mother was always telling me to be quiet and get on with the chores, so I used to compensate by telling my stories to all the other village children and my sisters and brother.

'You must tell Martha some of your stories,' she says. 'She'll love that.'

The day seems to fly away and we've made good progress. Joseph and Philip are pleased and think that at this rate, if we keep it up, we'll be in Alexandria within the week. However, it's not always so easy. Simeon stayed awake a long time on a couple of nights – Dora thinks he must be teething – and we were slow to get going in the morning and needed a long midday rest. We did meet and chat to other travellers from time to time but by the end of the week, as we sensed we were nearing our destination, we had become inseparable as if we were just one family.

One night as Joseph and I lay awake, after parting from Philip and Dora and getting Joshua off to sleep, I raise the subject that had been vexing me for several days.

'Joseph,' I murmur, 'can't we tell Philip and Dora why we are really leaving home? Dora has been so open with me and I feel I'm holding something back all the time. I don't know if she senses something, but I feel as though I'm not being as honest with her as she is with me.'

'I know they seem totally trustworthy, but what if they tell someone else? And we've had time to get used to the idea that Joshua is so special. You don't realise just how extraordinary our claim might seem to Philip and Dora. It might destroy our friendship.'

'Surely not. They'll be thrilled by our news, won't they? As a nation we've been praying for the Messiah for so many years. Why can't we let them share our anticipation and excitement?'

'As I said, you've got too used to the idea. You don't realise just how shocking our claim will seem. You ought to remember. You know the awful fuss your uncle and his fellow rabbis made in Nazareth and the suspicion of the other villagers. You seem to have forgotten how nearly you succumbed to the threats and the last minute miracle by which you escaped their condemnation. You don't want to start that sort of persecution all over again, do you?'

'But Philip and Dora are not like that. They're not bigoted and angry like Uncle Eli. They'd be interested and supportive, I'm sure, and sometimes I feel I'll just burst if I can't say something to someone. It's such a huge secret to have to keep. And we don't talk about it much, do we? You do believe, don't you, Joseph? All that the messenger told me coming so true and the findings of the synagogue court and everything those strangers from the far east told us the night before we left Bethlehem?'

'Of course I believe, Mari. But we can't live all the time in a state of excitement. There are mundane things we have to do. You must know that – just trying to survive these last few weeks is enough to occupy fully anyone's mind. I have responsibility for you and Joshua and I have to think all the time what is best for us. I don't think spreading the message that we have the future Messiah with us is going to be very helpful at the moment.'

'Oh!' I'm quiet for a minute. I feel put down. I feel so wound up so much of the time by what God has entrusted to us and I want to shout it from the rooftops. I suppose, looking at it rationally, Joseph is right. So what do I do to express my frustration?

'Go and tell God about it then!'

I think he said that with some irritation, but I realise that he's hit on something that I should have thought of before. Of course, I still say my prayers every day, but sometimes they've become a bit routine, a duty rather than a joy I get up and open the flaps of the tent and stand under the date palms looking up at the black sky. The moon is waning now and the sky is full of myriad stars. The sight is magnificent. I wonder just how many there are and what they are. What are they made of that they shine so brightly?

I shout to the universe. 'God,' I say, 'you are wonderful. The psalms say that you made all this and yet you want our little Joshua to shine as brightly. Why did you choose us? Why are we so different? Are we different or did you choose us because we are ordinary so others may recognise a special miracle one day and not just assume that his regal status or abilities were natural?'

I'm quiet for a moment just looking at space through the palm fronds. They are waving gently in the breeze still coming off the sea. I seem to hear them whispering to me. I can feel a surge of emotion overwhelming me. God is here in Egypt in this very place, I think, just as I used to find him under my special fig tree in Nazareth. He's everywhere in a gentile country, not just in the Jewish synagogue in Alexandria. The realisation of this truth fills me with joy. I dance. I do huge swirls. I begin to sing. 'Why me, why us?' I shout to the tree tops. I don't care who hears me. They'll think I'm mad. I don't know how long I stayed there, what I said, what I did. I feel liberated. It's just like it used to be when I shared secrets with God in the grass under that tree.

Eventually I calm down, say a big thank you and crawl back into the tent. Joseph is fast asleep. He is snoring loudly. I poke my head outside the flap of the tent. All is silence. There is no movement from Dora's abode, which I can just see silhouetted in the darkness. No-one is watching wondering what I've been doing. Perhaps it's just my imagination, in my head. I go back and stare at Joshua lying there. He is so beautiful. One day, will he be a king? Will we live in palaces and will he lead armies, drive the Romans from our shores? It seems so improbable looking at the vulnerable child breathing so softly. Yet God can do anything, I know he can.

'Believe, Joseph. Believe with me.'

Chapter 22
Mari

When I awake the next morning, I find everyone else is nearly ready. Joseph has fed Joshua some bread and figs and has let me lie, because, he says, 'You looked so peaceful there with a big smile on your lips. I hadn't the heart to wake you, but we need to get moving soon.'

Philip and Dora are already packing their things and Martha comes looking for me. I feed Joshua quickly while Martha shares my lap, then we are on our way once more.

'You look radiant this morning,' says Dora looking at me with something that appears to be a tinge of jealousy in her eyes. She winks at me. I'm sure she thinks Joseph has just been the loving husband. Not much room to do that sort of thing in our restricted space, certainly not with Joshua crammed up against us. I suddenly realise that I don't feel sick. Usually by this time the nausea is welling within me even if I'm not actually physically sick. I look up at the friendly palms. They are absolutely still this morning. There is not a breath of wind. The horizon inland is already shimmering in the heat. Only the line of the land against the sky toward the sea is clear and distinct. I strain to look in that direction and imagine I can see the sea, hear the waves, but I think it is just my mirage. I must get on and cease my daydreaming. Joshua is making a nuisance of himself getting in the way of Philip who is leading their donkey. I must pull him away from the animal's legs before he gets kicked.

Dora tries to engage me in conversation as we walk, but I'm only half listening. The ecstasy of last night has not yet evaporated and I can't tell her. I wish I could but Joseph has said no, and I must try to submit to his instructions even if they're hard. He doesn't often make demands on me like some men I know. I don't think Philip is like that either, I haven't heard him speak a harsh word to Dora or his children since we met them. Dora is telling me about her pregnancy with Simeon and the pleasure of her parents when they found he was a boy. I find myself telling her about my pregnancy now and immediately she shows some excitement and quizzes me about all the telltale signs, when I last had my period, how sick I've been and when the baby is due. She asks me what we are going to call the child although Joseph and I haven't even discussed that yet. I'll let Joseph choose – he had no say at all about Joshua's name because I was so sure that was what we had to call him. It was his idea to use the 'Joshua' form of 'Yahoshua' though – more common and the boy wouldn't feel so conspicuous using the less archaic name. It's all the same anyway so I'm sure it doesn't matter. When she's extracted from me everything I know – and more – we walk in silence. She keeps glancing at me as though she now worries about my state and the strenuous marches each day towards the big city. I look back at her and grin. I'm stronger than she thinks. After what I went through with Joshua's pregnancy and survived, this should cause few problems.

And so we continue our journey together each day. We grow totally accustomed to each other's presence. It is as if Dora and Philip and their children are part of our family now. Joseph and Philip seem totally relaxed with each other. They don't argue or dispute over anything. Even our children play together without any childish squabbles or tantrums. Both Martha and Joshua are gentle with Simeon and when we stop, spend ages trying to amuse him by pulling faces and making gurgling sounds at him and tickling him.

'Not too rough,' I admonish, but my words are really unnecessary for they both have a natural tenderness when they play with him. Martha sings and Joshua tries too. I thought once or twice that he'd picked up the tune Martha's singing, then his voice trails off and he laughs and looks at Martha or me for approval.

Dora is delighted. It makes her job so much easier when the two older children keeps Simeon amused and in good temper.

Of course we get tired and hot, but we have frequent rests and stop each day to let the children sleep in the hottest part of the afternoon. We don't always find an ideal site and on one occasion we had to put up the tents on a bank beside the road and tolerate the lack of shade but usually we find somewhere more suitable. We take longer than Joseph had predicted. I suppose we are slower as a group as we move at the pace of the slowest. Dora lets Joshua ride on their donkey with Martha sometimes while she carries Simeon. I offer to carry him sometimes but Dora points at my belly and laughs. She needn't be so solicitous for me. If we had been on our own I think Joseph would have been impatient at our rate of progress, but we are frugal with our money and spend just enough each day to meet our minimum food requirements and no more. Philip and Dora are equally careful. I'm sure they have more cash than us but they are careful not to buy loads of things that they know we cannot afford.

One evening, after we've pitched camp and I've returned with water for both families while Dora cares for all the children, Joseph looks animated and when I place the pitcher on the ground, he speaks.

'We're nearly there, Mari. We met some merchants coming from Alexandria who paused here for a short while to adjust the loads on their beasts and they said that the outer gate of the city is but a half day's march away. We should be in the city by tomorrow evening.'

A moment of uncertainty and even fear overtakes me for a moment. I've got used to the daily routine of travelling. We are with friends. We feel safe. We feel in control. What awaits us in Alexandria? Will we be disappointed? Will we find the things that we anticipated are wrong? Will we find ourselves in slums rejected by the city inhabitants as we'd experienced in Pelusium? Why am I always asking so many questions, I ask myself. Why, I'm even asking a question then! I must trust God. Each night I've slipped out of the tent to share time with God. I've not had that feeling of exuberance again, but I've felt an inner peace and gone back to sleep dreamlessly. I've not felt sick any more. If Philip and Joseph are nervous about what lies ahead of us, they are not showing it. So I stay quiet and say nothing.

I haven't seen any sign of the city yet when we stop for our midday rest. It is hotter than ever, as each day brings us nearer to the zenith of the summer. Philip and Joseph chide us to move on after our shortest break yet, they want to be in the city with plenty of daylight still left. It is another couple of hours though before we spy the ramparts in the distance. There are villages and roadside shacks lining the highway almost continuously now and some men have stalls of fruit or cloth and bid us buy, but we don't heed them. It is becoming clear that we will not reach the main gate until it is nearly dark and Philip and Joseph confer and tell us that we should try to find a secure resting place and enter the city first thing in the morning to give ourselves all day to find our way around and fix a temporary dwelling place.

In view of our experience in the approach to Pelusium, which I know Joseph has shared with Philip, they are insistent that we find as safe a place as possible. I don't think they trust some of the traders and other people we've seen hanging about the highway now. There are soldiers about, I don't think anyone would attempt a major robbery but I could imagine we might lose some belongings while we sleep. Then we find a small lake on the marine side of the road and see a number of tents set up around its edge. I expect they're people who've had the same concerns as us and are waiting for the morning before entry. By joining them I feel at least that we have some sense of security and are unlikely to be singled out for attention by people intent on harming us.

That night I see Joseph counting the money we have left. We haven't much, I think he's concerned in case the officials at the gate charge us more tax than we can afford. Philip apparently has said that they only charge tax on goods being brought in for sale or barter and not for our own use, but you never can be sure. Tomorrow is going to be a big day and I'm restless and can't get to sleep quickly for once. Joseph keeps turning over also and in the confined space keeps bringing me back to a state of alertness when I'm beginning to feel drowsy. I suspect he's not sleeping properly either although he doesn't let on. Joshua however has no cares and sleeps well now going through the night quite often without waking hungry. I'm both excited and nervous. I suppose I eventually sleep but I dream a lot although I've already forgotten the substance being left with a vague sense of unease.

We are just one of the many groups making our way in the morning towards the imposing Canopic Gate (I didn't know that is what it was called then, but of course I find out later). It is the only gate facing east to which the Roman highway comes directly. On our right after the small lake is a grove of trees that lies outside the city walls and a large crowd is assembling around the Gate itself seeking entrance to the city. The walls are high and obscure most of the buildings inside, but there is one staggering edifice that towers over the city, its white surface glinting in the morning sun, its topmost point glowing a dull red. It's huge even though it must be some distance away and I'm awestruck. I've never seen anything like it, not even the Temple in Jerusalem.

'What's that building?' I cry out pointing. 'Look Joshua, look at that. What is it, Joseph?'

Joseph is as astonished as I am and Philip comes to our rescue.

'It's the famous lighthouse, the 'Pharos', the tallest building in the world. You can see the light at the top. Its purpose is to guide ships into the harbour, large ships that come from Rome and all its colonies.'

I hold Joshua up to see, although I don't think he's as impressed as I am, as he's much more interested in the crowds of animals congregating round the gateway, especially the number of camels that are being forced to kneel so that their masters can dismount.

'We'll go and see it one day, Joshua. It seems to go right up to the sky. This must be a very rich city to have something like that.'

We cling to each other in the throng, fearful of losing our children in the crush of those waiting to enter the Gate, being knocked and barged out of the way by men and beasts coming out. It's a big muddle and the only way forward seems to push and shove like everyone else. Then a couple of Roman soldiers emerge and try to create some sort of order and I grab Joshua before he can escape again. Martha is frightened and is clinging to her mother's hem and Simeon is whimpering. At last we are at the Gate itself and find ourselves being questioned by a couple of very officious looking men in some sort of uniform. I don't understand what they're saying at first. I recognise some Greek and then they realise that we're Jews and revert to our language. I'm beginning to wish they hadn't for what they're saying to us is not very nice. One oath follows another and I wish I could stop Joshua's ears as I don't want him being curious about some of those words. They're cursing the Jews and I catch the gist. They don't want us here, they obviously believe they have too many Jews already.

'Why do you want to come here? What's your business?'

Joseph and Philip explain that they're skilled artisans come to help with construction work in the city, but the officials ask them who they will work for and which building they are contracted to, and of course they can't answer that. They ask to see the men's tools but Joseph has nothing to show because they were stolen in Pelusium, however Philip still has his equipment and he manages to unpack some carpentry tools from the bags on the donkey's back and the official grunts.

'How many women and children?'

They peer at Dora and me and Martha tries to hide behind her mother. Joshua is unabashed and gives them a beautiful smile, oblivious of the contempt they seem to feel for us. In the end they seem to give up, one of them even gives Joshua a playful tug and we are waved forward.

'Stay in the Jewish quarter of the city unless you are an approved contracted worker. Have you lodgings?'

Philip says that we will stay with friends. I'm sure that's a lie, he hasn't said he knows anyone here previously. He later explains that if we can't demonstrate where we will stay there's a risk we would not be allowed in. It was all a bit unpleasant and a rude shock after things had been going so well, but at least we're now through the Gate and they made no attempt to try to charge us anything. The highway widens out into a broad avenue with a watercourse running beside the road and stretches as far as the eye can see. Dominating the view to the north west of the city is the lighthouse, which seems even larger now the bottom of the structure is not obscured by the city wall. Both sides of the highway are narrow streets leading off at right angles, all dead straight and all looking exactly the same.

'I think this is the Jewish area,' says Philip. 'I was told that it's in eastern part of the city and that the Jewish houses are around a series of roads that criss-cross each other. We'd better look for the synagogue and see if anyone there can give us advice.'

I couldn't see any building that looked like a synagogue. I'd imagined the Jewish quarter to be a small settlement that we'd soon be able to find our way around, but if this is all the Jewish area, it's huge, stretching as far as I can see in all directions. What do we do now?

Philip and Joseph are asking the way from various bystanders and I can see arms waved in the general direction of the south. We've been walking slowly towards the centre of the city – at least following the main avenue – and we come to a canal, which passes under the roadway. It looks sluggish and oily and smells unpleasant, I guess much sewage finds its way here. The city odours are strong but not as bad as in the area we inhabited in Pelusium.

'Down here I think he said,' opines Philip to anyone who is listening and we follow him into one of the narrow streets lined with simple houses, where many women are busying themselves emptying slops into the drainage ditch that follows the contour of the street.

'Is this the way to the synagogue?' he calls out to a group of women and they point in the direction that we are going, confirming that we have got it right. It seems very crowded. It doesn't look to me like the prosperous community I'd been led to expect. We continue down the roadway and keep passing intersecting alleyways narrower even than the road we are in. The city must be huge for we've been walking now for nearly half an hour. We eventually see a white walled building at the end of a row of dwellings, larger and grander than those we've passed. It must be the synagogue.

We halt outside. It is shut up. The men walk round looking for an open entrance. Dora and I and the children sit on the steps and wait. People are passing to and fro, but none are taking any notice of us. They all seem to be Jews, I hear the odd snatch of conversation, but some must be Greek-speaking despite their appearance. I do catch odd words of Aramaic but the accent seems harsh and I only understand the occasional word. Joseph and Philip come back, shaking their heads. They confirm that the synagogue is closed, something I find unusual and worrying, as by this time in Bethlehem the synagogue would be a hive of activity with boys streaming in for their schooling. Perhaps it is earlier than I thought. Philip stops one of the pedestrians, a man walking purposefully towards the city centre and comes back to say that the synagogue staff will not come until later as the school is closed today for it is some Egyptian festival and the Jews respect the customs of the native Egyptians – apparently they do not want to cause offence to the citizens of their host country. I've always been taught that we Jews do not bow to the religions of other races – it's a theme that comes through the writings of the prophets that I learned from Joel in the synagogue in Nazareth. The Jews here must be very nervous of the Egyptians or else they've been corrupted and seduced into the ways of the Gentiles – I can just imagine what Uncle Eli would have had to say about that.

So we have to wait. We can't think of what else to do. We've got no contacts here. There is no obvious place to start looking for a way to begin our life here, apart from in this building. The children are getting bored. They'd run round for a while, chasing each other, then Martha trips and cries and Joshua has come back, climbs on my lap and needs a cuddle. They get a new burst of energy for a while, but the sun is now high and the shade given by the building has all but disappeared. They are hot and fractious and I wonder how much longer we'll have to wait. I begin to fear that perhaps the synagogue will stay closed all day, then what will we do?

Eventually our patience is rewarded. A rabbi wanders up, gives us a fleeting glance and unlocks the heavy doors to the small courtyard and we follow him in. Joseph immediately asks if we can speak with him, but he tells us to wait and disappears into the main building of the synagogue. Another rabbi appears soon afterwards and follows him in, giving us just a quick glance as he passes us. Our waiting continues, until eventually the second rabbi reappears and comes up to us and asks us what we want. Before we can answer, he looks at the children and suddenly scoops Joshua up and stares at him. I think Joshua is a bit frightened at first at the sudden movement of the man who is staring fixedly into Joshua's eyes. Then Joshua relaxes and chuckles at the rabbi, whose face softens and returns Joshua's grin.

'Well, you've a bonny lad there, a bit special, I think. Let's see what we can do for you.'

Philip and Joseph tell him of our situation. He questions us for a long time. He wants to know where we are from. When Joseph says we are from Bethlehem – he seems more ready to admit that now – the rabbi seems to increase his interest and asks us to calculate when we left that village. Then he starts talking about King Herod and the politics and I'm beginning to worry that perhaps after all Joseph was unwise to say where we had come from. The rabbi just keeps nodding as Joseph and Philip talk and all the time he is watching Joshua who is back in my arms. He seems to ignore Dora's two children. She must be feeling a little hurt that he is so taken with Joshua and is ignoring her own children. I put Joshua down and draw little Martha to me and give her a cuddle and look to see if the rabbi will redirect his attention to us, but his eyes are following Joshua's movements all the time he is listening to our husbands.

He finally holds up his hand to interrupt the story that the men are telling, and says:

'I think I can help you. It will not be all that easy for you, but if you are skilled craftsmen as you claim, you will find work, but you'll need to seek support among the Gentiles here. There is a lot of new building work for which labour is in short supply, but it's mainly at the instigation of the Roman occupying force. I trust you will not find that unacceptable. We Jews have to adapt to the ways here if we want to survive and prosper. We have our own community and you will find that we can treasure our customs and culture in this Jewish city enclave but we are dependent for our prosperity on the goodwill and opportunities allowed us by the Greeks and Arabs and especially the Romans who've been in charge here this last generation. You'll find some of the works where you might find employment strange to Jewish eyes and not what you think we should be doing. However, you have young children to nurture and their future and wellbeing must come first. Accept what is necessary even if sometimes it might offend your consciences. Abide your time – we Jews are good at waiting. The day will come …'

The rabbi suddenly looks hard at Joshua again. It gives me a funny feeling, a tingling in my spine. I shudder involuntarily. I think of what some of those men said when Joshua was born and the strange visit of the rich sheiks from Babylon. I know of course, I've always known, but has this rabbi suspected something? He is looking at me now as if he knows my secret.

'Now,' he says, 'let's see what we can do for this family of yours!' And he gives the boy a playful shove and a big wink ...

Chapter 23
Mari, BC 4

I'm sitting in the doorway of our little house rocking James in my arms. He'll be a year old next week. Time seems to have flown so quickly yet so much has happened – it seems an age since we lived in Bethlehem and my life in Nazareth seems worlds away. Joshua has gone with Dora and Martha into the market and Simeon is playing quietly in the roadway in front of me where I can keep an eye on him. Baby Sarah is asleep in her cradle – Dora has left her with me while she is in the city.

My mind is wandering as I laze here in the shadow of my home. Simeon is quite safe, this alleyway is too narrow for much through traffic and I can see clearly in both directions for all the streets and alleys in this city are dead straight. The boy will get dirty playing in the street, but Dora and I have given up trying to keep the children clean each day. We are resigned to the constant need to wash their clothes to remove the stains from the dust and filth that this city seems to exude everywhere. No-one seems to clean up the muck from the animals and slops although I try to keep the area in front of my own house as clean as possible.

I say my own house – it's not really ours, we rent it from the synagogue for the rabbis there administer a large number of dwellings whose profits help to maintain the buildings and the rituals and I'm sure pay the rabbis themselves, as they do not seem to want for much. When we first came here they forced a couple of families to move in together so that Philip's family and we could find somewhere jointly to live. It was very crowded and I felt bad about the other two families who had to move to make room for us, but we were pretty desperate and the rabbis were insistent. I quickly learned that the decisions of the rabbis counted for everything in the Jewish community here and little happened without their permission and support. Joseph told me that there is a council of elders for most important decisions affecting our race, but decisions about things like housing seems to rest with the rabbis of our local synagogue. The big synagogue is the other side of Canopic Street – I think the council must meet there, but we don't have anything to do with them. The richest Jews seem to go there.

We have our own place now, it used to belong to a couple but the husband was killed in an accident in the royal harbour and the widow was persuaded by the rabbis to move in with one of her sons and his family. The rabbi, Malthus, who was the one that met us on our first day here, seems to have had a soft spot for us and has fallen over backwards to give us every opportunity to prosper. He found work for both Philip and Joseph together in the construction of new villas in the Rhakotis area for Roman officers and officials on the far side of the city. It takes them a long time each day – it's nearly an hour's walk to the site of their labour. They work long hours as they're under pressure to finish their work and move on to the next villa. Apparently there are Romans queuing up for transfer from Rome to this city, for they find the trade here so profitable, and that part of the city near the sea and the royal palace is very pleasant.

Dora lives in the next street to us, still in the small house we were allocated at first. When this slightly larger house became available, I argued that it was only fair for Dora and Philip to have it as they had two children already and a third on the way, but the rabbi had decided we should move and that was that. This is a better house, I'll admit that, and there is more room, but I feel guilty sometimes that we should be so favoured. I'm surprised Dora and Philip aren't jealous or resentful, but they seem unaffected and count us still as their best friends although we've both extended our contacts and acquaintances to many families in the neighbourhood. We all go to the synagogue every Sabbath and Dora and I stay with the children in the Women's Court, just like we did back at home, but most of the priests here seem to gabble through the rituals as though their heart is not in it and they want to finish as quickly as possible. Afterwards, though, everyone hangs around for a long time and gossips – it seems more of a social occasion.

Only when Malthus teaches do I feel that he is believing what he says – for the others it seems just words. Sometimes I hardly recognise the faith I was taught back in Nazareth. They use a lot of Greek words and seem keen to emphasise how similar our religion is to that believed by the Greek philosophers. It seems odd to me and Joseph shakes his head sometimes but we do keep all the Jewish festivals. But several times recently Malthus has talked about the coming of the promised Messiah. He almost appears to be courting danger by being outspoken, for he prophesies the end of both Egyptian and Roman rule. I hope he checks that there are no spies in our gathering, for what he says must be considered provocative in this city. Anyway he's got away with it so far. He still makes a point of seeking us out afterwards and giving Joshua his blessing. Other people stare at us then and wonder what our connection is with the rabbi. I've been asked several times if we're related.

I nearly blurted out the truth once for I've become increasingly certain that Malthus has guessed our secret. Dora hasn't usually said anything about his apparent favouritism, but one day after the Sabbath meeting when Malthus had taken the scrolls and interpreted from the writings of the prophet Isaiah, she commented that the rabbi seemed to be staring at us while he was saying that the prophet was describing the character of the Messiah to come. Joshua had pushed himself to the front and was peering through the grill, so Malthus could see him and suddenly the rabbi almost shouted that the time was coming soon. Everyone started from their reveries and some looked quite shocked and Dora asked me if I knew why he seemed so certain. I almost told her then everything that had been promised to us and just stopped myself in time. Surely Malthus can't know anything, can he? He just seems to like Joshua and think him special.

Well, even though I say so myself, he is special. Even if you were unaware of all the promises and miracles we've experienced so far, you'd notice Joshua is an exceptional little boy. His vocabulary for a three year old is remarkable – he seems at least as fluent as the five year old Martha to whom he is very attached. And Malthus has even begun to teach him a few Greek words when we see him and more remarkably, Joshua remembers them. I've noticed too how all the other children seem to flock round Joshua and laugh at his antics. Some of the older ones seem to enjoy asking him lots of questions. I thought they were teasing him at first, but he always gives them answers and sometimes the other children break into roars of laughter and other times I can see that they're astonished at his replies. I do find him very demanding – he exhausts me sometimes. It's not his physical energy – he's just the same as any other little boy of his age. It's just that he's so inquisitive, his mind never seems to let up for a minute. I can't ever relax except when he's asleep or off with Dora and Martha, as he is now.

Last week he asked me who God was. He must have heard the rabbi talking about God in his address and he kept asking me. I tried to think how I could explain to him, how I could make him understand. I told him God made everything and he promptly spent the next two days pointing to every object that came into his view and asking, 'Did God make that?' The stars and sky were easy but he pointed to our house and wanted to know if God built it and when I said that a builder had made the bricks and put them together, he asked me again that if God made everything, didn't our house count? I replied that God gave men the skills that enabled houses to be built and he said no more then – I'm not sure if he bought that argument. The river was easy but when he pointed to the canal, I said that men had dug the banks but God had put the water in it. When he pointed to the drainage ditch that ran along our alleyway with its sludge and waste, I felt on unsure grounds as I couldn't really ascribe to God the creation of such filth and disgusting excreta of men and animals. Then one day, he asked, 'Did God make me?' and I answered yes, but with a little help from your mama too. 'And Papa?' he asked. Surely he's not been hearing the other children talking about the way babies are made? We'll have to watch our words carefully if he's around because he seems to pick up everything and absorbs it into his mind for brooding over.

I haven't said, have I, that there are periods when he seems to just stare fixedly at something as though his mind is far away. Sometimes it can go on for several minutes – it's quite disturbing really. The first time it happened, I thought he'd had a fit and I got really alarmed. I waved my hands in front of his face and he didn't appear to even notice. I picked him up and touched his face and still he was lost in thought. Then, just as I was panicking and determined to seek out Dora and ask for her help, he suddenly clicked out of his seeming trance and carried on as if nothing had happened. Dora doesn't seem to notice. I think she's just too busy all the time trying to keep an eye on her children to worry overmuch about mine. She's just got Martha with her now, I wonder what Joshua will get up to in the market.

James has woken up. He'll be wanting a feed soon. At least he seems a perfectly normal little boy. He doesn't walk or talk yet although I think he's trying to say 'papa'. His dad dotes on him, well I suppose that's natural because he is fully the father this time. The boy gets really excited when his father returns home each evening and they spend time together playing while Joshua pretends he's helping me cook the evening meal. Sometimes though, Joshua goes and handles his father's tools while Joseph is messing around with James. I'm worried that Joshua will hurt himself. Some of the tools are very sharp – Joseph has a good set now, he's been able to get really good ones with the wages from the Roman building works. Joseph seems relaxed though. He points out how careful Joshua is, he seems to love just feeling them and pretending to use them. Some of them are quite heavy, but he must be a strong lad for the weight doesn't seem to bother him.

I wondered how Joshua would regard James. At first I worried that he'd be jealous and might harm the baby, so I watched him carefully. I soon realised he was quite safe but I was a little puzzled. He seemed to accept James without any special question, it was just natural. He didn't pay him any more attention than he paid to Simeon or baby Sarah. It was as if all children were of the same value to him. He paid just as much attention to the children of our neighbours or those whom we see each week at the synagogue. His only special friend is Martha. A year ago she was his heroine, he followed her about and learned much from her. Now despite their age differences, they seem to be equals. It's odd. I can just imagine Dora now – the two children will be entirely absorbed in each other, she needn't worry about them, yet they'll notice everything and ply us with questions hours later about what they've seen.

I hope Dora will be home soon as Sarah's woken up and will be hungry. She's crying now and that's disturbing both Simeon and James. Simeon tries to drag me to his sister and I pick her up and now have a child in each arm. Sarah quietens a little but I can see her little mouth is searching and she'll soon be screaming again. I'm relieved when a bit later I see Dora turning into our alley with Martha and Joshua, hand in hand, trailing behind her.

'Sorry to be so long,' she says breathlessly. 'I've been hurrying as best I can, but these two want to stop every few yards to go and look at something or try to tell me all about what they're looking at. I thought I'd never get home.'

'You're too indulgent with them,' I venture, smiling, 'you should keep them moving.'

'I tried, but you must know how difficult that is. They're both so curious. We had to look at everything on the stalls and they quizzed me until I was exhausted mentally. Then we were just about to leave the market square when a fight broke out between two men. I wanted to leave quickly but a crowd soon developed to watch and I found we were hemmed in. Both the children wanted to know why the men were fighting, and I told them they both wanted the same thing from the market stall – that they were being silly squabbling like little children. The real reason seemed to be racial though, I heard them swearing at each other and the Greek-speaking Arab was insulting the Jew who got angry and tried to hit the other who then retaliated. It was quite nasty and some of the crowd began to takes sides. As Jews, we were definitely in the minority and I got worried in case it turned into a wider skirmish in which the Arabs in the crowd would round on any of us that were Jews. I tried to find a way out, then Joshua and Martha escaped my clutches and wriggled their way to the front. Then, just as the fight was getting vicious, Joshua suddenly planted a smacking kiss on Martha's cheek and the crowd fell about laughing and the fighting stopped and everyone drifted away just like that. It was most peculiar. It was almost as though Joshua had done it single-handed, casting a spell on them!'

I told Joseph about this incident later, because of how Joshua had acted, but Joseph became quite agitated and said that he could sense a growing antagonism between the Jews and especially the Greek-speaking Egyptians. It seemed to spring from the increasing prosperity of many Jews – not us unfortunately – who were taking quite influential roles in the city government, although everyone in the end had to obey the Roman governor. I hoped that it would not lead to Joseph being thrown out of his job as had happened in Pelusium, but Joseph said that most of the craftsmen working on the villas for Romans who worked in the Brucheum area were Jews and the Romans would not allow these tensions to delay the completion of the building work.

Anyway, when we awoke this morning I knew we were going to be able to spend the day together as it was one of the many Roman festivals and everyone had a holiday. The Egyptians and Jews have festivals too but we have to celebrate these in our own time, because the Roman supervisor in charge of the building of the villas does not recognise them and won't let Joseph or Philip have the time off. I had assumed that we'd have a quiet day at home, but Philip came round and proposed that we all went together into the city centre and see the many wonderful sights there. We've been nearly a whole year here and neither Dora nor I have seen anything except the huge shining synagogue on the far side of Canopic Street and, of course, the Pharos – you can hardly miss seeing that looming over us all, the glare from its topmost mirrors causing us to squint if we looked directly at it. When I told Joshua he became very excited, and Martha popped in a few minutes later and the two children were so bubbly that I had to try to calm them down. Dora followed with Simeon and with Sarah tucked in a cloth slung round her waist and I held James while Joshua and Martha were very happy to walk hand in hand as usual.

Joseph and Philip know the city of course and lead us into the wide Canopic Street and there we turn west, opposite the road, which leads to our chief synagogue. We reach the Gate of the Sun, which neither I nor Dora have ever passed through, and I'm astonished for the street widens into a magnificent thoroughfare with colonnaded buildings of white stone on either side. I've never seen anything like this before, not even in Jerusalem. There are many people in the street but it is so vast that it swallows us up. It's quiet at the moment, though Joseph says it will be noisier later when the festival gets going. It's called Floriania apparently and is to welcome new life and all the flowers blooming in the new season. That seems a nice idea, perhaps we shall see some of the decorations and celebrations later. Joshua and Martha seem oblivious to the magnificence around us and start chasing each other and hiding behind some of the marble columns. I worry that they might get in someone's way and cause anger, but people seem relaxed and unbothered.

Philip suggests that we go to the maritime wall where we can see the whole of the Pharos and I can get my first glimpse of the sea itself in the Great Harbour as it's known. We come to a great crossroads. Another street of equal size and magnificence called the Street of the Soma is here and opposite us is another huge stone edifice, polished and glinting in the sun. Joseph says it's the monument to the Emperor Alexander who founded this city hundreds of years ago and this is his burial place in what he called a 'Mauseleum'. The children are not the slightest bit interested, and Philip tells us to turn right into this new street which will lead us straight to the waterfront. The Pharos is straight ahead of us and I stare at it in amazement. We can see it all because there's no other building obscuring the view now. Even Joshua stops and gawps at it. 'It reaches right up to the sky,' he exclaims. It does indeed. I tell him not to look at the light itself for it will dazzle his eyes and already he's rubbing them, for our eyes are drawn to the brilliance.

We soon reach the harbour wall and there before us is the sea. I've never seen so much water before, it's quite frightening. There is a strange smell, I can't quite place it. It's salty, fresh, not nasty like some of the smells we get round the canal and the water-ditches near our house. It's quite windy too, which makes the heat much more bearable. Philip is pointing out more magnificent buildings on the waterfront to our right and saying that it's the royal palace where the pharaohs used to stay and where the Roman Governor now lives. There are many ships to our left loading and unloading their cargoes and Joshua wants us to go that way and watch all the activity. We can see the causeway with lots of movements - people and animals – linking us with the island on which the lighthouse stands.

I just want to stare at the Pharos, my mind cannot take in such a sight. I count the windows up the sides of the building, it's like twenty houses built on top of each other and there are sculptures of magnificent beasts, which you couldn't see from our home. Eventually we tear ourselves away from the sight before us and move towards the ships unloading in the docks, but I keep turning around and looking at the lighthouse. We pass another imposing building on our left and Philip tells us that it's a famous library with more books in it than any other place in the world. I don't know how he knows this – I suppose the Romans who work with him tell him those sorts of things. I wonder what all those books can be saying. Are there some, which would tell me more about God? That would be good, but I doubt if they'd be in a language I could understand. Perhaps Joshua will one day learn to read and become a scholar. I wonder if he has to learn much to be our Messiah?

It's becoming hot despite the breeze and I'm getting tired carrying James all this way. He's too heavy to carry like Sarah and not quite walking yet – perhaps another couple of months.

'Let's walk onto the causeway,' says Joseph. 'We can sit down there and watch the ships coming and going and eat our food.'

We walk about a league onto the Heptastadium and find a patch of rough grass where others are seated looking at the view. Joshua is too interested to want to sit down and eat, he's putting questions to his father all the time. I'm glad Joseph is listening to him, because I don't know half the things he's asking. I keep turning round and staring at the Pharos. I still can't believe it. I would think something as high as that must soon fall down, but Philip says it's stood there for over a century. There are more and more people coming onto the causeway now, many have brought food and some have garlands of flowers draped around their necks reminding me of the festival today. Some are drinking wine. One man seems already to have drunk too much and is shouting at everyone. Joshua looks at him and I can see he is puzzled. I'm quite pleased when Joseph suggests we move on.

'Would you like to see where I work?' Joseph is asking Joshua and he nods vigorously. Dora and I would like to see too, so we pick up our things and retrace our steps, the wind now on our backs. When we get back to the main crossroads we turn right towards another big gate we can see in the distance, the Gate of the Moon according to Joseph. I've heard him say that he works near there, although we turn off to the south just before we reach another canal into the area called Rhakotis where Greek speaking Egyptians and Romans live. Many of the villas look new and there is space round each one, not like the houses in our street. A bit further on there is open ground and I can see half-built villas and newly dug foundations. We stop opposite one that looks nearly finished and Joseph tells us that they have still to construct the doors and some of the outhouses behind the villa – I can see some huts behind villas that have been completed and the wooden structures look as big as our house.

'What do they use those for?' I ask my husband and he tells me that these are where the servants and slaves live. Apparently all the Romans here have many servants because they are army officers or rich merchants or government officials. Joshua and Martha are playing hide and seek in and out of the incomplete villa and Joseph chases after them to make sure they don't trip over the timber lying ready for their next day's work.

'When you've finished that villa, will you be out of work?' I ask nervously. Joseph points to the incomplete house next to it and a row of ditches that he tells me are just the foundations of more still to be built. I breathe more easily. That means we are guaranteed income for at least another few months. We carry on walking past the new construction site and come to some smaller houses.

'Who lives in these houses? Do Romans live here too?'

'No,' says Philip. 'Some of the richer Egyptians live in this area. These houses have been here for some time. There were poorer houses where the new villas are being built but the inhabitants were moved out to clear the site for the Roman immigrants.'

'What happened to the previous people who lived here?' I ask. 'Were they allocated new homes?'

'I don't know,' says Joseph. 'The site was already razed when we started work here. But the Egyptians who still live here don't like the Romans. And the Romans don't like living next to the Egyptians. I've heard some of them complaining, but the land in the best environment in the Brucheum nearer the sea and the royal palaces is all used up, and there seem to be more Roman officials and merchants arriving here every month.'

We carry on and can hear the sounds of a crowd, which seems to be getting nearer. Ahead of us is a hill and I can see what looks like a big temple on it with masses of people packed together on the slopes in front.

'What's happening?'

'It's the annual Floriania festival. Offerings are made to a god they call Serapis of wine and flowers. The temple there is the Serapium, it's one of the most important in Alexandria. It's the time of resurrection and new life after the winter, the Egyptians worship another god called Osiris – I get a bit muddled, they might be just be different Egyptian and Roman names for the same god. A procession is garlanded with spring flowers at the temple and they go down to the Stadium and there are games, races and trials of strength, and much dancing.' Philip is trying to tell us everything he knows, but I'm getting confused.

'How many gods do the Egyptians worship? And do the Romans worship the same one? Do they include our God, Jehovah as well?'

'There's lots here – there's the temple of Artemis whom the Romans call Diana and there's a temple near the sea for Poseidon or Neptune who's the god of the sea ... oh, and lots more, I can't remember them all.'

As we get nearer I see that the crowd is singing and swaying and all are looking at the temple waiting for something to happen. Philip asks one of the men who is just watching rather than singing and he comes back to tell us that in a few minutes the temple doors will open and the priests will lead men, women and girls who are the dancers along the street and into the Stadium where they will perform. Dora and Philip seem quite keen to go into the Stadium to see the fun, but I can tell that Joseph is dubious. I'm not sure that we Jews should take part in pagan rituals like this. Philip cajoles Joseph, saying it's not serious, the Egyptians just like any excuse for celebrations especially since the Romans came. Their daily life is much harder now and this is one of the few festivals when the Romans join in and permit everyone to relax. We go past the Serapium therefore and stand among the crowd lining the street near the entrance to the huge Stadium. I can see inside and the tiers of seats are well occupied, especially the lower levels. A lot of the men are drinking, in fact there seem to be few women about and I begin to feel a little out of place among the many Arab men. There are only a few children and no-one that I recognise as Jews at all. Joshua, Simeon and Martha manage to squeeze their way into the front of the throng and I'm watching them carefully to see they don't get lost.

Suddenly I hear a great shout and the word goes round that the procession is coming. People in the crowd begin to laugh and scream, and I see many are drunk. I'd back out if I could, but I can't get to the children, so I'll have to wait until the procession has passed. They're coming. I can't see everything for the men in front of me are tall and Joseph and Philip are straining to see as well. Then I see them. The priests in their white robes are leading but I'm shocked by what I see then. The girls and women are nearly naked, they are dressed with flowers and just a transparent thin sliver of material which scarcely covers their bodies. The girls are cavorting shamelessly and the crowd is egging them on and the men dressed only in cloaks, which are flapping open with no modesty at all, are caressing and dancing with the garlanded women and stripping off their remaining veils even as they pass us. I try to cover my eyes but I'm frightened of losing sight of the children – heaven knows what they are making of this. Then I see that men at the front have lifted Martha and Joshua high so that they can see better and one of the young girls trips forward, swirls and throws out her arms to touch Joshua and plants a kiss on his cheek. The man holding Joshua rips the girl's remaining veil from her shoulders and she screams with mirth and runs stark naked back into the dancers where many others have been uncovered as they run into the arena. Meanwhile the man has thrust the flimsy piece of cloth into Joshua's hands and above the din I hear him shout, 'Here's a momento for you, young man. Your first virgin! May you enjoy many more!'

Philip and Joseph are now trying to hustle us away, but we are still impeded from reaching the children. The crowd is surging after the dancers who now have thrown off all decorum and nearly all are twirling naked waving the floral garlands over their heads. The crowd has gone wild and I'm really scared. Joshua and the other children could easily get crushed in the stampede. Philip fights his way to the front and takes Joshua from the man holding him and grabs at Simeon but Martha is somewhere under the trampling feet and Joseph hurls himself at her when he glimpses a sight of her, now crying out in panic. Thank heavens someone in the crowd sees her in time and lifts her over the charging herd into Joseph's outstretched arms.

'Joseph, please let's get out of here.'

'Yes, Mari,' he shouts, 'I'm trying my best. I didn't realise it would be like this.'

Eventually we are able to extricate ourselves from the stream of men and youths pouring into the Stadium and reunite on the far side of the road. I find I'm shaking all over and Martha is crying. Dora is trying to comfort her and I try to get to Joshua who is still clutching his trophy. However, James has now begun to cry too so Joseph goes to Joshua and tries to wrest the veil gently from the boy, but he clings onto it and cries when Joseph begins to tug at it to tear it away from him.

'It doesn't matter, Joseph. He doesn't understand what it is. He just thinks it's a toy. Don't make an issue of it.'

We make our way home as fast as we can. It seems a long way and we are tired and upset. Neither man says anything and Dora begins to say something, then decides against it. When we eventually get home we feed the children and get them to bed as fast as we can. Philip comes to our house later that evening and apologises to me.

'Mari, I'm sorry for taking you to the temple – I should have known better. I heard the Romans and Egyptians on the building site talking about the festival as a sight to be seen, but I didn't realise that they were looking forward to a drunken orgy. Apparently it's not only celebrating the harvest of the wine but it's a fertility rite as well. The Romans and the inhabitants here don't see nakedness as something shameful. No wonder we didn't see many Jews the other side of the Sun Gate today.'

I hear Philip and Joseph talking about it with some of our neighbours the next day but they don't seem shocked at all. That's what the locals do, seems to be their attitude and the Romans encourage them. Apparently the Greeks and Romans wrestle and race naked and no-one thinks it unseemly. Our neighbours don't seem bothered. They don't partake themselves but don't seem to think it wrong. Their advice is just to keep out of the way especially when the wine and beer is flowing as the mob can be unruly when drunk.

I thought about it all as I tried to sleep that night and imagined the horror of Uncle Eli and the rabbis back in Nazareth. Was it really so shocking? The drunkenness and violence unleashed by the alcohol was clearly wrong, but on the whole the people were good-natured and having fun. The girls and young women didn't seen upset by what was happening. I thought about the threats and violence they did to me in Nazareth because they judged me to have stepped outside their rules. I thought about the time I used to lie naked in the sun under the fig tree and talk to God – well no-one ever saw me, at least I don't think they did. I remember though the horror and scandal when the Roman soldier brought me back to the village on his horse and people were shocked because my clothes were torn and indecent, so they said. Was what I'd seen today worse and more to be condemned than that? I don't know.

When I put Joshua down to sleep he is still clutching the veil. I try to take it gently from him, but he's wound it round his fist, so I leave it with him. When I look in later, he is holding its softness against his cheek and sucking his thumb. Oh well, I might as well forget how he'd got it and let him comfort himself in his sleep. I wonder if that girl will ever realise that her veil has comforted the future Messiah!

Chapter 24
Joseph, BC 2

I really think I must talk to Mari about going back to Bethlehem. She won't be happy about it. We've really settled here now and she has made many friends she won't want to leave. Dora in particular. She's been such a help to Mari especially when she was so sick when Salome was on the way. It seems hard to believe we've been here nearly three years now. Joshua will be five soon, James is chattering away and getting into all sorts of mischief, and Salome has just taken her first steps. But I see some problems ahead and I wonder if we should not try to make our escape back to our home country before worse befalls.

Last night there was a very nasty confrontation between the Jewish and Greek workmen in the Rhakotis area where I work. The Greeks accused some of the Jews of pinching their overtime payments. It was their fault really, the opportunity for additional work on more villas in the south of the area cropped up, and someone told the foreman they didn't want the extra time, so he gave it to Jews who then worked long hours several days at a stretch. When some Greeks saw our earnings, they got jealous and tried to say we'd cheated them and fights broke out which turned into a brawl. I got away with Philip before a bevy of Roman soldiers waded in and cracked a few heads open.

Unfortunately this has been simmering for sometime. When we first arrived, I was agreeably surprised and thankful when I saw good relations between many races in this very cosmopolitan city, unlike our experience in Pelusium. Life has been difficult but I've worked hard and earned enough to look after my family. We have not gone short of food or clothing even in the early days for the rabbis at the synagogue and other rich Jews ensured that newcomers were helped until they were self sufficient. I was loaned money to buy some decent tools and was therefore able to join Philip in working in my own trade, even though it was mostly for the hated Romans.

Then last year visiting Jews from Jerusalem brought us the news that at last the tyrant Herod had expired and his son, Archelaus had taken the throne. My immediate thought was to return home, but Mari was pregnant and I didn't want to subject her to the strains of that long journey unnecessarily. It was different when we came here. I felt we had no option then, our lives were in danger. I still wonder if that was true. I couldn't risk it though. But now we were not in danger, we had friends and a good livelihood. There was no urgency to return.

Then messages began to filter through of turmoil in Jerusalem. I suppose the usual arguments over succession – these princes seem an ill disciplined lot. I thought it best to stay out of harm's way until things settled down a bit. I didn't say any of this to Mari and she seemed quite happy with her lot here. The three children were occupying her pretty well. Joshua in particular was happy here and thriving among other children and often played at the synagogue where one of the rabbis seemed to take a special interest in him and had – even at his young age – begun to teach him about our scriptures and the patriarchs. So I said nothing, and we progressed for another year without too many scares or tribulations. Salome was quite ill when she was only three months old and frankly I thought we were in real danger of losing her. She had such a high fever and cried so much except when Joshua held her. It was very strange, the power that the lad seemed to have over her. He would ask his mother if he could hold her and she would immediately calm down and stare into his face. Mari would then fetch a little water and bathe her while Joshua rocked and sang to her – it was extraordinary. Before you could realise it, Salome would be fast asleep and breathing easily.

So we stayed. I saw that all was not peaceful in the city, but it didn't affect us. The Romans were everywhere and generally disliked. They threw their weight around but it was mainly the richer Greeks and Jews who resented them most – people who, but for the presence of the Romans, would have been the rulers here. Parts of the city were terrorised from time to time by a rowdy group of youths they called 'the Mob'. Apparently they were in thrall to some of the merchants and advisers to the rulers who paid them to take out some of their rivals or pay off an old score. It was threatening to get out of hand – there was an incident somewhere in the city almost every day. Then last week the Mob attacked a Jewish shop – apparently a Greek-speaking Egyptian reckoned he'd been overcharged. I heard during the brawl yesterday someone shout for the Mob to beat up Jewish homes. To cap it all, we found that overnight our synagogue had been disfigured with painted slogans defiling the Jews and telling us to get out of their country. It's not an emergency yet, but I can see the writing on the wall. I'm going to work this morning, but I shall keep a sharp lookout for brewing trouble and make myself scarce if necessary. I can't risk being involved and getting injured or arrested and leaving Mari to bring up three young children without support.

Philip and I walk though the city in the early hours amid streams of other workers going through the Sun Gate to the Brucheum and Rhakotis districts. But we are subdued, furtive even. There is tension in the air. Groups of men are watching us. Perhaps it's just my imagination, perhaps they're always there and I just don't notice them. When eventually we reach the building site where we are currently working, there is chaos. Someone during the night has systematically destroyed the work of our last few days. Oaken beams lie strewn about, wooden doors have been wrenched off their hinges and lie splintered on the ground. The supervisor is casting around for someone to blame and we are met with insults, not sympathy. We are instructed to clear the site up and told to repair the damage without pay – in fact we are told that we will get no further pay until we have restored the villas to the state they were before the culprits struck. Who were they? The Romans don't care. We are all the same to them. Jews, Greeks, Egyptians, any of us are the criminals and so any and all of us will repair the damage. If not, we will be dismissed, as simple as that.

So we slave all day in the heat for no pay. We are too afraid to protest, we know what will happen if we do. We are angry and tired and bad-tempered, but there is nothing we can do about it if we still want paid employment tomorrow. On the way home, Philip and I discuss the situation.

'What are we going to do about it? It could be three or four days without pay before we're back to where we were. And that's assuming there's no more damage. This could go on for weeks unless someone is paid to guard the villas overnight.'

Philip grunts. Then he shakes his head.

'Who knows who did this? What do you think their motive is? Is it someone wanting to get at the Romans and delay more coming here to take over the city or is someone trying to cause mischief?'

Philip has hit on my fear.

'I think someone is deliberately causing strife between the Greeks and Jews. You'll see, it won't be long before we're accused of being behind the damage. Then the Greeks will have a perfect excuse to get us laid off.'

'Will the Romans fall for that one? They're keen to get the villas finished, there's still a queue of wealthy immigrants ready to pay good money for these houses.'

'I don't know. I'm not optimistic. I'm wondering whether we shouldn't return to Judea while I still have enough savings to cover a lean period while I build my trade back up again.'

'It's alright for you. You're near a large city where I'm sure there's plenty of work. If I went back, what would I do? My brothers were struggling to make a living where they were. I would not be welcome back.'

'Why don't you come back with us? You could go into partnership with me.'

'That's generous of you, Joseph. But how do you know there'd be enough work for the two of us. How long have you been away? It must be three years surely. How do you know that no-one's taken your place?'

'I don't. That's a risk I'd have to take. I suppose if I couldn't make a go of it in Bethlehem, we could always go back to Nazareth up in Galilee where Mari's family is. When we got betrothed, one of Mari's relatives gave me contacts and put work my way. There was a lot of new construction work in Sepphoris which was only an hour or so distant.'

'There's a lot of imponderables. It would be a big decision to take. I'm not sure how we would manage now that we have four youngsters. I think Dora will be very sceptical.'

'I'm sure Mari will be too. I'm not going to rush it, but if relationships in the city deteriorate any further, I'm going to give it serious consideration. Why don't you think about it, Philip?'

We didn't discuss it any further then. I said nothing to Mari that night, and went back to work the next day. I noticed with relief that a night watchman had been employed and that our previous day's work was undisturbed. We worked for three more days for nothing. Then there was another attack on the synagogue. A mob of Greeks – rumour blamed the Greeks anyway – came one night and smashed one of the outer walls and smeared pigs' blood over the courtyard and the walls of the inner sanctum. The synagogue was closed for several days while the mess was cleansed and the synagogue purified. Everyone was angry and there were some in our midst who wanted to retaliate, but no-one was quite sure what target might be most appropriate and nothing happened. People bottled up their anger and quietly seethed.

One evening Mari seems upset and I ask her what is wrong. Apparently some children had been chased out of the city centre back into the Jewish quarter and one boy had been injured, hit by a stone thrown by a Greek youth. The Romans had ignored a plea for help. Mari knew the boy's mother and had helped her dress his wounds – a bad cut on his forehead.

'I'm getting nervous about the violence here,' she said. 'It seems to be increasing every day. When are we going to go back to Judea? I know Herod's been dead over a year now.'

She'd brought the subject up herself. I'd misjudged her. I thought she'd be loath to leave her friends and the stability we'd enjoyed here. Although, I now realise, this stability is but a veneer, skin-deep. This evening I watch Mari as she goes about her domestic duties. I watch how she cares for the children with infinite patience. She's become a mature woman, in the prime of her life. At eighteen years of age, the strains of childbirth and poverty have not yet coarsened her features. She does not nag or shout at the children as some women do. She listens to them. She seems to treat Joshua as a little man whose opinions are worthy of respect. She is kind and generous to our neighbours and, I discovered, very popular. I'm guilty of taking her for granted, underestimating her because she stays here in the community while I venture into the city each day seeing the wider picture, meeting and mingling with the many races in the huge metropolis.

And I watch her moulding the lives of our children – is not that of great significance? Some men's wives are submissive and dumb before their husbands and take out their frustrations in petty jealousies and in their constant scolding of their children. Mari is certainly not that. I treat her as an equal. I value her opinion and I listen to her often, especially on the Sabbath after our meeting in the synagogue. She surprises me often by her comments about what the rabbis have pronounced. She disagrees with them sometimes and when I reflect on what she's said, I can't help but think she might be right. But then, of course, she was privileged to have Joel and the other scribes and rabbis in Nazareth teaching her as well as the boys. I know Eli used to think that made her too rebellious.

I'm sure she's not, but she does think for herself and she's not afraid to voice her opinion.

We don't often talk about Joshua's mission. He is a bright boy and despite the attention he gets from rabbi Malthus and the adoration from the other children here and their parents, he's not spoilt. Mari does talk a lot about him, but she refrains from any claim that he is fulfilling our prophecies, that is apart from an occasional quiet reference to me alone. I watch him playing with James sometimes. James can get very tiresome and sometimes does things deliberately to wind his brother or mother up and I caught him the other day teasing Salome although she is too young to understand much. I suppose it's normal behaviour for any small boy but I don't remember Joshua being so awkward or annoying. Perhaps I just forget.

So I broach the subject of going back home to Bethlehem with her tonight. As I said, I'd expected resistance from her. But her comment about the increasing violence in Alexandria had caused me to rethink. She is quite animated.

'You think we should go home? You think it's time we should be preparing Joshua for his destiny? It keeps coming to me – I keep feeling that the time is drawing near when we should take that step.'

'Are you ready to go, Mari? It's a long way and we've three small children to keep safe and healthy on the way. It's a risk. You know how we nearly didn't survive on the way here.'

'But we did survive, Joseph. God looked after us. He'll look after us again. He's given us a promise and many signs. You believe it, don't you?'

'I thought you'd be reluctant to leave here. You'll be parting from Dora and Martha and all the children. You were sorry to leave Naomi and Anna in Pelusium. I thought this would be much harder for you.'

'It will be a wrench, of course it will be. She's become such a friend. But I still miss Rachel back in Bethlehem – I wonder if Benjamin has younger brothers and sisters now. And Joshua loved playing with Ben so much – I wonder if we go back whether they will pick up where they left off. And perhaps we can go back to Nazareth, Joseph. I miss my sisters and our Benjamin – he'll be having his 'bar-mitzvah' soon. I worry about my mother. Is Eli still looking after them all?'

'Hold on, Mari,' I say. 'We've only just begun to talk about going home and you're ahead of me already. We must think about it. I've not decided yet.'

So the decision to go home begins to grow in my mind. Although we resumed paid work in Rhakotis, the tensions remain and I often feel that violence might break out at the slightest provocation. After we have got the children to sleep we often return to the topic and several nights we chat into the early hours about the possibility until it becomes not whether, but when. I begin to save money more stringently for our journey and tell Philip about our intentions, inviting him and his family to join us. However, it seems just a step too far for Philip. When Dora learned of our intentions, she was quite upset and tried to persuade Mari to convince me to stay. I don't think Mari was ever seriously tempted, although she admitted that she disliked the thought of leaving her friend here.

One night I can tell Mari is wanting to tell me something but is strangely hesitant. This is most unlike my Mari so in the end after several near starts, I push her and she comes out with it. She had been regaled by Dora's doubts on the wisdom of leaving their well established life here and trying to strengthen her argument for being determined to go, she'd hinted that there was one special reason that overshadowed everything else. Once she'd said that, of course, there was no way that she could get away with not revealing the full story behind her loose statement. So, she says, she'd told Dora everything. Dora had been shocked. Mari is wondering if she'd done the right thing after all. They'd always been very frank with each other and Dora had never dreamt that Mari had such a secret. Mari isn't sure if Dora feels let down, not to be trusted with such an astounding message earlier, or whether she is truly shocked at what Mari has said and disbelieved her, treating her with some caution in case she got enmeshed in some fanciful tale that is mad and dangerous.

'I'm just worried that somehow I've spoiled our friendship,' she says to me, resting her head on my shoulder. I'm in two minds whether to try to reassure her or chide her for revealing our secret. After all, if we are just about to go back to Judea, isn't it dangerous to risk alerting someone who might spread the tale with the risk that it might upset Herod's successor.

The next day, Philip tackles me about it.

'Dora told me the most amazing thing last night. She said that your wife claims that Joshua is to be Israel's long awaited Messiah. I know Joshua's very bright, but isn't that a mite arrogant? I always thought Mari was very sensible, but surely that's a delusion and a dangerous one at that? You don't believe it, do you?'

He's put me on the spot. I hesitate for a long time, searching for the right words. He looks at me and suddenly says,

'You do believe it! You of all people! What possessed you, Joseph, to listen to this rubbish? I've always found you the most rational of beings, I certainly never thought of you as a romantic mystic. And how come now, after we've known each other for nearly three years? Have you only just come to this conclusion?'

We stop near the Gate of the Moon and I tell him everything we've experienced together, Mari's pregnancy and my belief in her innocence and her call, the judgment of the Nazareth rabbis, the birth in Bethlehem, the signs there and the exotic visitors who confirmed our vision that he was indeed the Messiah and our flight for fear of Herod's possible reaction.

Philip doesn't know what to make of it all. He thinks he knows me. His instinct is to believe me, but it's just too much. He shakes his head. He doesn't want to hurt me by openly expressing his doubts but he can't hide his scepticism. He is silent as we resume our walk together and we work without exchanging a further word. Later he tries to resume our normal relationship but our conversation is laboured and artificial. There is now a barrier between us. From that day on there is no further talk of him and Dora and their family joining us in Bethlehem. I raise it once, but he just replies that it was too dangerous – if we were to repeat to others what I'd told him, we'd be marked men. He couldn't put his family at risk. He'll stay here and take his chance that the growing enmity between the Greeks and the Jews will come to nothing more serious.

I notice of course that they watch Joshua with increasing, even obsessive interest now. It is as if they want to catch him out in something underhand and say to us, 'that proves you're wrong, the Messiah would never do that!' And that spreads to me too. I find myself watching Joshua and looking out for any sign of his miraculous future. But he seems just a normal boy. He plays with the other children. He is popular but at that age most children play happily with each other. They only draw back from those who are obvious bullies or are too boisterous. Joshua is neither of those. I do see that he seems to have a very special bond with his mother. At first that seemed quite normal. All children have that bond as long as the mother follows her maternal instincts. Then I began to feel guilty. Had he somehow sensed that I was not his real father? Had I distanced myself, so that he compensated by becoming closer to Mari? I didn't think I had. I've always tried very hard to treat him as my own son and I don't think I've shown any favouritism to James or Salome.

I therefore have no evidence whereby I can say to Philip or Dora, 'Look, can't you see he's special?' He is a good lad, yes, but I don't ever remember him doing anything another child can't do. He cries if he falls over, he keeps us awake at night, he gets sick, he dirties his clothes, he doesn't want to go to bed if he is busy doing something that interests him. He is bright and has learned already more than most boys his age, but isn't that because Rabbi Malthus has singled him out for extra attention? Perhaps that is a sign that he is special. That rabbi has seemed to join the list of others who have recognised his destiny. But Malthus has never said as much and in other ways I don't find the rabbi particularly spiritual. In fact he seems a very worldly sort of guy who appears to make more accommodation with the religions of the Greeks, Egyptians and even the Romans than the other rabbis who are more traditional and conservative. But at least he is lively and takes an interest whereas the others seem dry and get through their rituals and duties as though they are bored and want to finish as soon as possible.

One thing I do notice about Joshua is how often he asks 'why'. I suppose children of a certain age begin to question everything, but I'm sure 'why' is Joshua's favourite word. It annoys me sometimes, it seems as if I can't conclude any conversation with him quickly without also stumbling against that tiny word again. He'll look at me with those huge brown eyes of his and I think he's teasing or making fun of me, but I've come to the conclusion that he's serious. He's just a boy full of abnormal curiosity.

Then it happens. It is the Sabbath and we are resting. Philip and Dora and their children have visited us on the return from the synagogue and while the other children are playing in the street outside, Joshua has stayed with us appearing to follow our conversation although we are discussing the rabbi's interpretation of one of the Mosaic laws – I'm sure Joshua cannot have understood our discourse. His eyes are fixed on Philip and never waver. Suddenly Philip become aware of his scrutiny and begins to feel uncomfortable.

'Why does that child stare at me so? It's disturbing. Is there something wrong with the boy?'

Joshua does not bat an eyelid but maintains his scrutiny.

'Joshua, why are you looking at me like that? Is something wrong?'

I tell Joshua to go outside and play with the others, but before he obeys me, he looks Philip full in the eyes and says,

'Why don't you want to leave here and go home? Are you afraid?'

He doesn't wait for the answer and trots outside as if unaware of the consternation he's caused. Philip looks at me in dismay.

'What have you been telling the boy? That was most embarrassing. You've no right to criticise us for wanting to stay here.'

I protest most vigorously that I've said nothing of the sort to him. As far as I know I've never mentioned going back to Bethlehem in front of him and certainly not discussed Philip and Dora's reasons for staying. Then, as I'm thinking about it, I'm curious that Joshua had talked about going 'home'. How did Joshua know Bethlehem was 'home'? Surely he'd only known our house here in Alexandria – he was less than two years old when we left Israel. And what on earth had given him the idea that Philip was 'afraid'? Children do not ascribe fear to adults unless they witness some obvious incident such as a violent storm or fight involving those they love. I search my brain and the only time I can think of when Joshua would have seen my fear was when we were robbed in Pelusium. He was not two but perhaps it made a big impression. But that was a different sort of fear. Is he right in thinking Philip is actually nervous of returning to our homeland? And if so, how has he garnered that? Perhaps this incident will, after all, indicate to Philip that he is someone special. However, it causes Philip and Dora to be even more wary of him and creates more tension when we met up as families. I am on tenterhooks that he will say something else that might upset them. I'm sure he didn't mean to hurt Philip. He had somehow ascertained the man's emotions and was just curious, as usual.

So we decide finally to go. Mari is fully with me on that. We tell Joshua what we have planned, since he seems to guess so much and he becomes very excited. He chatters incessantly to James about the fact that we are going home, and plies me with questions about our town and Jerusalem, facts once gleaned that he passes on to an incurious James.

We decide to go as the heat of the summer is subsiding a little but before the winter rains can come. We've been in Egypt three and a half years. We pack all our belongings and make safe all the money I have saved. I calculate that it will fund our expenses on the return journey and give me three months to build my carpentry business up to the level where it could maintain us with our minimum requirements. I'll make sure to travel with experienced merchants to avoid putting ourselves at risk and I speak to Malthus - he knows most of what was going on. He tells me that a group of rich Jews are returning with offerings for the Temple in Jerusalem - he's got this information from a colleague at the big Temple the other side of Canopic Street - and they have agreed that we could accompany them as long as we can maintain their pace. I purchase a good-looking ass that seems strong and we are ready.

We make our farewells to Philip and Dora - tearful despite our recent strains. Mari and Dora hug each other and both give us their blessings, but I have a feeling they are almost relieved to see us go. Rabbi Malthus comes to greet us just before we leave. He chats with all of us, then takes Joshua on one side and gives him a special blessing and embrace.

I am suddenly moved to ask Malthus why he's paid so much attention to Joshua. Has he any premonition of what Joshua might become? Malthus looks at me most puzzled. He obviously has no inkling of what I mean. It seems that all the attention, all the singling out of the boy has been nothing but chance, the recognition perhaps of a bright lad. Nothing more than that. He is just a favourite as teachers have their 'pets' and he's sorry to see him go and that is all. I am disappointed. I'd been thinking that perhaps here was another sign that Joshua is indeed the Messiah elect. But no, I can't quote this seeming special relationship between the rabbi and the young boy as another insight or revelation. I wonder if this will change when we get back to Bethlehem. Should I take him to Jerusalem, seek out a special education for him with the city's best scholars or should I let him grow up in obscurity, attend the local synagogue with the other local boys and help me in my work as he gains the necessary strength?

Part 3
Mari's Child

'But Mary kept all these things, and pondered them in her heart'

(Luke chapter 2, verse 19)

'And the child grew, and waxed strong in spirit, filled with wisdom: and the grace of God was upon him'

(Luke chapter 2, verse 40)

Chapter 25
Mari, BC 2

We're home. It was a long journey and tiring, but we had company all the way and the merchants had a couple of youths with them who helped me with the children, particularly with Joshua and James, so that I could concentrate on looking after Salome. She's just begun to walk, but only a few steps before she totters and falls, so that was not a lot of help on our long march. However, she did enjoy riding the donkey and she had quite a good balance although I stayed close in case she slipped. The merchants chose to use the route via Bethlehem to Jerusalem instead of the Roman road all the way, which was good of them. We'd developed quite a friendship with them though we'd said nothing that might have hinted at Joshua's special status.

It was nearly dark as we approached our village and I was nervous that our home would have been wrecked or taken over by others in our absence and we'd find ourselves with nowhere to stay. Joseph was more confident, however. He was sure that our neighbours would look after our interests until we returned.

'We did leave without any intimation of where we were going or why', I said, 'so they had no idea of how long we'd be gone.'

At least the house is still standing. Joseph pushes at the door and it screeches open – the hinges are rusty and need some oil. At first it's too dark to see much. I find and light a candle – there are some lights aflame in the street and I take the candle from one of the bags on the donkey and ignite it from that source. I hold it up and look around our room. It's empty. Completely empty. Even our large water pots have gone. I know we had taken many things with us, as much as we could pack, but everything we'd left has disappeared. I follow Joseph as he walks through to his workshop at the back. That's empty too. All the stacks of timber have gone, even the rough table and bench where he rested wood for sawing. His tools are not there, of course, he'd taken those and had them stolen at Pelusium. He has new tools now, but he'll have to start again from scratch for everything else.

Luckily I have brought most of our belongings from Alexandria with us. We'll make do tonight with what we have – the same as we've used on our journey, of course. In the morning I'll assess what we need and think of the priorities to buy. I feed Salome and get her to sleep as quickly as I can and James is soon asleep as well, but Joshua is excited and wants to go out into the night and explore. Joseph has to chase after him and promise to let him roam the town to his heart's desire in the morning before he allows us to steer him towards his bedroll and sleep. At length we are able to rest ourselves and although we are exhausted, both of us lie awake for some time, thinking about all we've been through. I've been so concentrating on getting us home safely that I've hardly given any thought to what we'll do on arrival. I suppose I've assumed we'd just carry on where we'd left off, but of course I soon realise that that was very naïve of me. Lying on our bed in the empty room, I begin to think seriously about the future.

First thing tomorrow I'll need to deal with the practicalities. I'll need to find a water jar. I've a couple of cooking pots and a small jar that will have to suffice initially – I've left the large pots with Dora as they were too bulky to bring. I have some food we'd purchased earlier in the day but I'll need to see if Ishmael, the baker, still has his stall in the market. I realise that our return will be news and will soon reverberate around the village, so I might as well go to the well at the usual time for all the women and tell them our news. I'm curious to meet my former friends, especially Rachel and see how Benjamin has grown and whether he has brothers and sisters. I think Joseph is a little worried at the possibility that other carpenters might have moved in and taken care of the trade he once had. It might take time to build up trust and confidence again but I know that he's a good craftsman and others think highly of his skills. I'm sure he'll reassemble the equipment he needs for his trade and when news gets out of his return, his old customers will flock back.

These thoughts are flowing through my head and keeping me awake. I think Joseph is still awake too, for he is silent. When he is asleep I can hear his steady breathing. I wonder what he is thinking. Is he nervous about our future or is he just relieved to be home? I wonder now if we can just slip back into routine with everything the same as before or whether there have been big changes. I'm sure there'll be new children to admire. I can show them James and Salome and won't they be surprised to see how Joshua has grown and how intelligent and articulate he is. I wonder how he'll compare with Rachel's Ben. Will the two boys immediately resume their friendship?

Perhaps Joseph can go to Ein-Karem and see Zechariah and Elizabeth. We must meet them soon and find out what news they have of my mother and brother and sisters. It's been a long time with no news. We must get a message to them to say we're back in Judea. I wonder what they've made of our absence. Perhaps they came looking for us at the Passover Festival and found our house empty. What would our neighbours have told them? Perhaps they think we've been taken by Herod and killed. We've not told anyone where we've been, for fear of news getting back to Herod. We must find a way of letting them know we are alive and well as soon as possible. The more I think about these matters, the wider awake I become. And just when I'm becoming drowsy at last I hear Salome whimpering and rouse myself and go to her. I suckle her, but she is slow and I nearly drop off while she is still at my breast. Then I notice that her eyes are closed too and I risk laying her down before I have winded her properly. Perhaps I'll pay for this when she wakes me again, but I'm too weary now and I must have fallen asleep as soon as I'd settled her, for I remember no more.

I'm lucky. Salome is still sleeping when James stirs, then Joshua. Joseph is already up and moving around out in the courtyard behind his workshop. I can hear scraping and wonder what he is doing. I peer out of the door and find him digging in the earth using a chisel for apparently our spade has disappeared as well.

'What on earth are you doing?' I shout to him.

'I'm looking for the gifts the sheiks brought before we left. Don't you remember? We decided it was too risky to take them, so we buried them – here I thought, but I can't find them at the moment.'

'It was just as well we didn't take them. They'd have been stolen with the rest of our goods.'

'Well, I can't find them. I thought I buried them here, though perhaps they're deeper than I can reach with this tool.'

'It doesn't matter now, does it? There's lots of other things we must do. Can't that wait?'

'I just thought I'd reassure myself that those valuable things were still here. You were still asleep. I'll try again later. I'll borrow a spade from someone and dig a bit deeper. I'm sure it was about here I buried them.'

Joseph comes back and helps me feed the two boys. He promises to look after James and Salome if she wakes while I pick out our largest pot from the pack we'd just untied from the donkey's back and venture forth into the daylight and the stirring village.

I think I'll get water first and come back via Ishmael in the hope that he has fresh bread I can buy. As soon as I set foot outside our house I nearly bump into Susannah who is obviously making her way to the well too.

'Well, bless my soul, if it isn't the disappearing Mari! It is you, isn't it? You've changed a bit, but I'd know you anywhere. Where on earth have you been? We thought you'd left us all for good.'

'We've been in Egypt.'

'Heavens above! Why on earth did you go there? I suppose you knew what was going to happen. You got out just in time, I must say.'

'What do you mean? What's happened?'

'That's your Joshua there, I suppose. I shouldn't flaunt him before the other women if I were you.'

'Why not? What's wrong?'

'Do you mean to say you don't know?'

Before she can say any more we're joined by a couple of other women, one of whom has a young child in her arms. Then, coming up the road, I see the familiar form of Rachel and my heart leaps. I grab Joshua and rush to meet her.

'Rachel, it's you. I am so glad to see you again. Here's Joshua. Where's Ben? How is he?'

'Mari, it's really you? You've come back to us? We thought you'd abandoned and forgotten all about us. You sent us no message, we couldn't imagine what had happened to you.'

Rachel seems changed. She looks older, lined, more careworn. Well, she is older of course, so am I. But she looks much older than I feel. Perhaps she has many children now.

'I'd not forgotten you, Rachel, how could I? But we had an emergency, I'll tell you all about it soon. But first tell me, how's Ben? And have you other children now? I have two more, I left Joseph looking after James, he's three and I have a little daughter, Salome, who's just walking.'

'I've two daughters now, Ruth and Esther.'

'And how old is Ben now? Where is he? Joshua'd love to gang up with him again, I'm sure.'

'Do you really not know, Mari? Do you really not know what happened when you went away? We thought that's why you'd gone.'

'What happened, Rachel? Will no-one tell me? You're all talking in riddles. I don't know what you're talking about.'

'He's dead, Mari. Days after you left us. Dead with all the other children.'

'What! How? Was there an epidemic? That's awful. I'm so sorry, Rachel, I really am.' I'm shocked. She's looking at me accusingly as though I should have known. How could I know?

'No, Mari. He was killed. Murdered. Slaughtered by Herod's soldiers along with all the other boys in the village. Do you mean to say you really didn't know? We thought that's why you'd gone. That someone tipped you off and you fled to save Joshua's life. Why didn't you tell us, Mari? Why didn't you tell us? We could have escaped as well.'

I'm horrified. Dumbstruck. I can't look her in the face. I feel her eyes boring into mine and look down while I try to compose myself. She's saying something more, but I can't take it in. I feel hot and flushed, dizzy. Joshua has run off somewhere. When eventually I compose myself and look up, Rachel is cradling Joshua in her arms. Tears are pouring down her face and Joshua is looking at her in great puzzlement. The other women are now crowded round us in a circle staring at me and Joshua. They are waiting for me to say something. What can I say?

'I didn't know, Rachel. I swear to you I didn't know. Joseph thought we might be in danger, so we left by night, but it never occurred to me that you might be at risk because you knew me.'

'It wasn't just me, Mari. Everyone in the village suffered. All the boys ...'

Rachel breaks down in mid sentence and weeps piteously once more. Other women start crying too. What on earth have I stirred up here?

'Please, please tell me. I don't understand. What has all this to do with us?'

The women start whispering among themselves. No-one says anything further to me and they begin to walk slowly towards the well. I don't know if I should join them or hang back. Are they angry or ashamed at my return? Am I not welcome? I don't know what to do.

Rachel has put Joshua down and beckons me to follow.

'If you really know nothing, Mari, I'll tell you later. It's a long story. Come and get the water. Then come to my house afterwards and I'll tell you what has happened. But don't be surprised if some women are suspicious or want nothing to do with you. For three years now many have blamed you for their misfortunes. It'll take time for feelings to mend.'

So I follow in silence. I can tell everyone is watching Joshua closely. The boy seems oblivious of the attention focused on him and trails after us cheerfully, being diverted whenever some point of interest en route – a stray chicken or lizard or an interesting rock – comes into his line of vision. We arrive at the well and a group of women, including Susannah and Miriam, Barthaeus' wife, stand in a huddle whispering to each other while one of their number draws water. I can't help but feel that they are excluding me deliberately. Rachel stays with me and my friend Rebecca joins us along with a girl who must be her daughter Miriam and a couple of young lads. Miriam is carrying a bundle and I see suddenly through my confusion that it is a tiny baby. When the girl sees me staring, she comes over and pulls her shawl back and I can see that the child is older, perhaps six months.

Miriam looks up at me and says succinctly, 'It's a girl.'

Then Joshua wants a look and the girl bends down and shows the child to him. Joshua laughs and tries to make faces to the child who responds at once, wide eyed, to Joshua's attempts at communication. Despite the apparent embarrassment over Joshua's presence emphasizing his rude survival, his interest and laughter make it impossible for the women and other children to ignore him and I let him drift away to play with a few who are a little older than him. Rachel and Rebecca do not quiz me any more and we wait our turn patiently. When most of the women have drawn, they set off back to the village without waiting for us. Rachel and Rebecca stay with me. Rebecca begins to say something on our walk back, but it is difficult with the noise and distraction of the children and she gives up. As we reach Rachel's house, she just says,

'Come and see me later when you can. I'll tell you everything that's happened. Then you'll understand.'

I busy myself with James and Salome who are now both awake and seeking my attention. Joseph has managed to borrow a spade and I can hear him shovelling in our yard, disturbing our donkey, which is braying loudly. My mind is still in a whirl from the bare news that has been imparted to me and I am brimming to say something when Joseph returns into the room a few minutes later. I don't get a chance. Joseph looks red in the face and flustered.

'I can't find any of the gifts I buried. I know where I put them, I'm sure of it. But everything's gone. I can't believe our neighbours would stoop to stealing from us. Perhaps it was just too much of a temptation. The gold would have been too obviously of significant value. I'm not sure if anyone here would have known what the other gifts were or even hazarded a guess at their worth. It's really disappointing. I had thought that we could sell the objects for a sizable sum and give Joshua a first class education with scholars in Jerusalem, to fit him appropriately for his destiny.'

I'm not really listening to him. Who worries about such trifles? After what has been hinted at, I don't want the further guilt of riches received from the very people who may unwittingly have been the cause of the problems that seem to have swamped the village women. I stop him from carrying on further about the loss.

'Joseph, it's awful. Rachel's Ben is dead and many other children. Rachel says that Herod's soldiers killed them. They seem to think it was our fault. I can't look them in the face.'

Joseph stops in mid stride and stares at me.

'Why, Mari? How could they blame us? How is it our fault? What actually happened? Tell me properly.'

'I can't. I've only had hints that something terrible happened. I know Rachel's Ben was murdered and so were some other children, but I don't know how or when. Rachel said she'd tell me the full story sometime, but she seemed too upset to say more now. When she saw Joshua she burst into tears.'

Later that day Rebecca calls round and tells us everything. Miriam comes with her and takes Joshua and James to play so Rebecca just has her little one – Sarah she calls her – and I nurse Salome while she tells me what had happened. Joseph comes in from the yard having abandoned his search for the gifts brought by the sheiks and swills the mud from his hands and listens. We sit there speechless as she describes the action of Herod's soldiers and tells of the rumours that the king had got it into his head that there was a potential claimant to the throne living in Bethlehem, a young child. Apparently the priests had foolishly drawn his attention to certain scripture prophesies and the king, who'd grown superstitious in his illness, believed them and would not rest until his soldiers had eliminated any possibility that the rumour might be true. She doesn't mention that the sheiks had visited the king first and probably sowed the idea in his head and therefore she is not inclined to believe that we have been even an indirect cause, but she tells us that some of the villagers had guessed that Joshua had been the subject of the prophecies and blamed us for the calamity which overtook them.

'I don't believe a word of it,' she says, 'of course, it's foolish superstitious nonsense and you mustn't take what some of them are saying about you to heart. Some idiots tried to find out why we'd suffered so and I think the soldier they asked just told them some cock and bull story about a rival king just to get them to shut up and go away. Anyway, why did you go away? You obviously left in a hurry – some of your customers, Joseph, were very upset with you. I told them it must have been an emergency, probably someone in your family seriously ill. But you mentioned Egypt, Mari, I didn't know you had relatives there.'

'We don't,' I say, 'it was an emergency but not the one you guessed. Perhaps the other women were right.'

From the corner of my eye I see Joseph making frantic signs at me, which I interpret as a sign that he wants me to reveal nothing more, but how can I stop now? Rebecca's eyebrows are raised and she is waiting for me to continue.

'We had visitors the night before we left. They came because they'd dreamed that they'd find Herod's successor here in Bethlehem and for some unknown reason they seemed convinced it was Joshua. They'd apparently told Herod they'd look for him and as soon as we knew that we thought we might be in danger and decided that we couldn't risk staying where Herod's guard could find us. That's why we went to Egypt.'

I pause. She's gaping at me. Joseph now realises there's no point in keeping it secret any longer.

'It never occurred to us that Herod would be so mad that he'd kill so many children just to stop one. I persuaded Mari that we should move just in case Herod was jealous and I was really scared that we could be arrested at any time and tortured, that was why we left in such a hurry.'

'So it was not a fanciful tale after all? There is some substance to this story? I thought you were humble folk like us. If you have royal blood in you, why did you live among us? Did you not think that you were endangering all of us by just being here?'

'We're not related to Herod or any other possible line that might conceivably have a claim on the crown. The priests and Herod must be wrong. It is tragic but you can't hold Mari and me responsible for it, surely?'

I'm unhappy that Joseph dismisses our calling so lightly even if it means that it might increase the antagonism I'm feeling.

'Joshua is special,' I say 'We've had lots of signs. Our rabbis in Nazareth where I come from told us so. I've always known and risked many people's wrath because I insisted on telling them. They called me a blasphemer and threatened to kill me once before. When our visitors came late at night and told us that Joshua was a future king, we became frightened and that's why we fled. I thought we were in danger, not you!'

'What strangers came to you? Who were they? Did you believe them?'

Joseph says nothing and looks at me. He knows I'm going to tell her everything and he's given up trying to stop me. He'll shake his head and later complain that I'm foolhardy, then he'll gladly put up with the extra trouble I've caused him. He's very good with me really.

So I tell her. She listens with an ever increasing look of incredulity. She's so sensible is our Rebecca, not in any way a mystic. This is way beyond her ken, but she won't ridicule me because she is my friend. However, when I finish, she does warn me.

'Mari,' she says, 'I don't know what to say. I do know this. If you repeat that tale to others, they will make fun of you. Some will be hostile, especially those whose children were murdered. I was lucky. My two boys were just too old to be victims of the massacre.'

'Where did it happen? How many children did they kill?' Joseph asks his question very quietly.

'Twenty seven,' answers Rebecca, 'every boy from the cradle to two years of age. Your friend Rachel lost her Benjamin. She was inconsolable for months. She was raped by one of the soldiers as well, I'm sure, although she won't admit it. She's only recently settled down. Your return is in danger of stirring everything up again, especially when she sees Joshua.'

'What can we do now? How can we help her?'

'I don't know. Perhaps she will take to Joshua, feel somehow that he will remind her of Ben, even if it upsets her. Or she might resent the child. You'll have to be very sensitive and play it by ear.'

We are both silent.

'Do you want to see where it happened? There will be no-one about now, everyone's cooking the evening meal.'

So Rebecca leads us to the plot of scrubland near the rubbish tip and we stand silent by the place she had described.

'They were all thrown into a pit the soldiers had dug right there. When they'd gone, we uncovered their bodies and washed and cleaned them and dressed them properly for the soldiers had ripped off their clothing in their haste to establish which were the males. We buried them together. It somehow seemed right.'

We stand there with Rebecca a long time. I imagine Joshua lying there broken and blooded and begin to weep. They let me cry for a while and then Joseph puts his arm around my shoulders.

'Mari, God looked after us and spared Joshua. His destiny is in God's hands. He will protect him and us.'

'But he didn't protect all those other children, did he?' And I begin to cry again. My mind says, 'Why God, why do so many have to suffer so. Is it really your will? I can't believe that'. And I stay there weeping for a long time staring at the abyss where those tiny bodies were once buried.

Then, suddenly, I realise I am alone. Rebecca and Joseph have quietly withdrawn from my grief. And my weeping stops. I get angry with God.

Chapter 26
Rachel

So she's returned. I'm shaking at the very thought of it. I suppose I ought to be glad to see my old friend again, but I have very mixed emotions. Just when I thought I had at last come to terms with the loss of Ben, seeing her has brought everything back. I find that I'm trembling and feel very tearful. I shouldn't let her return disturb me like this, after all its nearly three years since she disappeared without so much as a word to any of us. But I can't help it.

I'm lying on my bed now. The girls are at last both asleep and Nathan is pottering around outside, I don't know what he's doing. Earlier this evening Mari came and spent nearly an hour with me as I was suckling Esther. She told me some extraordinary stories about their life in Egypt and everything she saw there. I just can't imagine it. I've only been into Jerusalem once and that was awe inspiring, but some of the things Mari described, well I just couldn't visualise it at all. But it wasn't as though she was boasting. She seemed embarrassed, especially when she made me tell her about the death of the children and I swear she was crying then. And going back through it all again, that made me cry too. When she saw how upset I was becoming, she dried her eyes and apologised and quickly started telling me about Alexandria, which she said was a vast city, even bigger than Jerusalem. I asked her about the hardships of the journey, I could never face such an unknown massive change. She told me that they were at first nervous that they might be followed by Herod's men and then later how they were robbed and lived for a while as paupers almost on a rubbish tip. How awful that must have been. Yet she dismissed it as nothing compared with our ordeal. Well, I suppose she was right about that, though she must have wondered what was going to happen to her.

Despite all this, I still can't get over the fact that she and Joseph never said anything to us. I thought I was her best friend. Surely she could at least have said something to me? She said she didn't even believe that she was really in danger, although Joseph persuaded her to flee. Therefore, she said, it didn't occur to her that her act of running away might have repercussions for all of us left behind. I don't know whether to believe her or not. I never thought of Mari as a selfish girl and she says she wasn't really frightened, so why couldn't she have confided in me? It doesn't feel right.

Nathan comes back in and I tell him of the conversation I've had with Mari. He's tried to talk to Joseph but he says very little. Nathan says he thinks he feels guilty that they've let us down. Some of our other friends are angry and won't talk to them at all. I'm not sure that's very helpful. I wanted to know why they acted as they did.

Anyway, my thoughts are interrupted because Ruth has stirred and I go to her. I pick her up and sit her on my knee. She doesn't cry but she's disorientated and confused, rubbing her eyes. I don't know what woke her up, I didn't hear any sudden noises. I stare into her face. Her eyelids are already closing although she's trying to force them open. I look at her. I do love her, I really do, although it was hard at first. When I'm feeling low she reminds me of the rape and that horrible day and I have to tell myself over and over again that it wasn't her fault. Nathan's been marvellous about it and treats her just the same as Esther even though he knows she cannot possibly be his. I was very fortunate there. Other women who were raped have been shamefully treated by their husbands and the target of tittle-tattle in the village. Nathan has never let on that he was not Ruth's true father.

The next day Mari joins me as we make our way with the other women to the well. Rebecca and her brood come too and, hampered by all our children, we soon drop way behind Susannah and Miriam and the others. I can't help but watch Joshua and think that my Ben ought to be there playing with him. The poor lad has no other boys of his age to play with, he has to join in the girls' games. James follows his brother everywhere. I must say that Joshua seems very patient with him. As we walk I'm looking at Mari more closely. For a mother of three she still looks remarkably youthful. She was always a thin wiry one and bearing children doesn't seem to have changed that, not like me. I can't get my figure back since Esther's birth, Nathan says I'm more comely now but I don't think he means it. If Mari's been through all the hardships she described to me last night, she should show the outward signs of stress and worry but her face is unlined, her eyes look as big and lively as they ever did and she hardly looks the eighteen year old that she must be. Perhaps all that walking has kept her thin, perhaps it was the strange diet they ate in Egypt.

'What's Joseph going to do?' says Rebecca suddenly breaking my reverie. 'Is he going to be able to take up his former trade or will he seek work in Jerusalem? He'll find it hard to get his old customers back – they had to find other carpenters and they've now taken all the local trade. Joseph will find it hard to break back in.'

'I don't know,' Mari answers her. 'He was going to talk to some of the farmers today and see what his chances are.'

I'm not really listening to them. I'm too intent on watching Joshua playing with the other children and I can't help seeing Ben playing with him in my mind's eye. I must stop these thoughts. It won't do any good and will just upset me more. Rebecca's girl is making an awful fuss of him and he loves it.

Later on in the afternoon, I see Mari slip past my house. She must be going to the well again. I noticed this morning that she only had a small water pot – it couldn't possibly last her the day. I pick up Esther and Ruth trots after me. It's a good opportunity to get Mari on her own and ask her more questions. She's got James and Joshua with her. They can keep any eye on Ruth while we talk.

We draw our water. The children are playing happily, they won't come to any harm. Esther and Salome are both asleep in our arms, so we settle ourselves beside the well parapet sweating from the unshaded sun. There is something I want to ask Mari, but I don't know if I dare. It's something she raised herself once but then seemed to think she'd said too much and wouldn't be drawn further. I keep wondering if it's anything to do with the reason for their flight. I won't find out if I don't ask but she might be sensitive about it. In the end I pluck up courage. There won't be a better opportunity.

'Mari,' I say, 'can I ask you something very personal?'

She looks at me cocking her head to one side just like she used to. Perhaps we can get back to our old relationship.

'Mari,' I say again,' "you once told me that Joshua was a miraculous baby and that he was going to be our Messiah. Then you tried to tell me it was a joke. But I've always wondered. Was that why you thought you had to escape from Herod? Is there a proper reason why Herod really is afraid of you? Are you related in some way to the royal family?'

Mari is silent for a long time, then she sighs and begins to tell me things.

'Rachel,' she says, 'you'll laugh at this or find it absurd ...'

'No I won't. I'll believe you this time.'

'Well, listen to what I have to say first and then judge. I shan't blame you if you find it all impossible to believe. Sometimes it seems incredible to me, but I trust God and I have to keep on trusting him. You must have trusted him too to get you through the awful times you've had.'

Well, I'm not sure about that. I didn't see much to trust him about when the soldiers killed our children. Anyway, I don't say anything and let her carry on.

'It's a long story. It started when I used to take my uncle's sheep into the fields in Nazareth. I kept bumping into a stranger – well, he sort of kept appearing, it was most odd. Then he began to tell me some very disturbing things like I was going to have a baby. Well, I was only twelve and my mother and uncle hadn't even thought of finding a husband for me, so I was assuming he just meant that I'd have a baby one day. There was nothing unusual about that. But then one day he said if I was willing it was going to happen straight away and that the baby would be a great man, the Messiah everyone keeps talking about. I was scared then, I thought he was going to attack me or something, but he was so kind and gentle that eventually I believed him and he even asked if I was prepared to trust him and God to bear a child without any man being involved. Well, that seemed impossible, but he seemed so sure of God's plan for me that I said yes, without really thinking about the consequences. And then the world crashed about me.'

'Why? What happened?'

'I got pregnant just as the man said. And everyone accused me of adultery with him and no-one believed me. They even threatened to stone me to death.'

'How awful. Didn't anyone believe you?'

'Only my sisters and then eventually I think my mother did, although I was never quite sure whether she really believed or just wanted to believe.'

'What happened then?'

'My uncle Eli, he was one of the rabbis in the village, he had me tried and whipped and sent away. He told me to get rid of the baby. I had to go to my cousin near Jerusalem, a village the other side from here. And I found she was having a baby too despite the fact that she'd been barren for nearly thirty years and she said her son was a special child from God as well, so she believed me straight away.'

'Did you stay with her until the baby was born?'

'No, I went home. I thought God would protect me and my promised son if it was his plan. It nearly went wrong. I was on the point of being stoned after another trial in the synagogue when a miracle happened that convinced Joseph – in the meantime he'd been betrothed to me – and he convinced the rabbis that my baby really was the Messiah, and they released me and we came to Bethlehem and the rest you know.'

'And that was the end of it? Nothing else happened?'

'On the contrary. People kept coming up to us and telling us our child was special. The very night Joshua was born a crowd of dirty smelly shepherds burst into our room shouting that they'd been told to find our baby because he was going to be a great man. Then a week later when we took him to the Temple to be dedicated an old man said that he'd waited to see our child before he was ready to die and another old woman came and prophesied about him. It was extraordinary.'

She pauses for a moment and looks at me. I think she's expecting me to say something, but I just don't know what to say. Before I can think of anything, she carries on.

'Anyway, things settled down and returned to normal and I put it to the back of my mind. Joshua seemed a very ordinary baby just like other babies, nothing miraculous about him. He was bright, yes, but I couldn't see anything about him that proved he was the future Messiah. I suppose I was just too busy to think too much about it. Then the sheiks came ...'

'Who?'

'Sheiks. Rich men from somewhere to the East – Persia I think they said. They just arrived at our house one night, it was very late and they'd brought expensive gifts for us.'

'You're kidding me!'

Mari explodes into giggles and we both laugh until we nearly cry - when Mari laughs like that I just get a fit of the giggles myself, I can't help it. Then she pulls herself together and becomes serious again.

'They kept saying that Joshua was a prince and I said he wasn't, they'd made a mistake, and then they said something which really scared Joseph. They said they'd gone to the palace assuming that that's where a prince would be born.'

'How did they know a prince was born?'

'They said they could tell from the stars – Joseph said later they were astrologers. And Joseph said that he'd heard people say that Herod was very superstitious and had court astrologers who would test what these sheiks had said. Joseph implored the men not to go back to the king. Apparently they said that Herod had told them to return. I didn't hear that but Joseph did and it put the wind up him. In the end I think he must have persuaded them not to, but we didn't know it at the time. We invited them to stay the night with us, not that we had anywhere suitable for them to sleep, but they said they had servants outside the town and several camels so it was quite impracticable. So they left that very night and Joseph thought, despite his request to them, that they were committed to going back to Herod. That's why he persuaded me that we'd have to run for our lives. If Herod thought our baby was a threat to him, why, it doesn't bear thinking about.'

Then she stops for she realises just what she'd said.

'I'm so sorry, Rachel. We never thought that Herod would go as far as killing all the children to be sure he got Joshua. It didn't even occur to us. You must believe me, you really must. Of course, if we'd known that was what would happen we'd have warned everyone, but we could hardly believe ourselves that Joshua was not just called to be the future Messiah but was already being called a prince.'

I say nothing. I am just overwhelmed by her story. I don't know whether to believe her or not. The whole saga seems ridiculous, but Mari is ordinarily such a likeable girl. Part of me says she is just too fanciful and it is her vivid imagination, but obviously the king had taken it seriously.

'Do you believe me?'

What do I say now? Do I? I must have paused for a long time.

'You don't, do you Rachel?'

I protest, I say I'll really have to think about it. It is just too much to take in at first hearing.

We get up slowly and return to our homes. We don't say another word.

That night I toss and turn, wondering what to say to Nathan. The more I think about it, the more it seems as though she was telling the truth – at least I feel she believes it herself.

But if I tell Nathan, I'm sure he will dismiss such ideas as nonsense and I don't want him to think I am naïve and credulous. I don't say anything to him now but determine to watch Joshua carefully to see if I can discern anything so special about him.

So I watch him every day. I become obsessed with him. I encourage Mari to leave him with me to play with my girls when she is feeding Salome or making extra trips to the well, although she soon bought some larger pots to avoid that additional chore. I try everything I can think of to test him. Well, how do you test a five year old to see if he has princely blood? What am I looking for? Does he bleed if he cuts himself? Does he utter words of wisdom beyond the wit of a young boy? Does he instil fear and awe from the other children? No, he seems an ordinary likeable child, popular with the other children, sunny by nature. He is clever, very clever for his age, I think, but not unnaturally so. He is the sort of boy that I'd have liked Ben to grow into, I think darkly sometimes, upsetting myself again.

So I continue to watch. And I continue to find no proof one way or the other. He does nothing to show he couldn't be such a leader, but at the same time he does nothing to prove he is. I never see him do anything really mean or spiteful. He can be naughty like all small boys, getting dirty and into mischief and running away when his mother wants him in to wash or have his meal or go to bed. He is a good boy, full of life and fun and I realise that I am jealous of him and Mari. It is unfair. Why did my son have to die so that Joshua could live? Perhaps that's unfair but that's how my twisted mind thinks of it.

Chapter 27
Mari

Joseph is getting frustrated. He's spent three days trying to raise interest from his old customers, but they all use Ishmael now who moved in from Jerusalem when we left home and no-one wants to abandon him just because we've come back. Joseph says that some of his former customers, whom he thought friends, were quite nasty and not only accused him of letting them down before, but seemed to blame him for the catastrophe that overwhelmed the village. I think he'll have to search for work in Jerusalem itself which means a two hour walk each way every day hauling all the tools he might need with him. I don't think he's looking forward to that, but he hinted last night that if he can't get any work today, he'll have to try in Jerusalem.

I haven't told Joseph yet that I've spoken to both Rebecca and Rachel about Joshua and everything that's happened to us. I'm not sure what his reaction will be. I don't think he'll like it. I don't know what I think is going to happen either. I expected Rebecca and Rachel to be excited and really friendly, or to disbelieve me and be cold and antagonistic. It is strange, but neither reaction has taken place. Rebecca just carries on in her usual no nonsense way, as if I had never mentioned anything to her. Rachel seems cautious, as though she still can't make up her mind whether she believes me or not. I know she is putting Joshua under very close observation, trying to make up her mind whether he is different to other children. He isn't – why should he be? He won't begin to fulfil his destiny until he's a man, surely? If he, as a young boy, were to start challenging the Romans, or showing his true colours, he'd come to grief. He's just not old or strong enough yet. I don't know what Rachel expects to see. She keeps telling me that Joshua is such a nice ordinary boy, as though she was challenging me to deny it and tell her some new miracle or astonishing skill that would prove my words. But it's not like that. What do I expect anyway? Reading our scriptures does not give me many clues. Should I dedicate him to the Temple like Hannah did with Samuel? I don't think I could make that sacrifice. I'm proud enough to think he needs me.

I do spend a lot of time with him after James and Salome are both asleep, even though he is sometimes so tired after a full day playing that he nearly falls asleep as he snuggles on my lap.

I tell him lots of stories, tales I learned when Joel spent time with me and his daughter, my friend Hannah, at the synagogue in Nazareth. Joshua seems to know them by heart because if I leave out any bit, even if I think he's only half listening, he stops me and insists I get it right! Sometimes I tell him about the stranger who told me that I would bear the Messiah and about some of the problems I had. I don't tell him the really nasty bits as I don't want to distress him. I'm not sure if he understands any of this yet, but I think it'll be easier if I get him used to some of these strange things rather than springing it on him when he's really old enough to understand. I tell him about his cousin John. Now we're this close I've got Joseph to promise me that we'll visit Elizabeth, Zechariah and John soon. They might have news of everyone back in Nazareth. I'm anxious, it's been so long since we were in touch. They must think we've disappeared off the face of the earth. I wonder if the news of the killing of the boys in Bethlehem reached home – if so, they'll have assumed Joshua was murdered too and will be grieving for him, perhaps even fearing that we're dead too. I must try to see if I can find anyone up from Galilee at the next Passover and get a message home if Elizabeth and Zechariah aren't in touch.

Joseph comes back tonight very despondent. He's still had no success in finding any work. He'll have to go to Jerusalem tomorrow and see if he can find a carpenter who needs assistance or seek new construction work with the possibility of a contract as he did in Alexandria. He's worried though that such work, which would almost certainly be for the Romans, would not go down well here. The local people are much more antagonistic to Roman building developments than the Egyptians, and he's heard Jews calling such men who work for the Romans 'collaborators' and shun them. I suggest to him that we might do worse than go back to Nazareth, but he is of the opinion that he might face the same problem there as in Bethlehem and says we must wait and see how he gets on in the city. He does, however, think that a visit to Elizabeth and Zechariah in Ein-Karem might be worthwhile. Zechariah with his contacts and influence at the Temple might know of some opening.

After a couple of days of searching in Jerusalem with still no prospects of employment, we decide to pack and pay my cousin a visit. We take the donkey and our tent as Elizabeth might struggle to house all of us – for all I know she might have had further children after John despite her age. Joshua is ever so excited when we tell him that we are going to visit John as I'd told him so much about him. Despite being a popular child in the village, I think Joshua misses playing with other boys of his own age. We set off early as it is a good day's trek to Ein-Karem. We have to go into Jerusalem itself as there is no route to Elizabeth's village other than the direct road from the city, and I remember my long walk with Zechariah when I was already tired, after the walk up from Jericho with the crowd of us going to the Passover celebration five years ago.

Of course Joshua is fascinated with the sights in the city. He's heard me talk about the Temple and is overawed by its vast bulk. He's seen bigger buildings in Alexandria but not been quite so close to them and we go right up to its walls towering above us. I think he is a bit frightened by the noise and bustle too, it's pandemonium there with everyone jostling each other and traders shouting out about their wares. James seems oblivious to it all, he just wants to ride on the donkey's back all the time, while Salome is fast asleep in my arms.

Anyway, we get to Ein-Karem in the middle of the afternoon. I remember the way to her house and I can't help wondering what sort of reception we'll get. How surprised will they be? I'm really looking forward to the reunion as Elizabeth and Zechariah were, I'm sure, the first persons – apart from my sisters and brother – who really believed in me. Even my mother seemed unsure although she clearly wanted to believe. At first I'm worried as their house seems to be shut up. I can't hear any movement. Surely they've not moved away? Has something dreadful happened to them? Joseph goes in search of someone and comes back with the message that Elizabeth and John are probably at the well. I assume Zechariah must be at the Temple, back in Jerusalem – he used to serve there two or three times a week.

So we wait outside Elizabeth's house and eventually we are rewarded as I spot Elizabeth and a small boy hand in hand coming up the road towards us accompanied by a couple of other women, all bearing large water pots. When she spots us, she puts her water jar down and scoops John up and comes running to me.

'Mari, Mari, my dear, is it really you? After all these years? I was so afraid for you, I wondered what on earth had happened. I thought something must have gone badly wrong or you'd have been in touch earlier.'

She flings her arms around me and cradles Salome and hugs us with all her strength. Then she looks down questioningly at my family.

'Joshua?' she says looking at the boy. And before I can answer she points to James and Salome. 'And these? All your family? You lucky girl. You are well blessed.'

'And you?' I manage to blurt out whilst the breath is being squeezed from me.

'This is John. You know John, you helped to deliver him. He's a great comfort to me, especially as Zechariah has passed on.'

I start. 'You're alone? Zechariah is dead?'

Elizabeth nods. I see her eyes water.

'Over three years ago. He caught a fever. There was much disease in the city. I think pilgrims brought it when the city was crowded at Passover time.'

'I'm so sorry, Elizabeth. I didn't know. We've been out of the country. It's a long story and I'll tell you later, but you must tell us if our visit is upsetting for you.'

'Of course not, Mari. I'm delighted to see you all. And Joseph too – I presume this is your husband?'

Joseph greets her and lifts Joshua, then James to be given a hug by my cousin whom I still think of as an aunt as she is of a different generation to me.

'Come inside and make yourselves at home. You'll stay a while with us, won't you?'

'Only if it is convenient for you. We've brought our tent and food.'

'Don't be ridiculous, Mari. Of course you're welcome. Nothing will give me greater pleasure than getting to know all your family and hearing all your news. Come inside and let me get you a drink. You must be tired and hot? Where have you come from today? Are you all the way from Nazareth?'

We go inside her house – it somehow seems smaller than I remember. John has already taken Joshua out to their backyard and is showing him their chickens and a couple of goats. James trundles behind them. She pours Joseph and me a jar of wine and takes a little herself.

'How are you managing?' asks Joseph. 'Is anyone caring for you?'

'The Temple people are good. One of the rabbis visits me every month and sees that I have need of no essentials. I cannot grumble. The priests look after their own.'

Salome wakes up at that moment and Elizabeth immediately comes to look at her. I offer her and Elizabeth beams and takes her into her own arms. Luckily Salome gives her a smile and for the next minute or so they commune in silence. Joseph goes out into the yard to check that the lads are up to no mischief and I get a chance to ask Elizabeth what I've been dying to say ever since we arrived.

'And news from Nazareth, Elizabeth? Do you have any? We've been in Bethlehem and earlier in Egypt, I've not heard from my family since we left Nazareth five years ago. Do you have any news? How is my mother?'

'You've been in Egypt, dear? My, what experiences you have. You must tell me all about it. But yes, you'll want to hear such news as I have first I'm sure. I don't know a lot, but Susannah and her husband called last year when they were up for the Passover festival. They said your mother was well and also your brother and sisters, but they were distressed in not knowing what had happened to you. However, your uncle, the Rabbi Eli, had apparently died a couple of years ago. That's about all I know.'

I start a little at this news. It is strange to think my biggest critic and latterly almost embarrassing supporter is no more. That such a momentous change has happened and I've known nothing of it is disconcerting. I think about it with mixed feelings. My immediate thought is the impact on my mother for he had helped her despite his misgivings about us.

As if she guesses my worries, Elizabeth adds, 'Clopas has apparently taken over all his father's responsibilities. Susannah said that your family was very grateful for his continuing support – in fact they found Clopas more congenial to live with than old Eli had ever been.'

At that moment Joseph comes back into the room with the boys and all efforts at meaningful conversation come to an abrupt end. The boys are in a boisterous mood and wrestle with each other and Joseph, until Elizabeth calls Joshua over and asks him some questions. Clearly he doesn't want to leave his new friend, but he is polite and answers Elizabeth to the best of his ability without volunteering anything other than a direct and succinct answer to her queries. She sees the sun is beginning to set and busies herself with making a meal for us. I give her the food we have brought which she reluctantly accepts for she has insufficient to feed all of us. I need to feed Salome now and watch the three boys playing as she suckles from my breast. It's only after our meal and the children go up onto the roof to play and then sleep that we are able to resume our exchange of news.

Elizabeth is agog to hear absolutely everything and between us Joseph and I spend over two hours recounting everything we can remember – which is most of it for so much is printed indelibly on my mind. She'd heard that I'd married Joseph so she knew there must have been a happy outcome as when I last saw her I was in disgrace and facing a showdown with Eli and the rabbis over my refusal to get rid of the baby I was carrying.

'Zechariah and I prayed hard for you,' she says. 'You were so courageous. You were a lesson to all of us in your steadfastness and trust in God.'

She makes me describe my ordeal in the synagogue when I was examined by the rabbis and accused of blasphemy and even makes me recount my humiliation – but only to marvel the more that I maintained my faith. That is what she says, anyhow. And Joseph tells her how he with my mother interceded successfully at the last moment. The birth and the strange visitors in Bethlehem are met with delight on her part.

'Oh, Mari, your mother will be so pleased and relieved to hear news of you. You can't imagine how much she's worried about you all these years. It'll be as though you're back from the dead for her. You must go back to Nazareth and visit her. I can't wait to see her face when you meet up again.'

Then I tell Elizabeth why we fled to Egypt and the dreadful consequences for those left in Bethlehem.

'Had you heard about Herod killing all the boys in Bethlehem and did you fear we had been caught up in it?'

'What's that Mari? What killing?'

'You haven't heard about it? How King Herod feared that a Messiah had been born who would threaten him, so he ordered a slaughter of children who might claim the throne?'

'No. I hadn't heard anything about that. Were you involved, Mari?'

She hasn't heard anything. Now I realise that Zechariah must have died before that massacre and therefore it's obvious that no rumour has gone back even the short distance to this village. She is appalled when I recount to her what Rachel and Rebecca had told me. At least, if she hadn't heard, the chances of the news having got back to Nazareth and my mother and sisters worrying about that and fearing the worst was less likely.

When she recovers from the shock of what I've just said, she wipes a tear from her eye.

'God has truly watched over you,' she says although I am reluctant to think God rescued me but condemned our neighbours in Bethlehem to that murderous tyrant. We skim over our time in Egypt for it is getting late and she insists we tell her more of that in detail on the morrow.

'But you have said little about your life,' I say. 'Your John is special too. What signs and experiences have you received? Your story is as miraculous as ours.'

'Nonsense, my dear. I was an old woman with the belated and much treasured gift of a child. He'll support your son, I'm sure he will, but yours is the Messiah, not John.'

'But the vision of Zechariah in the Temple. The restoration of his speech. The prophecies – all these mean nothing to you?'

'Of course they do, Mari, but they are insignificant compared with your destiny and that of your son. I know it.'

'Don't belittle yourself, Elizabeth. John will be important, I'm sure of it. We were joyful together when we met that first time, it was an equal joy we both shared. God values you too and honoured Zechariah.'

'Thank you dear for saying so. You haven't changed much have you? I know you've grown up and had three children – not that it's so obvious – but you're still the same old Mari, humble and so enthusiastic, full of life despite your experiences which would have burdened many a soul and made them bitter or tired or too self-centred. No wonder God chose you. And your good husband, of course,' she adds hastily, looking suddenly at Joseph who's been silent for most of our long discourse.

Joseph goes to fetch the tent, which is still strapped across the back of the ass, which is tethered in the back yard.

'You'll do no such thing,' Elizabeth exclaims, 'you'll have my space. I'll sleep with the children on the roof. It will be fresher up there and I'll watch to see that they come to no harm. We don't want Joshua or James falling because of their unfamiliarity with the place. You can tend Salome here. I guess she will disturb during the night and need another feed.'

There is nothing we can do about it. She insists and we give in with good grace. It does make sense even if I feel guilty about it. We are tired, it's been a long day and we fall asleep very quickly. Salome does wake later, but I'm unsure how long I've been asleep and she only spends a few minutes at my breast before she's fast asleep again and I can resume my rest.

The next day we are presuming to return to Bethlehem, but Elizabeth will not hear of it. She wants the rest of our story and has to wait for some time until the children rest after the midday meal. In return I try to get her to tell us more about our family back in Nazareth, but she is vague and I come to the opinion that she really doesn't know much more than she's already told us. So we spend a second night at Ein-Karem. Joshua and John seem to have become bosom friends with poor James trying to keep up with them. John dashes ahead, he's not used to a smaller child wanting to join in, but Joshua is very good and protects the interests of his younger brother, even when he gets sulky or obstinate and spoils their games.

And Elizabeth takes the opportunity of plying us with more questions about our time in Egypt. She wants to know every detail. When I think we've exhausted the subject, she is quiet and, as I search for something more to say, she holds up a hand to cause me to hesitate.

'Now I think I understand. You too have been in the Egypt of our ancestors where you suffered hardship. And after a time God has called you back home, just like he did to Moses and those early Israelites. I see a parallel here. It is a prophecy that will come to pass when Joshua here sets forth on the mission that God is preparing him for. He will be a second Moses, to rescue and renew our nation.'

We listen in silence. No-one dares add anything while her words sink in.

Eventually Joseph asks, 'Do you mean that our Joshua will one day free our nation from Roman rule just as Moses destroyed the Egyptians?'

'I don't know. He will save us, of that I'm sure, but what sort of rescue it will be, that is in God's hands. Perhaps he will lead an army and he will be a true king like our ancestor, David. Who knows?'

'Should we be training him already in the military arts?'

'Surely not, Joseph,' I respond quickly. 'It is much too early to decide such things. If it is God's plan, we will know soon enough at the right time. Let's just teach him to love God's law and develop the character that is fit to fulfil all that our prophets foretell.'

After that, no-one feels capable of saying any more. We go quietly to our sleeping area, after checking that the children are sleeping soundly. I lie awake for hours thinking about all that has been said. It's Elizabeth's words that I ponder deep into the night. It's just like it was when I first met her and she knew instinctively that God had called both of us to serve him in a great mission. She gets to the heart of the matter. I must make some time tomorrow to be alone with her and share our thoughts and hopes. I can learn much from her.

And as I lie awake, my thoughts jump to my own family whom I miss so terribly. All evening we've been reliving our years in Pelusium and Alexandria. It's odd that it already seems so distant even though it's only weeks ago. But the more I think back about it, the more I begin to feel homesick, not for our Bethlehem home, but for Nazareth and my mother and Salome and Rebecca and little Ben – well, not so little now, I suppose. I wonder what he looks like. Will I recognise him if we meet again? That night as I lie awake listening to Elizabeth moving around above us, I push against Joseph and discover he's still awake as well. I whisper to him how I feel.

'Can we go home to Nazareth? You can't find work here. May be you will do better there. You worked in Sepphoris and Capernaum before. There must be a good chance now and Clopas can help you find work just as Eli did. Please, Joseph!'

'Go to sleep, Mari. You've worn your tongue out this evening. Leave it until tomorrow.'

'But please, Joseph, will you think about it then?'

'Alright, Mari, I'll think about it. But I'm not promising anything. I'm too tired to think properly now.'

Chapter 28
Mari

Joseph finally gave in and admitted that it would be worth returning to Nazareth to see if we could make a living there. For two further days since our return from Ein-Karem, Joseph has scoured the city unsuccessfully looking for work and I could see he was getting worried. The Passover Feast is approaching and Elizabeth told us that she is anticipating folk from Nazareth to stay over the holiday period as Jerusalem itself will be so crowded. Before we left, she suggested we have the Passover meal with her and John and if relatives from Nazareth come, we could return home with them, as it would be safer to travel in a crowd. And now Joseph has agreed, so we've been taking stock and I tell Rachel and Rebecca today that we've decided to go.

Rachel breaks down when I tell her. I'm most surprised. I thought she had treated me with great reserve and some suspicion since we returned from Egypt, but she confesses to me that my words in the last few days have left her thinking and she has come to the view that I really had been promised that Joshua would be the longed-for Messiah.

Between her tears, she says, 'Mari, I do believe you, I really do. Don't leave us now. After all this time I want to believe that my own son's death was not for nothing. Mari, do stay with us!'

I am confused at her reaction. I had persuaded myself of the rightness of the decision we had made and convinced myself that it was the best all round and that indeed our decision would be welcomed by our neighbours. Our presence and that of a healthy Joshua was too raw a wound for those women in the village who had suffered such grievous loss.

'Rachel, I don't know what to say. I thought our presence here was upsetting for you and that we'd be better back in my home village. I'm sorry if I got it wrong. We've told everyone now. I'm so sorry, Rachel. I really didn't think …'

I'm interrupted by Rachel sobbing and clinging to me. I stand there trying to imagine myself in her place. I can't change my mind, not now, but I feel badly about it. It seems impossible that I have so misjudged my friend. I stay at her home until she has recovered her composure. The children are watching us, perplexed, until Rachel calms down, then they resume their games, ignoring us. I eventually take the children home. Despite her continuing pleas, I stop myself promising to change my mind. I later tell Joseph about her reaction.

'Joseph, you do think we're right, don't you? You are sure it is best? You're not just agreeing because of my words, are you?'

Joseph just looks at me.

'Mari, you're not really reconsidering surely? We've talked about this decision at length. We've resolved to go. Don't be upset by Rachel. She's an emotional woman. You've been a good friend to her, but your duty now is to our children and yourself. We need to find a means of sustaining ourselves. I've failed to find work here. We know that there are likely to be opportunities back in Galilee and if not immediately, at least we'll be among family who will help.'

'I know, Joseph. You're right of course. I know you are. I just feel so desperately sorry for Rachel. I still feel for her. If it had not been for us she would have had a sturdy son to support her. I feel so guilty when I look at her, especially now she's pleaded with us to stay.'

'Mari, you're too soft hearted. You can't take all the problems of the world on your shoulders. Think of yourself for once. I know how much you long to see your mother and your sisters. Think of the joy they will have when they see you returned with Joshua and James and Salome. They'll be so proud of you. Will you deny them that opportunity just because you feel sorry for Rachel now?'

He's right, of course. But I remain silent.

'She'll soon get over it when we've gone. She has a fine husband and two bonny girls and another child on the way if I'm not mistaken. Perhaps that will be the boy child to replace her loss.'

'You're right,' I admit. 'But I can't help feeling sorry for her. I shall miss her although we've not resumed the closeness that I experienced with her when we first settled here.'

So we let it be known that we are leaving at the Passover time. Rachel said no more about it. When we meet, she puts on a false cheerfulness as though she is willing herself not to be upset. She makes a special fuss of Joshua. She has obviously decided he is the coming Messiah and treats him with undue respect that seems a little odd – after all, he is only a five year old child. Joshua does not seem to notice, but I'm sure some of the other women think she is acting a little strangely. The other women take our impending departure with little comment. Rebecca is her usual no-nonsense self – practical and down to earth.

'Good for you, girl! You'll be fine back with your own family. You've been away too long. I'll miss you and I know Miriam will miss the children, but she's plenty to do helping me and she's growing up fast. Next year we'll be looking for a husband for her. How time flies. You'll find things changed back in Nazareth, I'm sure. I hope you find that all are well. It's been over four years, hasn't it?'

Now we've decided to go, my mind fills with anxiety about what we'll find in Nazareth. Elizabeth has reassured me that all except Eli are alive and well – although it was Passover last year when she last had news and a lot can happen in a year. So I keep pestering Joseph with my thoughts. I'm surprised he doesn't get angry with me sometimes because I go on so, but I do rely on his calming sensible advice.

'Now Eli's dead,' I say, 'I wonder how they're all managing. Will they still be living in the same home?'

'You've no need to worry on that score,' answers Joseph. 'Clopas will have inherited his father's farm and home and all his responsibilities which he'll carry out with greater pleasure than Eli ever did, I'm sure of that. I know your mother always felt that Eli only helped because he felt it was his duty. You'll meet James and Jude and Mo when we go back to Nazareth together. They were fine lads, it'll be James's 'bar-mitzvah' next year. And Mo will probably be as cute as ever. They'll be so excited to see you again.'

'What about my sisters?' I ask with growing impatience.

'They'll be overjoyed to see you again. They'll have missed you terribly when we left home.'

'And Ben was very upset that he tore my shawl that Mother had made for my wedding garment. He was convinced that he had spoiled everything. And now it's been stolen. He'll be upset about that. Do you think that Salome or Rebecca will be betrothed or married by now?'

'I don't expect so. Don't worry about that. Clopas won't be in such a hurry as Eli was with you. Salome is only just of age and I expect the two girls will be spending as much time in the fields with the animals as you did. They were both good with younger kids just as you were. You were such a splendid example. They'll be pretty girls, well you don't need me to tell you that, you knew them well enough and you'll soon see them for yourself.'

'What about Benjamin?'

'He'll be growing up too. He must be ten by now. Perhaps Rabbi Joel takes him for special lessons just as he did for you. Perhaps he'll come with the Passover pilgrims from Nazareth. You'll have to be patient, Mari. We'll meet up with some of them at Elizabeth's home and you can get answers to some of your questions long before we get back to Nazareth.'

'Will they have heard about the killing of the babies in Bethlehem and think we're dead?'

'Mari, you heard what Elizabeth said. She didn't know anything of that, so how do you think such news would have got back to Nazareth?'

But perhaps some people from Nazareth stayed in Jerusalem and heard about the massacre.'

'Possible, but unlikely, I think. And what if they did? The news of your return with Joshua and the other children will be even more welcome news.'

Later that night I have a sudden horrid thought. I shake Joseph awake.

'What is it? What is it now, my love? Go to sleep before Salome wakes you again.'

'Joseph, we're not married. We've never had a proper ceremony. Mother will be shamed that we've lived as man and wife all these years and with all these children without getting married.'

It's as though we had forgotten. I'd put it out of my mind. To have gone five years and not even tried to put ourselves right. How could we have done? I feel a surge of guilt and fear.

'How could we have forgotten? How could we have done nothing about it? We'll be shamed.'

'Why have you suddenly thought about that now? At this time of night? Couldn't it wait until the morning? Stop worrying about things.'

'But we're going home. Everyone will ask us. How can we have forgotten such a thing?'

'I hadn't forgotten, love. But how could we have gone through a public ceremony in either Bethlehem or Egypt without our friends and neighbours finding out that we had been already sinning in their eyes and labelling our Joshua as an illegitimate bastard? We have been blessed by God. There is no need now to own up to our omission and expose us and our family to a shame that no-one need ever know about.'

'What are we going to do, Joseph? Should we get Elizabeth to arrange a secret wedding for us with one of her Temple contacts?'

'Why, Mari, why is it so important to you now?'

'Mother will ask. She will ask why we didn't come home to get married as soon as Joshua was old enough for us to travel back with him.'

'But at first you were so weak, you lost a lot of blood and I was worried for you. You had to look after your new baby and I wanted you to stay at my home while you recovered your strength again. Then we heard that travellers were being attacked on the roads north of Jerusalem, people said it was too dangerous to travel unless you were in a crowd.'

'I'm sure we ought to have gone back then to get married.'

'Mari, blame me if you like. At the time you pleaded with me to go home, you said that God would protect us, but everyone told me it was too dangerous even to go as far as the villages outside the city. Then I built up my workshop and was making a good living and wanted to save enough to live on for a few months before we could afford to leave everything and journey north. And everyone assumed we were married ... '

He must think I'm not listening to him.

'Mari, hear me out. You had the child and we lived together. Neither of us wanted to have to tell everyone about the child's conception and his destiny, it would have created so many problems for us. And we couldn't have a proper wedding without revealing to everyone that we were not already married which would have caused a great scandal. So we put it off until we could get home. Then we had to flee. So why tell everyone now and risk an unnecessary scandal?'

'Because Mother will ask when we got married and I can't lie to her.'

'Then blame me and not yourself. If you'd had your way you'd have rushed back to Nazareth. I feared you'd kill yourself. And if you hadn't succumbed to sickness and fever after your confinement, you'd have had us ambushed by marauding bandits. People told us that we were lucky to come through unscathed when we first went to Bethlehem, but of course we saw many people travelling to Jerusalem and surrounding villages for the census and we can't have been attractive targets for any thieves as we obviously had so little.'

I thought a lot that night about our marriage. We were husband and wife in all but name. I was sure we were in God's eyes, which is really all that mattered to me. But what will my mother think? Should we go through the wedding ritual in Nazareth? I have three children now – will admitting that we are not married be an even greater scandal and bring shame to my mother and all our family? If I have to explain to our new neighbours there, I shall have to tell the full story, and then everyone will focus on Joshua and he will not be able to be a normal little boy. It's bad enough already. I'm sure some will remember the judgment in the synagogue and look curiously at him to see if they can divine his forecast destiny.

Perhaps I should confide in Rabbi Joel at the synagogue and get his advice. He knows the full story, perhaps he will agree to conduct a private ceremony that would be attended by my mother, brother and sisters and Clopas and his immediate family only. Perhaps Mother will embroider a new shawl for me to replace the one that Ben ripped and was stolen in Pelusium. Perhaps it will be a first step in a new chapter of our life. Perhaps, perhaps, perhaps …

Chapter 29
Mari

We leave in the morning. We packed up everything last night, said our farewells to Rachel and Rebecca and their families. There was a lot of crying and hugging. I promised to see them again when we come to Jerusalem at Passover time. I wonder if I shall be able to keep that promise.

And now I'm lying awake in our little room here for the last time. The children are asleep and I can hear Joseph snoring softly beside me. It's five days now since we bade Elizabeth and John farewell. I still remember every word of the last long conversation I had with my aunt.

'Don't prejudge anything,' she told me. 'Let God show you in his own good time. You'll know, just as you did before. Even when Zechariah died, I felt God was near me, guiding me in the nurture of my son, because he too has been promised an illustrious part to play that will in time be subservient to your son.'

I tried to assure her that her son would be as blessed as mine but she was adamant. Joshua would be the Messiah, John was just to help prepare people to recognise him when the time was right. Elizabeth's words are so comforting when others are sceptical or disbelieve me outright. She helps me reaffirm my own faith when I begin to wobble.

It's very still outside. The sounds of movement have ceased at last. I'm restless and don't feel like sleep yet. I slip as quietly as I can outside without disturbing my sleeping family and gasp as the night sky embraces me into its unimaginable orbit. The vast expanse sparkles as myriads of stars illuminate the night, casting a pale glow over the little houses opposite with a couple of bare trees silhouetted darkly at the end of our street against the dim horizon. I feel God's presence here. I try to find some words but I am speechless. The awesomeness of my life, chosen out of this limitless universe pierces me. Why me, God, why did you choose me? What have I done to be worthy of all this? I don't feel equal to the task you've promised for me, my God. I have to trust you. I have to believe that everything I've already been through, experienced, was part of the plan you have for me and my son.

Yet it seems so improbable. Our nation has been praying and yearning for a saviour for centuries. Why now, oh God, why now? Are the Romans so bad that you want a king of our nation to arise to throw off this imposition and rule for the Jews alone? Will my son be a Moses, a David? They were of humble origins too, though both were plucked to be the children of pharaohs and kings. Will Joshua be taken from me by Herod's sons and made their brother, or will he even be adopted by the Roman Emperor or will he lead the freedom fighters just like my father, but drive all the foreigners off our soil? Which will it be, Lord God? Should I try to influence him or is it all in your hands?

Yet somehow, the thought of all this bothers me. It doesn't seem right. I know my father hated the Romans and our countrymen who supported them, but he wanted to avenge my grandfather and my uncles whom I never knew. But Herod is gone now, they say he died a horrible and painful death. And the Romans I know have not harmed us. Many Egyptians seemed to be pleased for their presence, I heard people say that they had brought order and peace and had reduced the lawlessness.

I still remember the Roman soldier who saved me and he seemed fair despite the fact that my father's band was scattered and killed, but that was done by Herod's soldiers. Am I really to go through all that turmoil again with my son re-enacting the actions and fate of my father? Or will he be different? If I counsel him into the ways of peace and love for his fellow human beings, will I be diverting him from his calling? Tell me, God, show me what I ought to say and do. If you really think I'm worthy to be the Messiah's mother, then surely you must expect me to influence him in the ways you want him to develop? Is it wrong for me to want peace? To want my people to be happy? To want my sisters to have a life that is not filled with drudgery? And what about the friends I met in Egypt? Are they included in God's plans? Will it just include the Jews in Egypt? What about those living in squalor in Pelusium? Can I help Nathaniel and Naomi and little Annie through things Joshua will achieve? Will he one day bring them home like Moses?

It's getting cool, I must have been out here longer than I thought. I slip back inside the house and note with relief that all is quiet. None of them has stirred. I lie down, but still thoughts whir round my brain. Tomorrow I may see some of my family when we meet at Elizabeth's home. Who will be coming? Will I see my mother and my sisters and little Ben again so soon or shall I have to wait until we reach Nazareth? How will we react? Will it seem just as though I'd never left or will all have changed so drastically that we are strangers? When we get home, will my mother accept me and the children with open arms and heart or will she blame me for being away so long and neglecting her? Will she see Joshua as special or will she just see everything that happened as the best way of obtaining my release from condemnation? Did she see the miracle of Joshua's conception and birth as a fairy tale that she had to go along with to obtain my rescue from the judgment of Eli and the other rabbis? Did she really believe the dream that appeared to so convince Joseph of my innocence or did they plot together knowingly to save me from an ignominious and shameful execution? My excitement is tinged with nervousness. After all this, I fear anti-climax, disappointment. My heart says all will be well, joyful, yet I worry. I know I will be happy to be back, but will they really be glad to see me after so long?

I try to picture my sisters and brother, but my image of them is still that of the farewell nearly five years ago, when tearful Ben had clutched and torn my precious shawl. Or of Salome and Rebecca curled up beside me in the fields as I reveal my secret to them and they are open mouthed in wonder – believing everything without any hesitation. But how much will they have changed – little Rebecca, a tomboy of seven will now be a demure young lady of twelve. Or will she? I try to think what I was like at twelve. A bit of a handful, I think my mother would have said. Certainly not a demure young lady. I know Joseph was quite shocked at my boldness and questions. I wonder if Rebecca is still the same or whether she has calmed down.

Salome was always the quieter and more serious one. Will she be pleased to see me again? She'll be thirteen now, I wonder if she is already promised in marriage. I suppose Clopas will be negotiating on the family's behalf now – that's better than Eli anyway. And thirteen is very young, though I say so myself. I was lucky in the end and was given to a man who was kind. I shudder to think of what my life would now be like if I'd been betrothed to that man from Father's rebel band that Eli tried to match me with. Will they let my sisters choose? I had to fight to get my way, just like Rachel and Nathan had in Bethlehem. But here in Nazareth, could one escape the traditions as easily as in the city of Jerusalem? I rebelled, but did tradition reassert itself once I had gone and normality reigned once more? Questions, questions, questions. My mind will not be still. I cannot sleep. Tomorrow will be a tumultuous day, I know it. But of what kind? I toss and turn and still the thoughts and questions keep coming? Will I ever sleep?

I suppose sleep eventually comes, for my mind has confusing pictures, as though I'm back in the synagogue arguing, running but my legs won't move, I'm trapped. Then I hear crying and I stir. I think it's Salome, but the child is still asleep. Then as I come round, I hear Joshua sobbing softly. What's wrong? He never wakes in the night. Is he ill? I take him in my arms and try to console him. He snuggles in my arms and goes straight back to sleep. Perhaps he was dreaming, a nightmare? I hold him in my arms and my confused mind ceases its incessant worrying. I look at his face, the muscles of which are relaxing under my very gaze. This is no warrior, I think. This is my lovely child, a little boy, my son, my life, my James' and Salome's brother. An ordinary little boy and precious member of our family.

I hold him until the dawn begins to break. There is no point in sleeping now. I am ready for the day ahead. It is in your hands, I pray to God, and am content to leave it there.

I don't tell Joseph how little I've slept. He would worry about my fitness to tackle the journey ahead. But we're only going as far as Ein-Karem today. Who shall we meet there? Will the pilgrims include Mother and my sisters and brother or will it just be Clopas and his boys? I must be patient, I really must.

We set off at dawn. The poor donkey is even more laden than when we left for Egypt and certainly more than when we arrived in Bethlehem five years ago. Joshua and James are both perched across the back of the animal surrounded by our baggage. Joseph is leading them while I follow with Salome in my arms. We reach the edge of the village and the rocky fields open out, filled with sheep and newborn lambs. There is much bleating as the tiny creatures seek their mothers.

I look back. The sun is just beginning to show above the roofs of the village. I can't see our house now for it's hidden on the far side. I wipe away a tear from my eye. I feel sad to be leaving my first home and my friends, but then I turn and look ahead. The sun's first rays are catching the distant walls of Jerusalem, and then I notice. A sunbeam has just caught the top of the head of Joshua riding high on the donkey. It's odd, the way it shines there, creating a sort of halo effect upon my son …

The End